John Millington Synge

John Millington Synge in 1906, from a crayon drawing by James Paterson.

John Millington Synge

A BIOGRAPHY

David M. Kiely

St. Martin's Press
New York

JOHN MILLINGTON SYNGE: A BIOGRAPHY.
Copyright © 1994 by David M. Kiely. All rights reserved.
Printed in the United States of America.
No part of this book may be used or reproduced in any manner
whatsoever without written permission except in the case of
brief quotations embodied in critical articles or reviews.
For information, address St. Martin's Press,
175 Fifth Avenue, New York, N.Y. 10010.

Library of Congress Cataloging-in-Publication Data
Kiely, David M.
John Millington Synge : a biography / by David M. Kiely.
p.   cm.
Originally published: Dublin : Gill & Macmillan, c1994.
"A Thomas Dunne book."
Includes bibliographical references (p. 239) and index.
ISBN 0-312-13526-2
1. Synge, J. M. (John Millington), 1871–1909—Biography.
2. Dramatists, Irish—20th century—Biography.   I. Title.
PR5533.K53   1995
822'.912—dc20   95-34750   CIP

First published in Great Britain by Gill & Macmillan Ltd.

First U.S. Edition: December 1995
10   9   8   7   6   5   4   3   2   1

For Jonathan 'nil desperandum' Williams

Ah God, we know that art
Is long and short our life!
Often enough my analytical labours
Pester both brain and heart.
How hard it is to attain the means
By which one climbs to the fountainhead;
Before a poor devil can reach the halfway house,
Like as not he is dead.

From Johann Wolfgang von Goethe's *Faust*
(Translated by Louis MacNeice)

Contents

Illustrations

Acknowledgments

The author wishes to thank the following, for their kind permission to use material, quoted or reproduced in this biography:

The Board of Trinity College Dublin and the J. M. Synge Trustees for permission to use the frontispiece, photos. 1-10, 19-21, 27 and letter 25, and extracts from the Synge Manuscripts in the Library of TCD; Winifrid Matheson for photo. 11; Anne Yeats for illustrations 12-15 and 17; Daphne D. C. Pochin Mould for photos. 29 and 30; National Museum of Ireland for sketch 26; Colin Smythe for photos. 16, 18, 22, 23, 24 and 28. My thanks, too, to Andrew Carpenter for permission to use material from the Stephens' TS; to Ann Saddlemyer for reading my TS, and for permission to quote from the Synge Letters; to Norma Jessop of the Special Collections, University College Dublin; to the librarians and staff of the National Library of Ireland; to Nicholas Grene, Cormac Ó Gráda, Ann Porter, Michael Kelleher, Kate Davis, Sue Naughton, Kathleen Reid, DK&A, and Clio.

A Wilder Altar

I

See Synge sitting in the Atlantic Hotel, overlooking the harbour at Kilronan. It is a poor hotel, even by the standards of Connacht in 1898. There is no other hotel here on Inishmore, the largest of the Aran Islands. The 'lady of the house' is Mrs Costello, who sleeps nights beside the fire in the kitchen. Down through the years, Mrs Costello has received a number of illustrious guests. There have been scholars: ethnologists, archaeologists, anthropologists and philologists. There have been poets too: men like the Englishman Arthur Symons, who came here in 1896 in the company of Ireland's poet-genius William Butler Yeats. Yeats insists that Synge is here on his recommendation: 'I said, "Give up Paris . . . . Go to the Aran Islands."' But Yeats remembers this in hindsight. Sometimes Yeats has a creative memory; sometimes Yeats believes his own myths.

Be that as it may, John Millington Synge is here in Aran. It is the evening of 10 May and he is sitting in his room on the first floor of the Atlantic Hotel. There is a public house below and, through the cracked panes of glass in his window, Synge is listening to the talk of the men who come from the harbour and enter Mrs Costello's premises. He understands little of it; the living Gaelic the men speak bears only a passing resemblance to the moribund Irish language he studied in Trinity College, Dublin. If Synge is to live, as Yeats put it, 'as if you were one of the people themselves', he must first learn the language of Aran; he must have a good tutor. Mrs Costello knows the very man: Old Mourteen. When dusk falls, Synge hears a shuffling on the stairs; it is the promised teacher. He is delighted to recognize the half-blind man he has spoken to this morning.

1

Synge sits over a turf fire in his room. The rain and mist, which have been his constant companions since leaving Galway some twelve hours ago, still shroud Inishmore. Old Mourteen warms himself on a stool on the other side of the hearth, and talks. He has been, he assures Synge, an intimate of many of Mrs Costello's distinguished guests. There was William Wilde, surgeon, eccentric, Renaissance man, and the father of Oscar Wilde, called—not without some justification, given his attitude to hygiene—'the dirtiest man in Dublin'; George Petrie, a brilliant fellow-antiquarian, was with him; there was the German ethnologist, Franz N. Finck, author of *Die Araner Mundart*, to whom Old Mourteen taught 'the Gaelic'.

Mourteen's English is odd; it is the fossil remains of the language spoken by the soldiers of Oliver Cromwell, who had a garrison in Aran in the mid-seventeenth century; the fossil remains are based on a rich substratum of Gaelic syntax. Mourteen tells his young visitor some of the stories of Aran. Synge will recollect this first evening in *The Aran Islands*:

> As we talked he sat huddled together over the fire, shaking and blind, yet his face was indescribably pliant, lighting up with an ecstasy of humour when he told me of anything that had a point of wit or malice, and growing sombre and desolate again when he spoke of religion or the fairies.

Yeats was right: the fairies are an intrinsic part of the islanders' lives. They are real; centuries of Christianity have failed to dislodge them from their homes beneath the pagan, Bronze Age forts. Some say they are the Fir Bolg, that semi-mythical race of men who were defeated by the warrior-magicians, the Tuatha Dé Danann, at Mag Tuired in County Sligo. The Fir Bolg went, literally, underground; it is a brave man, Synge learns, who will visit a *dún* or fairy fort after nightfall.

But John Synge has not come to Aran to hunt fairies. His interests are earthy: it is the flesh-and-blood existence of the islanders that has brought him here to these lonely lumps of limestone in Galway Bay. Morning finds Synge striding out along the only good road of Inishmore. He is a strong walker and can walk for hours without tiring, despite his sickly constitution.

Yet to look at him, no islander would imagine that John Synge at twenty-seven was anything but healthy. In her introduction to the first volume of the *Letters of John Millington Synge*, Ann Saddlemyer gives us this description: 'He was a strong, well-built man, muscular, with broad shoulders, standing five feet eight or nine inches tall and carrying his large, finely shaped head upright . . . . The nervous and virile face was pale beneath his summer tan, the cheeks rather drawn through constant illness; it was not a handsome face, but singularly expressive and sometimes almost sad. His light hazel eyes, at once smoky and kindling, gazed directly and frankly.'

On seeing Synge hatless, however, an observant islander would notice the black wig that he wears—a wig made from his own hair, which began to fall out last year, and has not yet grown back fully. The hair-loss was concomitant with a swelling that appeared on the side of his neck. They removed the swelling, but not the cause: Synge is dying slowly of cancer, of Hodgkin's disease.

The people of Aran stare at this unusual visitor; the children cluster around him. Word has gone out that Synge, like Yeats, Symons and the others, is a Protestant, a member of the land-owning classes—the old enemy, in fact. 'Synge, is it?' they whisper, for they are remembering another Synge. He too was a Protestant, and he came to Aran to convert the islanders.

John's uncle, the Reverend Alexander H. Synge, landed at Kilronan in the summer of 1851, soon after the end of the Famine, the Great Hunger that had decimated the population of the West of Ireland. Because of their isolation, however, the islands had been spared the full brunt of the devastation that the Famine had wrought on the mainland.

Alexander Synge was far from impressed by what he saw there: 'Here I am Lord of all I survey,' he wrote to his brother Edward, '—surrounded with dirt & ignorance . . . it is a very wretched Island . . . the soil very scanty almost all barren rock . . . . I get on with the people so far very well but how it will be when we begin to attack their bad ways and religion etc. I don't know.'

Reverend Synge lost little time. Offended by the islanders playing handball on the sabbath, he 'attacked them very sharply the other Sunday & the next Monday [and] went to them and spoke about it'. The next day, the parish priest began demolishing the wall used by the ball-players, 'though the rascal had seen them playing there a hundred times before'.

The following summer, Alexander Synge decided to augment his income by entering the fishing trade. He bought a motor-yacht, crewed it with three men and a boy, and proceeded to trawl in Galway Bay in direct competition with the islanders. He met with opposition from a fleet of boats from the Claddagh area of Galway city, whose crews attacked the Synge vessel with spears and stones. Until April 1853, the missionary fought a running sea battle with the Galway fishermen, once having occasion to fire a pistol above their heads. The matter was resolved at the end of July with the arrest of the fishermen, whom the Reverend Synge asked to be pardoned for their crimes against his person. He returned to Dublin some months later.

More than forty years on, John Synge moves among the islanders. But, rather than attempting to convert the people to his ways, he seems more intent on adapting his to theirs. He greets them in his halting Gaelic, transferring to English when the conversation goes beyond the pleasantries and chit-chat of the commonplace. All those he meets—men, women and children—are eager to talk. The farther Synge travels from Kilronan, the more unsure their English becomes. It is not the brogue of Galway; it is something 'foreign'.

II

See Synge lying in the grass near Killeany. There is not much grass on the island of Inishmore. Nor are there trees, turf or good soil; what little there is has been strewn on a shallow bed of seaweed, carried up on strong backs from the ocean. The wheel is used mainly for spinning in Aran;

burdens are carried by beasts, and men and women. In the summer they ferry the beasts northwards across the bay to Connemara, where the grass is marginally lusher and where the animals can fatten themselves against the harsh Aran winters. With his back to the sand dunes, Synge looks across the calm waters, past the lighthouse on Oileán na Tuí—Straw Island—to the distant hills of County Galway. He sees a small fishing boat, a hooker, bringing turf back from Connemara to fuelless Aran. Why would anyone choose to live in such a desolate place, when Bronze Age Ireland supported a population whose total would scarcely have exceeded that of Galway city? Were the ancestors of the islanders driven here, to the last landfall before America, by enemies who held the mainland; was the *dún* their final defence?

Synge, however, is not interested in the antiquities of Inishmore; he has shed this passion as he has shed so many others. All the same, he marvels at the proliferation of beehive huts among the limestone; the lonely retreats of the missionary monks of St Enda and others, those scores of holy men who earned for the islands their proud epithet Árainn na Naomh, Aran of the Saints. He sees the ruins of churches, oratories, monastic settlements, scattered among the boulders, loose stone walls, Bronze Age burial mounds and forts—the debris of this charnel-house of the Christian centuries.

One sacred place in particular holds his interest when Old Mourteen remarks on it. It is a holy well, close to a ruined church which bears the odd name of Teampall an Cheathrar Álainn, the Temple of the Four Beautiful Persons. As Synge and his half-blind guide sit staring into the well, an old man joins them. His is a strange story:

'A woman of Sligo had a son who was born blind, and one night she dreamed that she saw an island with a blessed well in it that could cure her son. She told her dream in the morning, and an old man said it was of Aran she was after dreaming.

'She brought her son down by the coast of Galway,

and came out in a curagh, and landed below where you see a bit of a cove.

'She walked up then to the house of my father—God rest his soul—and she told them what she was looking for.

'My father said that there was a well like what she had dreamed of, and that he would send a boy along with her to show her the way.

'"There's no need, at all," said she; "haven't I seen it all in my dream?" 'Then she went out with the child and walked up to this well, and she kneeled down and began saying her prayers. Then she put her hand out for the water, and put it on his eyes, and the moment it touched him he called out: "O mother, look at the pretty flowers!"'

That evening, Synge returns to his room in the Atlantic Hotel and records, as faithfully as he can, the story of the holy well of the four saints. The words are important, the words the old man used; they are perhaps more important than the story itself, which is, Synge has to admit, no better or worse than the anecdotes and folk-tales he has heard thus far on Inishmore. He reads his own poor version of the tale; it is not quite as the old man told it. Next time he will do better.

For Synge has stumbled onto something that has eluded him from the time he decided to shed yet another interest—music—and turn instead to writing. He thumbs through his old notebooks, making a mental check-list of those items that merit revision: poems complete, poems unfinished; snatches of dialogue meant for the stage; drafts of ideas; rough notes; a plan for a play, and the beginning of a novel, attempted in Würzburg, Germany, in 1894. There are fragments intended for a piece he has called *Vita Vecchia*, a veiled autobiography; some is prose, some poetry:

> I fled from all the wilderness of cities,
> And nature's choristers my art saluted,
> Chanting aloud to me their tunes and ditties
> And to my silent songs like joys imputed . . . .

It will do. He may revise it eventually. But Synge has heard, from
the moment he stepped onto the pier at Kilronan, other choristers
of nature. As each day on Inishmore passes, he hears more of their
song. He carries his notebook with him on his daily tramps and, as
the sea-birds screech above the Atlantic breakers, sits in the May-
time sun and jots down from memory passages of island speech.
The notebook swells.

He is not the only visitor enjoying Mrs Costello's hospitality
this summer. Returning to his hotel, Synge falls into conversation
with Mr Redmond, a Galway teacher with a passion for Aran. The
talk turns, as usual, to the beauty and strangeness of the islands.
What a shame, Synge remarks, that he had not thought to bring a
camera. Redmond arranges for his own to be brought over from
the mainland; it is Synge's for a good price. His nephew, Edward
Stephens, describes the camera, a small Lancaster hand model:

> It was an ingeniously designed instrument, beautifully
> made of polished mahogany and carried in a black leather
> jacket in which eye-holes were cut . . . for the lens and
> view-finders. When fully loaded, it held twelve quarter-
> plates, which were moved from one compartment into
> another—and when exposed, into another—by different
> mechanisms. It was heavy and conspicuous . . . .

Heavy or not, one cannot hide behind a camera; most certainly not
in 1898 when one is moving among a community for whom a
wheeled vehicle is a luxury, a community that calls all allochtho-
nous people *strainséirí*—strangers—even those who hail from the
relative closeness of Galway. And Synge is a shy man. Nevertheless,
he loads his twelve quarter-plates and makes his way down to the
harbour, there to join the women awaiting the steamer from the
mainland.

The women! Synge is captivated by the women of Aran. He is
struck by the 'strange beauty' of the tall girls. They are all dressed
much the same, in plaid shawls and petticoats of red or rose mad-
der, their brown feet shod in pampooties—moccasins of calfskin
which have to be wetted before they can be worn—footwear ideally

suited to clambering over the slick green stones of the shore, tough enough to challenge the fossil-encrusted limestone. The women cluster in groups against the pier wall, black eyes gazing out from behind the folds of shawls. Conspicuous behind the conspicuous camera, Synge removes the lenscap:

> I have noticed many beautiful girls whose long luxuriant lashes lend a shade to wistful eyes. They are amused to watch while I work my camera and observe keenly on whom I happen to light . . . . All the unoccupied women have thrown their shawls or petticoats over their heads and come down to sit in beautiful groups along the sea-wall and watch what goes on . . . . I am so much a stranger I cannot dare under the attention I excite to gaze as I would wish at a beautiful oval face that looks from a brown shawl near me . . . .

The men of Aran, in their flannel shirts, tam-o'-shanters and pampooties, do no more than 'harmonize with the limestone and the blue-grey' of their surroundings. It is the women who hold Synge's attention—in particular, a girl with a lovely oval face. He will meet her again:

> I saw suddenly the beautiful girl I had noticed on the pier, and her face came with me all day among the rocks. She is madonna-like, yet has a rapt majesty as far from easy exaltation as from the maternal comeliness of Raphael's later style . . . . The expression of her eyes is so overwhelmingly beautiful that I remember no single quality of her colour.

John Synge, aged twenty-seven, is still a virgin. To be sure, he has known love in the past; indeed, he has courted several eminently suitable girls of his own class. But Synge is a poor man; he has little to offer a wife in temporal terms. In spiritual terms he can offer even less: Synge has rejected the religion of his ancestors; no self-respecting young woman could think of marrying a self-declared agnostic. It would be so easy to acquiesce, to make a pretence of

accepting a belief in a narrow-minded and discriminating deity.
Synge has chosen the difficult path: the road that has led him, by
way of Wicklow and Würzburg, via Paris and Rome, to this desolate
place. He has chosen to worship at a wilder altar.

But Synge does not yet know how wild Aran can be. He is seeing the islands in summer, when the fish are plentiful and there is
sometimes a hunk of mutton boiling alongside the potatoes. He
observes, almost as a by-the-way, that the steamer from Galway
brings Indian meal 'as relief'. Has he looked within the poorest of
the poor cottages and seen the badly nourished children who may
not survive the winter? Does he know yet of the sicknesses that will
carry off the old and frail when no doctor from the mainland dares
hazard a winter crossing? Synge sees the benign face of Aran in the
clement season; he will never know at first hand how cruel the
islands can be in winter, when the sea claims its right to Aran's
young men. He does not yet know that his flight to this western
outpost of European civilization will reveal to him the other, dark-
er face of nature. The wilder altar at which the islanders worship is
one even Yeats dared not envisage. The God of Aran is one Synge
already knows: he has learned of him at his mother's knee, in the
safety of a sequestered suburban drawing-room. How distant, how
aloof the God seemed then. J. M. Synge, 'a man of ostensibly
mediocre talent', failed suitor, failed poet, 'a complete failure, in
fact', is to meet the God of Aran. In doing so, he will release the
genie of creation in himself.

III

In the closing years of the twentieth century, Dublin has
spread its urban sprawl far south of Rathfarnham. The green
of neighbouring Bushy Park and the old demesne of
Rathfarnham Castle still evoke the countryside, but, apart
from the latter, the area has become an indifferent, though prosperous, suburb of south Dublin. When Edmund John Millington
Synge was born here on 16 April 1871, his parents' home, lying

close to the castle, was one of a small group of rural dwellings, far
from the bustle and the smoke of the city.

Newtown Villas were built on a hill overlooking the river
Dodder. Kingstown (it would, in time, revert to its ancient Gaelic
name of Dún Laoghaire) lay to the east, and the gently rounded
hills of Wicklow were clearly visible to the south. Behind these hills
stood Glanmore Castle, ancestral home of the Synges.

The big house had been in the family from the late eighteenth century, and the accompanying estate had been developed
by J. M. Synge's great-grandfather Francis. In the early part of the
nineteenth century the property had occupied 4,000 acres of north
County Wicklow. Francis had let much of the land to tenant farmers, retaining some 1,800 acres for his own use. The rents paid by
the tenants, together with those on properties held in Dublin,
made Francis Synge one of Wicklow's wealthier landowners. He
sent his eldest son John to be educated in England, so that the
young man would be better capable of running the estates. John
was both an evangelist and a practitioner of Johann Pestalozzi's system of education. In order to answer both these callings, he
returned to Wicklow, bringing with him a printing press. He married a wealthy heiress, Isabella Hamilton, and his father made over
one of the estates to him. Soon, however, Isabella fell into bad
health and they moved to the more clement climate of Devon. The
choice was not an arbitrary one: John Synge was a member of the
Brethren (later to become the Plymouth Brethren), a religious
community formed in Dublin in the late 1820s. At the time of his
removal to Devon, the sect had gained in strength there, and John
Synge wished to play an active role in their ministry.

Isabella's health deteriorated rapidly and she died in 1830.
When Francis Synge passed away the following year, John returned
to Wicklow with his seven children and took possession of
Glanmore. He married Fanny Steele, the sister of his brother's
wife, who, like Isabella, gave birth to seven children.

John Synge devoted much energy to the family seat, making
many improvements to the beautiful pleasure grounds laid out by
his father. He borrowed freely for this and other ventures; reckless-

ly, it seems, because in 1845 he was declared bankrupt. He died that same year, leaving the estate and its debts to his eldest son, Francis, who managed to salvage both Glanmore Castle and a considerable portion of the estate. The need to earn their own living forced the younger sons into professional life. One of them, Alexander, chose the Church; another, John Hatch, became a barrister, and in 1856 married Kathleen Traill, the eighteen-year-old daughter of Dr Robert Traill, rector of Schull, Co. Cork. John and Kathleen lived first in Dublin, and six children were born to the couple in Hatch Street, of whom only three—Robert, Edward and Annie Isabella—survived infancy. In or about 1865, the Synges moved to Newtown Villas, where a third son, Samuel, was born, four years before Kathleen gave birth to her last child, John Millington Synge.

If the Synge family was a pious one—it had already produced five bishops and an archbishop in the eighteenth century—then that of John's mother, the Traills, was considerably more so. They were of northern Irish Protestant stock, and the family's antipathy towards 'popery' was extreme. Dr Traill, John's maternal grandfather, was a zealous evangelist who waged war against the 'thousand forms of wickedness' of the Roman Catholic Church. So great was this zeal that he had difficulty obtaining a living from his church superiors; the rectory in Schull was one of the few opportunities open to him. He died there of fever during the Famine years and his widow moved with her children to Blackrock, to the south of Dublin, in 1848.

John Synge's mother had grown up in an unusually suffocating and insular family circle. Such was the piety of Dr Traill's widow that any association with friends or neighbours whose Protestantism differed even marginally from hers was frowned upon. Her daughter Kathleen was nurtured on prayer and Bible studies; she was inculcated with an almost Manichaean view of the world, believing it to be ruled by the Devil until the Second Advent, after which time Satan would be chained for a millennium and Christ would rule the earth from Jerusalem. Much emphasis was placed on salvation, and precisely who should be lost and who

11

should be saved was the subject of frequent debate. The sabbath was stringently observed; books other than those which met with the approval of the Church were absent from the house; children were to be 'seen but not heard'. Some of the Protestant Ascendancy of the time lived the uneasy life of a garrison community in Ireland. Mrs Traill and her children found themselves to be a garrison *within* the garrison: their evangelical code condemned them to live in a society of which they could never be a part. They were 'saints' in a world of wickedness.

John Millington Synge's father died of smallpox when the child was not quite one year old. The tragedy was to have far-reaching consequences for his life; he would grow to adulthood in a milieu dominated by two women whose views were all but identical: Kathleen Synge and her mother, Mrs Traill. But John's enquiring mind was to cast doubt on much of what they held dear:

> When I was about fourteen I obtained a book of Darwin's. It opened in my hands at a passage where he asks how can we explain the similarity between a man's hand and a bird's or bat's wing except by evolution. I flung the book aside and rushed out into the open air—it was summer and we were in the country—the sky seemed to have lost its blue and the grass its green. I lay down and writhed in an agony of doubt. My studies showed me the force of what I read, [and] the more I put it from me the more it rushed back with new instances and power. Till then I had never doubted and never conceived that a sane and wise man or boy could doubt. I had of course heard of atheists but as vague monsters that I was unable to realize. It seemed that I was become in a moment the playfellow of Judas. Incest and parricide were but a consequence of the idea that possessed me.

This passage is from Synge's *Autobiography*, a short work written—and revised several times—between 1896 and 1898. Charles Darwin's *On the Origin of Species* was one of several books of natural history he had brought to the country for his summer reading.

Synge subsequently smuggled it out of his mother's home; he recognized 'perfidy' when he saw it. But the seeds of doubt had been
sown, and, by the time he was sixteen or seventeen, he had, as he
puts it, 'renounced Christianity after a good deal of wobbling,
although I do not think I avowed my decision quite so soon'.

Clearly, Synge's chancing on Darwin's theory of evolution
upset him a great deal, as it would any boy brought up in the belief
that man is a creature infinitely superior to, and utterly different
from, the rest of the animal kingdom. And yet it is not Synge's vis-
ceral reaction that intrigues, but the conclusions he drew from his
discovery, when his writhing in agony had subsided. He found himself allied with Judas, the betrayer of Christ. This is understandable
too—Darwin himself was accused of as much, and more. But what
to make of that last sentence: 'Incest and parricide were but a consequence of the idea that possessed me'? Incest is defined as sexual
intercourse with a member of one's immediate family; parricide is
the act of murdering a parent or a near relative; both are the most
dreadful crimes possible in relation to one's kin. It is interesting to
note that Synge wrote these lines the year he visited Aran for the
first time, where he heard the story of a young man who had slain
his father on the mainland and had been hidden by the islanders
until he could make his escape. Synge could have used the term
'patricide' which, in the circumstances, might have been more per-
spicuous. But he had never known his own father and so it seems
unlikely that he could have borne either a conscious or unconscious animosity towards him. When John Synge chose the path of
agnosticism, he was rebelling instead against the surviving members of his family, and he was hurting his mother in the most pec-
cant way possible: he was rejecting her deity.

Synge never lost his belief in God; rather, he sought the
Creator in places where his family would not have cared to look.
His mother's God was a vengeful one, a God who brooked no back-
sliding or apostasy. The punishment meted out to the 'wicked' was
impressed on Synge at an early age. 'One night', he recalls in his
Autobiography, 'I thought I was irretrievably damned and cried
myself to sleep in vain yet terrified efforts to form a conception of

eternal pain.' He was, by his own admission, 'a painfully timid' boy and thought that 'the well-meant but extraordinary cruelty of introducing the idea of Hell into the imagination of a nervous child has probably caused more misery than many customs that the same people send missionaries to eradicate.'

Unlike his mother, John Synge was not prepared to wait for the Second Coming, when the glory of God on earth would be made manifest. He went out into the world beyond the family drawing-room with its eschatological books and its narrow code of conduct. He wished to discover a more benign God, one closer to man, and one he could understand. Science, Synge decided, might hold the answers he was seeking.

IV

S ynge's dilemma, his dissatisfaction with conventional religion, was in keeping with the *Zeitgeist* of the century's latter years. In 1885, two twenty-year-olds—W. B. Yeats and his friend Charles Johnston—established the Dublin Hermetic Society; five years later, in London, Yeats became a member of the Hermetic Order of the Golden Dawn. The latter was a secret society founded by Freemasons and theosophers with the intention of engaging in practical work in the realms of Higher Magic. They sought to bring together the magical traditions of East and West, under the aegis of Hermes Trismegistos, the Greek messenger of the gods and teacher of mankind. Yeats and his associates—the infamous Aleister Crowley was numbered among them—made much use of Rosicrucianism, the tarot, and the cabbala.

The Golden Dawn and similar societies emerged towards the zenith of the Victorian age, when many young men of Synge's class had begun to question the values and ethics of their elders. The British Empire had grown mighty on the fruits of the Industrial Revolution; vast fortunes had been made through commerce and trade—not least of which was the sordid trade in human beings. London had become the richest and most powerful city in the world. Made blasé by the trappings of wealth, ostentatiously flaunt-ed, some offspring of the successful industrialists turned away from Mammon. They did not, however, revert to the humdrum religion of the indigenous Christian Church, but instead embraced more exotic beliefs. Buddhism came from the Orient, often in the per-sonages of holy men of India, who were the toast of theosophical circles like that of Madame Blavatsky. (One such philosopher, the Bengali Brahmin, Babu Mohini Chatterjee, visited Dublin in 1886 and made a lasting impression on the young W. B. Yeats.) Numer-ology and astrology came from the Near East, and there were those who claimed to have found evidence of an advanced occult system buried in the ruins of ancient Egypt. Taken together, these mys-tery-filled traditions made a pot-pourri that was irresistible to the jaded palates of the young. W. B. Yeats, though born in Dublin, spent much of his life in the London of the cabbalists MacGregor Mathers, Annie Horniman, Alan Bennett and others; when he met Synge in Paris on 21 December 1896, the poet, at thirty-one, had assimilated an impressive knowledge of magic, mysticism and mythology.

But Yeats had returned to the Irish mythological canon for his finest inspiration. He had read William Allingham, who stimulated his interest in the fairies, and Samuel Ferguson, whom he called 'the greatest modern poet Ireland has produced'; Ferguson's work served to introduce Yeats to the spirit of Celtic Ireland. His friend-ship with the Fenian John O'Leary encouraged him to read the poetry of the nationalists—J. J. Callanan, E. R. Walsh, Thomas Davis and James Clarence Mangan—whose work was concerned with a more immediate and vital Irish past. Their sentiments coaxed the young poet away from the classical themes of his early verse: sphinx-es atop Mediterranean rocks were replaced by Irish lake isles and home-grown sprites and heroes. He had unearthed a glorious past about which few of his Anglo-Irish contemporaries were aware, and his aim was to 'unite the radical truths of Christianity to those of a more ancient world'. Yeats had looked for poetic inspiration both in his own dreams and among the traditions of other nations, and had discovered it almost on his doorstep. He had found it at a time when Ireland stood on the brink of acquiring, at last, her own cultural as well as political identity. Yeats felt that the one was a prerequisite of the other, but he knew that he alone could not effect the intellectual awakening of his people to their past. He knew, too, that the nuts-and-bolts of political activism could best be entrusted to the likes of Maud Gonne, but he also needed other poetic voices that would complement his own. 'I am always ransacking Ireland', he wrote in 1895 to Olivia Shakespear, 'for people to set writing at Irish things.' Yeats was attempting to stimulate the Celtic muse in Eva, youngest daughter of the Gore-Booths of Lissadell, a Big House outside Sligo. 'She does not know', he went on to Mrs Shakespear, 'that she is the last victim.'

She was not. That honour went to J. M. Synge.

William Butler Yeats had been in Paris for some time in the winter of 1896 before he learned that another Irishman was staying at the Hôtel Corneille. The poet had spent that summer in the West of Ireland with his friend Arthur Symons and they had visited Aran; he had also met Augusta, Lady Gregory for the first time. Maud Gonne was lately returned from a lecture tour of the United States, where she had used her considerable powers of oratory to fuel transatlantic support for the cause of Irish home rule. Yeats had joined the Irish Republican Brotherhood (the forerunner of the IRA) *circa* 1886, but he and Maud Gonne resigned their memberships shortly after the outbreak of the Boer War. When Synge met Yeats, the poet and Maud Gonne were recruiting members for a new endeavour, *L'Association Irlandaise*, the Paris branch of the New Ireland Society, whose immediate aim was to draw attention to the Irish land struggle; the ultimate goal was home rule. In a preface to *The Well of the Saints*, Yeats records the meeting:

> Six years ago I was staying in a students' hotel in the Latin Quarter, and somebody, whose name I cannot recollect, introduced me to an Irishman, who, even poorer than myself, had taken a room at the top of the house. It was

J. M. Synge, and I, who thought I knew the name of every Irishman who was working at literature, had never heard of him. He was a graduate of Trinity College, Dublin, too, and Trinity College does not, as a rule, produce artistic minds. He told me that he had been living in France and Germany, reading French and German literature, and that he wished to become a writer. He had, however, nothing to show but one or two poems and impressionistic essays, full of that kind of morbidity that has its root in too much brooding over methods of expression, and ways of looking upon life, which come, not out of life, but out of literature, images reflected from mirror to mirror. He had wandered among people whose life is as picturesque as the Middle Ages, playing his fiddle to Italian sailors, and listening to stories in Bavarian woods, but life had cast no light into his writings. He had learned Irish years ago, but had begun to forget it, for the only language that interested him was that conventional language of modern poetry which has begun to make us all weary. I was very weary of it, for I had finished *The Secret Rose*, and felt how it had separated my imagination from life, sending my Red Hanrahan, who should have trodden the same roads with myself, into some undiscoverable country.

If Yeats had, as he insisted, urged Synge to visit Aran in the course of this meeting, his words seem to have had little immediate effect: almost eighteen months were to pass before Synge made that first, fateful voyage. What is certain is that Synge's interest in primitive societies quickened during the following months.

Thinking that his future lay in literary criticism, he had enrolled for a series of lectures at the Sorbonne in the autumn of 1896, in order to study Petrarch and French literature. In April 1897, however, Synge attended a lecture given by the folklorist Anatole Le Braz, several of whose books on life in Brittany he had already read. The similarities between Breton life and that in the West of Ireland were striking, but Synge was not yet ready to commit himself to writing about his own country. Instead, he delved deeper into the works of Breton writers like Pierre Loti and Ernest Renan, who had highlighted the rapid decay of the language and customs of this Celtic province of France.

That is not to say that Ireland's plight was far from Synge's thoughts. He was one of the first expatriate Irishmen to join Yeats and Gonne in *L'Association Irlandaise*, which was officially inaugurated on 1 January 1897. Synge threw himself with a will into the work of the organization.

Its membership was small in Synge's time; the society was hardly more than a coterie of friends. There were Yeats and Maud Gonne; Yeats's old mentor John O'Leary; Arthur Lynch, the Paris correspondent of the *Daily Mail*, and his wife; John Synge, and Stephen MacKenna, a man one year Synge's junior, who was to remain a lifelong friend and confidant.

When Synge moved, on 29 December 1896, from the Hôtel Corneille to lodgings in rue Léopold-Robert, MacKenna was living on the top floor of a house in the nearby rue d'Assas. Near starvation himself, he was generously sharing his room, rent free, with a penniless Armenian scientist. Stephen MacKenna was, by all accounts, a colourful figure. Son of a Catholic British army officer, he had attended school in England and for a short time had entered a religious order. He had subsequently worked for a Dublin bank, and as a reporter for a London newspaper. When Synge befriended him in Paris, he was earning a small stipend as a correspondent for an English Catholic journal, though he was eventually to become an atheist. A brilliant Greek scholar, he devoted some twenty years to translating the *Enneads* of Plotinus.

Stephen MacKenna was a committed socialist; moreover, he shared Maud Gonne's antipathy towards the English. He also had a lively interest in spiritualism. He and Synge were drawn to one another immediately; they had much in common, not least being the almost constant hunger and deprivation which they both endured at the time. But there was more. Before he left Ireland, Synge had read *The Communist Manifesto*, Marx's *Das Kapital*, John Hobson's *Problems of Poverty*, and other books related to socialism, anarchy and the poor; indeed, his mother wrote to John's brother Samuel that he 'has gone back to Paris to study Socialism, and he wants to do good'. MacKenna stimulated this interest, and others close to Synge's heart; they 'talked days and nights through, and mainly on literature and the technique of it'.

MacKenna appears to have been stamped out of the Byron mould: when war broke out in 1897 between Greece and Turkey, he left Paris to fight on the side of the Greeks; however, the conflict had ended before his arrival. Edward Stephens describes an incident in Paris which occurred at the outbreak of the hostilities; it may well have been J. M. Synge's only brush with violence:

> In the month of April, feeling in Paris was running very high about the issues of the war . . . and extreme Irish nationalists were passionate in their support of the Greeks. John, who was drawn into the public excitement by his friends in the Irish League, was nearly knocked unconscious . . . by the police who were laying about them with their batons . . . . He turned very white, but said nothing, and none of the party knew that he had been hit until Stephen MacKenna, when seeing him home, discovered that he was bleeding from the baton wound.

Synge's association with the 'League'—the New Ireland Society—is curious in one respect. As David Greene points out, Synge 'was, after all, an Irish landlord, even if he had partly liberated himself from the convictions which that implied'. Greene is referring to the fact that the young aspiring writer was living off money sent by his mother, part of whose inheritance was some land in County Galway, worked by tenant farmers.

In the event, Synge's association with the Society was short-lived; he resigned on 6 April 1897. According to Yeats, he disapproved of the 'Fenian turn' Maud Gonne gave the movement, and believed that 'England would only do Ireland right when she felt herself to be safe'. Maud Gonne's solution to the 'Irish Question' was a bombing campaign in England, which must have horrified Synge, a convinced pacifist.

So his association with Yeats was not—ostensibly at least—to be a political one, but was to concern itself with Irish literature and Celtic mysticism.

V

Soon after their first meeting, Synge began reading Yeats's work. At the same time, he was exploring the esoteric worlds into which the elder poet's membership of the Golden Dawn had led him. One of Yeats's reasons for visiting Paris that year was the making of a ritual for an Order of Celtic Mysteries and there seems little doubt that he saw in Synge a future member. He had discovered Castle Rock on Lough Key, Co. Roscommon, and wished to make this a holy sanctuary for the new religion; a religion that would not be rooted in Palestine, but, instead, would unite the perceptions of the spirit with those of the natural beauty of Ireland. Synge was already a passionate lover of nature; now Yeats was to introduce him to magic and to psychic phenomena. In his diary of 19 February 1897, Synge records seeing 'manifestations', but does not elaborate. He was also reading works like Paulam's *Le Nouveau Mysticisme* and the *Proceedings of the Society of Psychical Research*. In a short piece, entitled 'Under Ether', written after an operation he underwent in December 1897, when the swelling on his neck was removed, Synge describes a vision he experienced and the subsequent, heated conversation he had with the surgeons, whom he imagined were mocking him: '"I'm an initiated mystic," I yelled with fury; "I could rend the groundwork of your souls."'

Some time later, he felt the full effects of the ether:

> Another paroxysm of frenzy, and my life seemed to go out in one spiral yell to the unknown.
>
> The next period I remember but vaguely. I seemed to traverse whole epochs of desolation and bliss. All secrets were open before me, and simple as the universe to its God. Now and then something recalled my physical life,

and I smiled at what seemed a moment of sickly infancy. At other times I felt I might return to earth, and laughed aloud to think what a god I should be among men. For there could be no more terror in my life. I was a light, a joy.

This passage would not have appeared out of place in Yeats's *Rosa Alchemica*, with its 'shapes trembling out of existence, folding up into a timeless ecstasy, drifting with half-shut eyes into a sleepy stillness', published in April 1896, the year of Synge's meeting with Yeats. That the subject of psychic phenomena interested Synge greatly can be adduced from a letter Stephen MacKenna sent to him from Paris—Synge had returned to Ireland by this time:

> There is no doubt Paris is the place for these studies—an immense richesse of the literature of the subject from the elementary matter of Magnetism, Hypnotism *etc.* to deepest Magic. I have some rough bibliographical notes made in Paris which I will look up for you. But we must meet and talk this business over much . . . . I have several purely practical works on Magnetism and Hypnotism—Binet and Féré of the Salpetrière, Moll of Nancy, Gregory (1851) of England (with much on clairvoyance by crystal-gazing, *etc.*) and a really good little book—a general, non-selfcommitting study from the *Bibliothèque de Merveilles* (Paris). These I do not send, since they are *applied mysticism*—if mysticism at all—not pure, like the theosophical things. But ask and you shall have . . . .

So Synge was not concerned with 'applied mysticism'. Rather, Yeats and MacKenna had introduced him to an interpretation of things divine that he had failed to find in the family Bible. It was not for want of Mrs Synge's trying.

As the youngest, and frailest, child, Synge was the apple of his mother's eye. She called him Johnnie, and he was a source of concern to her from his early childhood until her death in 1908. She had brought up five children: Robert, Edward, Annie, Samuel and

John. Robert went to his uncle's ranch in Argentina in 1883, not returning to Ireland until 1900; Edward became a land agent and managed the Synge properties in Wicklow and Connacht; Annie married the solicitor Harry Stephens in 1884. Only Samuel and John remained in their mother's home.

It is difficult to say exactly when Synge's religious doubts began to be obvious to his mother, but it may have been soon after he first read Darwin. In any event, Mrs Synge noticed her youngest son's reluctance to accept her faith. Family prayers were said each day in the Synge household, in conjunction with the reading and interpretation of the Gospels. The Synges attended Zion Church in Rathgar, whose curate was possessed of great evangelical zeal. His Bible classes impressed Mrs Synge, and she hoped that these, together with her own scriptural lessons, would encourage John towards the world of Christian belief.

Summers were spent in Greystones, Co. Wicklow, where Mrs Synge could rent houses cheaply. Like John, she loved the out-doors, and they would stay at this seaside resort each year for six-teen years. It was also some twenty kilometres distant from the Synge estate of Glanmore, home of John's Aunt Editha and her hus-band, Major Theodore Webber Gardiner. Known to the Synge chil-dren as 'the Major', he was a member of the Exclusive Plymouth Brethren, a sect which was to cause much distress in John Synge's life.

His mother engaged a tutor for Synge when he was eleven; chronic ill-health had played havoc with his schooling. Spending so much time within the family circle had two very different influ-ences on him. The first concerned religion, and Edward Stephens writes that Mrs Synge

> could not feel certain that other children at school were well brought up and John, while he remained at home, was under the good influence of her household, and had the company of his sister, his brothers, and his cousins.
>
> John received religious instruction from both his mother and his grandmother. They were in complete

accord in carrying on the teaching of the evangelical revival, as it had been preached by the Rev. Dr Traill . . . .

Mrs Synge conducted her household by a rule as strict as that of a religious order and supposed that her children would acquiesce without question. She was very well versed in the doctrine to which she adhered, and could support every tenet by citing scriptural authority. She believed the whole Bible to be inspired and its meaning to be clear to anyone, who read with an open mind and faith in the Holy Ghost.

The second effect of Synge's isolation from schoolfriends was the cultivation of an enquiring mind. Left to himself, and having ample time on his hands, he soon discovered the delights of the countryside near his home. The hills to the south were his goal, and great was his joy when he reached them on foot for the first time. Synge became an avid naturalist and when the Dublin Naturalists Field Club was formed in 1885 he enrolled as one of its youngest members. School subjects were relegated to second place, and he threw himself into the study of the natural world. At the same time, he was reading difficult books on theology. It was a queer mixture for a boy of fourteen.

In the meantime his brother Samuel, while learning to play the concertina, had sparked off in Synge yet another interest: music. He learned to play the violin, an instrument, which, according to Stephens, 'fully aroused his enthusiasm'. In 1887 he persuaded his mother to engage a music tutor: Patrick Griffith, one of Dublin's finest violin teachers. Synge decided that his career lay in music, and others soon recognized his talent. 'Johnnie's ear is wonderfully good now,' his mother wrote, in 1888, to her son Robert in Argentina; 'he hears if the piano is at all out of tune . . . . I have to practise the accompaniments as they are not easy: there are too many sharps and flats.' Mother and son regularly played duets together: she on piano, he on violin. Their collaboration was not altogether satisfactory: Mrs Synge complained that John 'at first

. . . never left with me and he still runs away when he ought to rest, so I have to try and watch him as well as play my own part'.

When he was sixteen Synge sat his entrance examination for Trinity College, Dublin, and was accepted in June 1888. University life did not suit him. His isolation from people of his own age had turned him into a shy boy, who did not mix well with others.

When Synge's grandmother, Mrs Traill, died of bronchitis in 1890, his mother moved her family and servants to Crosthwaite Park in Kingstown, in order to be close to her daughter Annie and son-in-law, Harry Stephens. They had adjoining houses, and some years later a door was made in a dividing wall, so that the families lived on a very intimate footing.

At this time, Synge was pursuing, if rather half-heartedly, his studies at Trinity College; half-heartedly, because a career in music continued to occupy his thoughts. In later life he would say that he regarded his years at university as wasted time, and in some respects they were. But Trinity, that bastion of Ascendancy values, was to influence Synge in a way that would have dismayed the college authorities, had they known it. Synge took Irish. That the language was taught at all at Trinity College is not so surprising as it may seem; it was taken mainly by the sons of clerics, and youths who aspired to the collar—youths who one day would go out to attempt the conversion to Protestantism of the Gaelic speakers of the western areas. It was taught as one of the 'Divinity School subjects', using, as a textbook, a poor and what Synge called 'a crabbed version of the New Testament'. Taking Irish at Trinity had one great advantage for Synge: few of the first-year students sat the special examination; Synge took first prize in June 1892 and was awarded £4. It would be tempting to conclude that the prize money was his motive, were it not for these words of his, written on or about the time of his first visit to Aran:

> Soon after I had relinquished the Kingdom of God I began to take a real interest in the kingdom of Ireland. My politics went round from a vigorous and unreasoning loyalty to a temperate Nationalism. Everything Irish became sacred

24

. . . and had a charm that was neither quite human nor divine, rather perhaps as if I had fallen in love with a goddess, although I had still sense enough not to personify Erin in the patriotic verse I now sought to fabricate. Patriotism gratifies Man's need for adoration and has therefore a peculiar power upon the imaginative sceptic, as we see in France at the present time.

In France, yes. Sentiments such as these could not have been more alien to both the English and the Irish ethos. A soldier or a gentleman did his duty 'for God and country'. Synge chose the one above the other; he chose godless socialism. It was strange baggage to carry to Aran of the Saints.

VI

The curagh is large, one of the largest used in the islands, and four rowers man the oars. Pat MacDonagh pulls strongly, exchanging talk with his passenger. He has heard good reports about this fellow Synge, and on inspection the young man strikes MacDonagh as being a cut above the average ethnologist or folklorist, of whom he has seen a great many these past few years. Synge may have the manners and soft hands of a gentleman from Dublin, but his clothes—apart from his old, worn boots—are those of Aran. He speaks a smattering of Gaelic too, though not yet enough for a satisfying conversation. That will come in time.

The curagh skims over the waves like a bird; it is the lightest craft Synge has ever experienced, but he knows that its timber stringers and ribs and its tarred canvasses are deceptively flimsy. There is no other boat that can challenge so successfully the seas off Aran. His portmanteau, books and camera are safe.

Inishmaan, Middle Island, is poorer than Inishmore. There are no roads, no priests, no doctors or officials of any kind; the modicum of cultivation that has touched Inishmore will keep the poorer sister waiting for some years to come. Synge has chosen well: there is little English spoken on Inishmaan, and that little is even further removed from the brogue of Galway city. Having come to learn Irish, John finds himself relearning his English. The syntax of this English is not that of Dublin; oddly enough, its structure resembles the German in which Synge became fluent during his sojourns in Koblenz and Würzburg. 'For no money at all would I do such a thing,' says a character in an Inishmaan story. 'Für kein Geld auf der Welt würde ich so etwas tun' is the German equivalent. This brand of English, Synge decides, is, well . . . dramatic.

Synge has chosen his new accommodation well, too. Pat MacDonagh's home is a three-bedroomed cottage, the biggest house on Inishmaan. It is also the post office and, as such, a favourite meeting-place for the islanders. Old and young, men and women, come to sit in groups beside the kitchen fire. Their Gaelic is rapid and difficult to follow, but Synge listens with an attentive ear, satisfied with picking up a word now and then, delighted by the sounds and cadences; content and meaning shall reveal themselves in due course. Synge will not learn much Irish during this summer of 1898, despite the tutorial efforts of Pat MacDonagh's son Martin. At the end of his visit, Synge confesses that his working knowledge of the language does not carry him 'beyond a few comments on the weather and the island'.

But Synge learns other things on Inishmaan, through the medium of the quaint English of the storytellers, prince among whom is old Pat Dirane. His English is excellent; he once spent some months in England. Synge listens, utterly fascinated, as Dirane repeats a story he is fond of telling. Dirane, it seems, was walking from Dublin to Galway when he took shelter for the night in a house whose master had just died. The corpse lay on the table; candles burned in the room. The woman offered Dirane a drink and a bed for the night and left the house, saying that she wished to inform the neighbours of her husband's death. When she had gone, the 'dead' man opened his eyes and told Dirane that he was feigning death in order to catch his 'bad wife' red-handed with her young lover; he asked Dirane to assist him in the deception.

Presently the wife returned in the company of her lover. She gave him tea and told him to lie down in the bedroom. Some minutes later, she stood up and informed Dirane that she was going to fetch a candle. When she did not return, her husband got up off the table and he and Dirane entered the bedroom, to find the wife and her sweetheart *in flagrante delicto,* whereupon the 'corpse' struck the lover on the head with his stick, delivering what was probably a fatal blow.

Synge is transfixed. The story resembles that of the Widow of Ephesus, written by the Roman satirist Petronius in the first century AD. Another story follows. Synge listens raptly. Again its plot strikes a familiar chord; he is hearing a retelling of *The Merchant of Venice.* 'It gave me', he notes, 'a strange feeling of wonder to hear this illiterate native of a wet rock in the Atlantic telling a story that is so full of European associations.'

English used with near-Germanic syntax; Shakespeare and Petronius transposed to an Irish setting . . . . What manner of place is Aran? The notebook swells further.

Synge and Dirane are inseparable. Each day, the old storyteller accompanies the young visitor on his walks around the island. The tales come continually. Dirane is keen to tell of the fairies; Synge would prefer him to repeat the tale of the fugitive, the father-killer.

'Here', says Dirane, as they sit in the sunshine on the walls of Dún Conor, the circular fort that overlooks the MacDonagh house, 'is where the young man was hidden from the peelers.' Dirane is pointing to a dark hole under the unmortared stones of the Bronze Age keep.

The young Connacht man, according to Dirane, killed his father with the blow of a spade and fled to Inishmaan, to throw himself 'on the mercy of some of the natives with whom he was said to be related'. They kept him safe for weeks, 'though the police came and searched for him, and he could hear their boots grinding on the stones above his head. In spite of a reward which was offered, the island was incorruptible, and after much trouble the man was safely shipped to America.' Yet another curious story; yet more grist for the mill that is turning in Synge's head.

He divides his time between listening to Dirane and sitting alone in the sun, watching the gulls and the sea, brooding. Now he knows for certain that he has stumbled on something utterly out of the ordinary. He has even come within the sphere of influence of the God of Aran. An old woman of the island has died, and Synge hears, for the first time, the 'keen' of the Aran women. Unearthly, other-worldly, foreign; it owes more to Arabia than to the British Isles.

But Synge is still not wholly aware of the nature of what he has found in Aran. The notebook is filled, the mind pregnant with images and impressions, which must be gone over carefully and classified, compartmentalized. 'Am I not leaving in Inishmaan', he writes as he prepares for the homeward journey towards the end of June, 'spiritual treasure unexplored whose presence is a great magnet to my soul? In this ocean alone is not every symbol of the cosmos?'

Synge is right on both counts. He does not know it yet, but already these first weeks in Aran have given him the plots of one half of what will one day be the Synge dramatic canon: his notebook contains the seeds of *The Well of the Saints*, *In the Shadow of the Glen* and *The Playboy of the Western World*.

Troika

I

Gort is a sleepy railway stop, a little market town some distance to the south-east of Galway. It is close to Coole Park, home of Augusta, Lady Gregory. Synge's train is somewhat late, but no matter: it is a fine summer morning, this historic morning of 27 June 1898. It is historic because it will bring together, for the first time, the troika who will decide the course of Irish drama.

Synge is delighted—and, it must be said, a little flattered too—to have received Yeats's letter, inviting him to visit Coole on his way back to Dublin. 'Lady Gregory asks me to ask you here for a day or two,' the letter reads, but Synge suspects that the invitation has come from Yeats himself. It is all part of Yeats's grand design.

Lady Gregory has driven personally in her phaeton to meet Synge. That is how Lady Gregory is: she is a practical, expeditious woman. She recognizes Synge at once as he steps down from the train; she has seen him the previous month. He is intensely bronzed, a picture of health; his cheeks appear less drawn. Aran has clearly agreed with him. He carries the old, heavy portmanteau with ease; Lady Gregory summons the station's porter to convey Synge's belongings to the carriage. She has got over her resentment towards him. Perhaps resentment is too strong a word. Lady Gregory too was on Inishmore when Synge had come in May. She assumed that he was doing as she was—'gathering folk-lore and talking to the people'. Lady Gregory is possessive of 'her' County Galway and was dismayed to discover another 'outsider' engaged in similar garnering. She felt angry, and 'jealous of not being alone on the island among the fishers and sea-weed gatherers'.

Yeats, however, has been keeping an eye on Synge—they have

29

talked in London since their Paris meeting and have kept up a correspondence. Yeats has persuaded Lady Gregory of the wisdom of making an ally of this man; they may have need of him in the taxing times to come. The Irish Literary Renaissance is in its seminal phase; Yeats and Lady Gregory alone, despite their formidable intellects, are not strong enough to awaken Ireland's Thespian psyche. They need a man such as Synge to complete the troika. And here is something curious. How does Yeats know that Synge is the man Yeats thinks he is? He had read only Synge's 'one or two poems and impressionistic essays' when the two men were in Paris. He was not too impressed by what he read, but evidently he saw something in Synge himself: the magma that seethes beneath the crust and mantle of this 'drifting, silent man, full of hidden passion'. Did Yeats foresee then 'the rushing up of the buried fire, an explosion of all that had been denied and refused', the smouldering of genius about to be made manifest?

The road from Gort to Coole backtracks on the railway Synge has taken from Galway. The carriage makes a right turn and, abruptly, the trotting horse is pulling its charges through a tunnel of green. Ilex trees flanking the long avenue stretch up and touch overhead, the sunlight through their leaves dappling the horse's back and flanks. Synge looks ahead, saying little. All the same, Lady Gregory, a widow of forty-six, finds herself warming to this young man; now that she has met him, there is no longer resentment. She likes men like Synge, men who listen, men who share her love of the countryside.

And Coole Park is lovely, 'a Sleeping Beauty palace in a thick forest'. Augusta is devoted to her County Galway home. 'There has always been', she says, 'a certain distinction about Coole.' Her fondness for the place, after the birth of her son Robert, 'has grown through the . . . years of widowed life, when the woods especially became my occupation and delight'.

There are seven woods at Coole, each bearing a different name. The names alone are poetry, irresistible to Yeats: Shan-Walla, Kyle-dortha, Kyle-na-no, Pairc-na-lee, Pairc-na-carraig, Pairc-na-tarav, Inchy. There is the lake, too, whose reeded shores are the habitat of fifty-nine wild swans. More prosaic is the fact that the lake also provides Coole's domestic water; sometimes guests will grumble about the weeds and parasites they find in their bathwater. It is not yet the twentieth century; this is rural Ireland *anno* 1898, when even a house like Coole has rats 'to a positively embarrassing degree'.

But, magnificent though Coole Park is, it does not possess the sort of beauty that can move Synge now. Aran has altered him. He is like the traveller who has visited wild, inhospitable regions of a distant continent and now is returning to civilization. The humdrum, the cultivated, the protected, the cosseted, can no longer awaken and hold his interest; he almost despises civilization because it is not raw reality, because life is most precious and prepossessing when it must be struggled for. Unlike Yeats, John Synge will not spend much time in the refinement of Coole Park.

The horse-drawn carriage quits the green tunnel, emerging on a track that twists through a forest. Synge sees the house, the ancestral home of the Gregorys, for the first time. Elizabeth Coxhead describes it thus:

> The house itself disappointed many . . . by its architectural poverty. It was an oblong white Georgian building with a plain little porch, the counterpart of hundreds in Ireland. The principal living-rooms, library and drawing-room, looked the other way, west towards the lake, through undistinguished but serviceable bays. All the house's distinction lay within.
>
> Four cultivated generations had filled it with books, pictures, statuary, records and mementoes of wide travel, all bearing the imprint of personal taste and personal achievement. It was the house of people who had never been afraid to use their brains.

People who had never been afraid to use their brains? Though speaking of Coole, Coxhead is calling our attention to Roxborough, the adjoining estate, where Lady Gregory grew to womanhood.

31

II

She was born Isabella Augusta Persse, and was a descendant of Henry Persse, Shakespeare's Hotspur. She was the fifth daughter of a large family: her father, Dudley Persse, sired sixteen children, three by his first wife and thirteen by Augusta's mother, Frances Barry.

Like the Synge family, the Persses—the daughters in particular—were strong on proselytizing. Augusta, however, would have no truck with these practices; she was not interested in turning 'the people to the written word of God in the Bible free from the interpretation of their church'. Augusta's interest in the written word was to take another course.

Roxborough, despite its 6,000 acres, its 'cow barns, dairies, stables, kennels, blacksmith shop, carpenter shop, carriage house' and its horde of servants, had no library. The seven Persse girls read now and then, the nine Persse boys did not. Augusta's brothers were a wild lot whose joy in life was the pursuit of country pleasures: hunting, fishing and shooting. They were the terror of the district; all were crack shots, and it was generally accepted that one did not harm a Persse son, no matter what his crime, for fear of retribution from his brothers. These brothers, Yeats remembers, 'were figures from the eighteenth century', half barbarian and without culture, 'ruling their tenants, as had their fathers before, with a despotic benevolence'.

There was *some* reading-matter at Roxborough. The Bible was there, as were Mrs Sherwood's wholesome books: *Stories on the Church Catechism, Henry Milner* and *Ministering Children*, works that were to be found in every self-respecting Low Church household. Some lighter reading came at Christmas; it was not unusual for a daughter to receive the occasional 'Monday', or ornamental, book. As in the Synge family circle, novels were taboo. By and large, the atmosphere at Roxborough was not conducive to the appreciation of literature or the printed word for its own sake. Given this milieu, it is not surprising that Augusta's first exposure to the traditions of

Ireland—rebel, Catholic Ireland—was an oral one. She had the good fortune to be nursed by Mary Sheridan, a woman who served the Roxborough household for some forty years. Sheridan had a vast fund of folklore and fairytales; she was also old enough to remember the cheers of a theatre audience at the news that the French had landed at Killala in 1798 to aid Ireland in her abortive attempt to rid herself of the English yoke. Augusta listened.

Soon she was bringing her sixpences, earned for her proficiency in scriptural knowledge, to a little bookshop in Loughrea which sold collections of national ballads—'Fenian' books. Like Synge, Augusta Persse was breaking with her family's traditions and beliefs, and embracing Irish patriotism. Her parents, mostly indifferent to their offspring's leanings, remained unaware of Augusta's burgeoning interest. Her siblings knew, but cared little.

At the age of fifteen, something strange happened to Augusta. It was the exact opposite, in fact, of Synge's experience at the same age: Augusta rediscovered God; she was, to use a later idiom, 'born again'. Deeply concerned about the welfare of the poverty-stricken tenants on her parents' estate, and the question of using violence to further rebel ends, Augusta became physically ill. Her family doctor sent her to the Persse hunting lodge on Lough Corrib, Co. Galway, where she had ample time and opportunity to meditate on things spiritual and temporal. Soon conversion—perhaps *re*version is a better word—came. Placed next to Synge's account of his Darwinian episode, Lady Gregory's description of this event (written in the third person) makes fascinating reading:

> Then of a sudden one morning . . . she rose up from her bed at peace with God. All doubts and all fears had gone, she was one of His children, His angels were her friends. Their ballads, and poems and patriotic songs had become as ashes; His word, the Bible, was her only book. She need no longer strive to do His will, it was her delight to do it. She was a little ashamed of this ecstasy, a little shy, unwilling to have it known.

From this moment on, Augusta plunged into a personal campaign to try to alleviate some of the dire poverty on the estate and the nearby village, going so far as to use her annual dress allowance of £30 to this end. But it was a secular crusade; she avoided scrupulously any taint of proselytizing.

Augusta Persse's life took a new turn when she was sixteen. Each Christmas, her parents had a box of books sent to Roxborough, from which the children could make a selection; that year it contained a two-volume work which aroused no interest in Augusta's sisters: Chambers' *Encyclopaedia of English Literature.* She grabbed it at once; in the evenings that followed, Augusta read the two volumes straight through.

Her appetite for literature whetted, she began to collect works by the great writers: the poems of Herbert, Burns, Keats, Tennyson; the essays of Matthew Arnold. What would set the stage for things to come, however, was her reading of Malory's great epic *Morte d'Arthur.* It rekindled her interest in the Celtic tradition: from Britain's legendary Celtic king, it was a short step to the heroes of ancient Ireland. Rebel songs and ballads once more stirred her imagination. Her cousin, Standish Hayes O'Grady, came to visit. He was a Gaelic scholar and translator, and stimulated Augusta into learning Irish. She learned German too, and French and Italian, going on to read Dante in the original by comparing the French translation with the Italian. She was eighteen when she discovered Shakespeare, and soon she was reciting to herself his sonnets as she walked in the mountains near her home. By the time her path crossed those of Yeats and Synge, she was immersed in the dramatic tradition. But first would come marriage, motherhood and widowhood.

Generally speaking, Augusta had been 'spending her time as women were supposed to—at the disposal of others'. Her own life proper began in 1880 when, not quite twenty-eight, she married the most eligible bachelor of the province: Sir William Gregory, late of Westminster, late of the Governor's mansion in Ceylon, master of Coole Park, and aged sixty-three.

The newly-weds went to London in March, where Augusta was presented to Queen Victoria. Rome followed, and more royal presentations; then Athens and Constantinople. Sir William's social circle was large and influential; Augusta, accustomed to 'dreary' Cannes, where she had nursed her tubercular brother Richard, and Cornwall, where her sister Gertrude lived, was seeing more of the world than she had ever dreamed possible. The couple passed the winter of 1881/82 in Cairo, where, not only did they become embroiled in a local rebellion, but Lady Gregory met Wilfrid Scawen Blunt, a cousin of the Duke of Rutland, with whom she later had a stormy love affair.

But for all that, Lady Gregory lived for eleven years in the shadow of her eminent husband, though he was sufficiently unorthodox to allow her considerably more freedom of expression than was the norm in his circle, and certainly he appreciated a wife who shared his love of art and culture. But only after his death in 1892 did Augusta attain that level of independence and liberty which enabled her to throw herself wholeheartedly into the Irish Literary Revival. Sir William had bequeathed her Coole Park. It had been little more than a *pied à terre* for him, a late summer hunting lodge, a repository for his books, paintings and oriental pieces. Let us give the task of describing Coole House to W. B. Yeats, he who loved it almost as much as its mistress did:

> It was perhaps Lady Gregory's husband, a Trustee of the English National Gallery, who had bought the greater number of the pictures. Those that I keep most in memory are a Canaletto, a Guardi, a Zurbarán. Two or three that once hung there had, before I saw those great rooms, gone to the National Gallery, and the fine portraits by Augustus John and Charles Shannon were still to come. The mezzotints and engravings of the masters and friends of the old Gregorys that hung round the small downstairs breakfast-room, Pitt, Fox, Lord Wellesley, Palmerston, Gladstone, many that I have forgotten, had increased generation by generation . . . . In the hall, or at one's right hand as one ascended the stairs, hung Persian helmets, Indian shields, Indian swords in elaborate sheaths, stuffed birds

from various parts of the world, shot by whom nobody could remember, portraits of the members of Grillion's club, illuminated addresses presented in Ceylon or Galway, signed photographs or engravings of Tennyson, Mark Twain, Browning, Thackeray, at a later date paintings of Galway scenery by Sir Richard Burton, bequeathed at his death, and etchings by Augustus John. I can remember somebody saying: 'Balzac would have given twenty pages to the stairs'.

Artistic, literary and worldly wealth from all corners of the planet, or, to put it another way, from every country where the British Empire had set marching foot. There was, of course, one notable exception: Ireland, the country in which Coole House actually stood. There was nothing of that nation at Coole, save, perhaps, the language of the servants.

When Sir William Gregory died, the house in Coole Park was just one more possession of a wealthy man's estate. His widow was to turn it into something rich and rare.

III

A national theatre. Coole House throbs with the excitement of the dream that is about to become a reality. Yeats and Lady Gregory can speak of little else; Edward Martyn is hardly less enthusiastic. Martyn, a Catholic, is the eccentric heir to Tulira Castle, a sprawling pile on the estate adjoining Coole, which he has rebuilt in the Gothic style, allowing his monogram to be incised in every renovation he has had a hand in. He is eccentric because he refuses to sleep in the Wagnerian splendour of his masterpiece, preferring the spartan comforts of an all but bare bedroom in the oldest part of the castle: a Norman tower built by an ancestor in the twelfth century. Martyn is a misogynist and appears to be a lay celibate. The celibacy, suggests his cousin, George Moore, stems from Martyn's abhorrence of marriage and his fear of being dominated by women. Moore plans to write a pamphlet entitled *Edward Martyn and his Soul.*

Martyn, nevertheless, has written two competent plays—*The Heather Field* and *Maeve*—which London has rejected; he has thought about having the first produced in Germany; he is convinced that Ireland needs her own theatre.

Martyn is eccentric—but which of this small band of zealots is not? Yeats with his tall, spare frame, floppy tie and unruly lock of raven-black hair—the poet personified. He talks easily and passionately (though talk, to use his own words, is merely 'creation without toil'), confident that all here see with the same eye of genius. Augusta Gregory: small, demure; seemingly a woman of her class, genteel and proper; but inwardly she burns with a passion that matches Yeats's.

And let us not forget the absent—if only temporarily absent—friends: Douglas Hyde and George Russell.

Hyde is the great Celticist, the man whose own grand dream is the revival of the Irish language. No, not only the language; Hyde would like to a see a return to pre-colonial times. He is an atavist of the first order, going so far as to advocate the abolition of trousers for Irishmen, believing (probably erroneously) that they are not of Celtic provenance.

Hyde is thirty-eight, a Protestant, son of a rector and landowner. He is the scholar of the Irish Literary Revival, invaluable to Yeats and Lady Gregory. He learned Gaelic at an early age by listening to the talk of the small tenants and farm labourers of County Roscommon, where he grew up. Later, he could read and write the Gaelic script with the aid of an Irish Bible. In 1890, he published the first of two books which were seminal for the Revivalists; this was *Beside the Fire*, a translation of Irish folk-tales, which appeared with the Gaelic original facing Hyde's English version. Similarly, in 1893, his *Love Songs of Connacht* carried both the original and translated poems in one volume. Never before had the rural tradition been treated with such love and scholarship. But, more important for Lady Gregory and John Synge, Hyde's translations employ *dialect.*

Thirty-one-year-old George Russell is the friend whom Yeats calls 'that myriad-minded man'. He likes to be known by his magical pseudonym: AE. In the true spirit of *fin de siècle* hubris, he wrote to Yeats in 1896, to inform him that the old gods were returning to Ireland. The New Aeon is beginning, he says, and he and Yeats are to be its high priests.

Russell is an extraordinary individual: painter, poet, philologist, theosopher, magician, draper's clerk, journalist; he will later organize the Raiffeisen banks in Ireland, in order to assist financially the farming cooperatives. His dramaturgical contribution to the Irish Literary Theatre will be modest. His work has, however, already attracted John Synge. Russell's volume of spiritual verse, *The Earth Breath and Other Poems*, was one of the books which accompanied Synge to Aran.

Synge feels somewhat uncomfortable on the occasion of his introduction to the inner circle at Coole; he is, after all, the lone wolf, the outsider, the man who feels uncomfortable in 'movements'. Yeats has seen this trait in Synge in Paris, when Synge resigned from *L'Association Irlandaise*.

John Synge hovers like a lost soul in and about the company. Coole contrasts too extravagantly and excessively with the Aran life he has shared until a day or two ago; Coole's art treasures and rich furnishings would surely dazzle an Islander, for whom even a clock is a superfluous possession. The English talk in the Big House is equally alien to Synge, accustomed as he has become to the Gaelic of the little Aran cottage. It is difficult to draw him into the conversation; it appears, to Lady Gregory and her guests, that he speaks only when spoken to.

But when Synge does speak, his every word is measured, thoughtful, graceful. He is, says Lady Gregory, 'a comfortable guest, good humoured, gentle, a quiet looker-on, a good listener'. She has the impression that he has no time for politics; he rarely even looks at a newspaper, shies away from Coole talk of home rule and the land struggle, as if these matters were of no concern to him, whose family's tenantry support him. It seems to Lady Gregory that Synge eschews human company—that of Coole, at any rate—and is more at home with the birds and other woodland creatures of the estate. Only when she and Yeats quiz him on Aran folklore do his hazel eyes light up and he describes with the eloquence of the poet the people and places that have touched him of late.

Synge is an enigma for Yeats and Lady Gregory; they suspect an artist here, but it is too early to tell into which waters Synge will channel his art. Neither suspects it will be the theatre. Synge dines next day with Edward Martyn, and arrives back in Kingstown on 29 June. Lady Gregory has lent him some articles on Irish folklore which Yeats has drafted with her help. Synge writes to her on 1 July, apologizing for having kept them so long. That same day, he goes to join his family at Castle Kevin, the Synges' summer retreat in the Wicklow hills.

At Coole Park, Yeats, Lady Gregory and Martyn are putting the final touches to their bold plan. Part of the undertaking had seen its completion before Synge arrived at Coole. The planners have appreciated that drama-making is an expensive business; Lady Gregory, ever the practical one, has proposed the drafting of a letter aimed at attracting subscribers to their cause. She knows a number of wealthy people to whom the letter should be sent and, with Yeats, composed the following:

> We propose to have performed in Dublin in the spring of every year, certain Celtic and Irish plays, which whatever be their degree of excellence will be written with a high ambition, and so to build up a Celtic and Irish school of dramatic literature. We hope to find in Ireland an uncorrupted and imaginative audience trained to listen by its passion for oratory, and believe that our desire to bring upon the stage the deeper thoughts and emotions of Ireland will ensure for us a tolerant welcome, and that freedom to experiment which is not found in theatres of England, and without which no new movement in art or

literature can succeed. We will show that Ireland is not the home of buffoonery and of easy sentiment, as it has been represented, but the home of ancient idealism. We are confident of the support of all Irish people, who are weary of misrepresentation, in carrying out a work that is outside all the political questions that divide us.

And so to the theatre, the bricks and mortar of the movement. On their arrival in Dublin, Yeats and Martyn encounter the first great obstacle. There are only three theatres in the city suited to their needs: the Royal, the Queen's and the Gaiety. All are prohibitively expensive to hire. Very well, then, they decide, let us give our plays elsewhere: there are any number of halls in Dublin where a temporary stage can be thrown up. Just so, but the friends are informed that it is illegal to perform a play on premises not built for that purpose: an eighteenth-century act of parliament thwarts the plan. The Rotunda Maternity Hospital is the only building exempt from the ruling. Yeats pauses; it is a tempting proposition—to give birth to the Irish Literary Theatre in such a place! It is tempting, yes, but the premises are unsuitable. The law itself must be changed.

Lady Gregory mobilizes her not inconsiderable forces. She writes to William Lecky, historian and Unionist MP for Trinity College. Lecky succeeds in getting a rider attached to the Act, whereby Dublin Corporation may grant licences for the production of plays. Once again, Lady Gregory shows what a formidable ally and influential woman she is.

IV

There is no doubt that George Moore is the *enfant terrible* of the Irish Literary Renaissance, but Yeats has need of him. Despite his eccentricities (yet another eccentric!), Moore is one of the few in Yeats's circle of friends who has practical experience of dramaturgy. Yeats's *The Land of Heart's Desire* was performed in London in 1894 as a curtain-raiser for 'a poor and pretentious piece' by John Todhunter. Both plays had a disastrous opening night; Todhunter's was replaced by Bernard Shaw's *Arms and the Man*. George Moore's comment on *Heart's Desire* was that the play 'neither pleased nor displeased; it struck me as an inoffensive trifle'. Moore can afford to be condescending; his own play, *The Strike at Arlingford*, had been produced the previous year, to very good notices.

W. B. Yeats and Edward Martyn have secured the Antient Concert Rooms in Dublin—a venue where Bernard Shaw's mother once performed in opera—for the week of 8 May 1899. Yeats's *The Countess Cathleen* and Martyn's *The Heather Field* will be the first plays given by the Irish Literary Theatre, and the producers need Moore's help in finding players.

The cousins George Moore and Edward Martyn are an odd couple, constantly at loggerheads; Yeats is convinced that it is a mutual contempt that keeps them together. Moore is, like Martyn, a Roman Catholic. He was born in County Mayo in 1852; his father died when George was eighteen, leaving him an estate of 12,371 acres. Moore spent his early twenties in Paris, where he tried unsuccessfully to become a painter and a poet. He took luxurious rooms in Montmartre, one of which was furnished as a huge scarlet Bedouin tent. In one corner was a python called Jack, which Moore, dressed in a Japanese kimono, fed each month with a live guinea pig, while a friend played the organ.

In 1880, problems arose with the Land League—an organization for the advancement of the interests of tenant farmers—and Moore returned to Ireland to negotiate with his tenants. He then moved to London and began writing. Success quickly followed; his second novel, *A Mummer's Wife*, caused a furore because of its uninhibited descriptive language.

Moore returned to Mayo in 1883 and wrote *A Drama in Muslin*, a novel that attacked the decadence of Dublin's Anglo-Irish society. Three years later, the native Irish were his victims, when he published a collection of essays entitled *Parnell and His Island*. It was a means of taking revenge on the Mayo tenants who had threatened his father's estate. Sentiments such as 'Ireland is a bog, and the aborigines are a degenerate race, short, squat little men with low foreheads and wide jaws' did little to improve relations with Moore's tenants. For one with such feelings of hatred and disgust of his fellow countrymen, George Moore seems a strange candidate for membership of the Irish Literary Theatre.

Moore's autobiography, *Confessions of a Young Man*, established his reputation as a prose writer; *Esther Waters*, published to great acclaim in 1894, sealed it. It also made him an influential man in London literary circles. If the word goes out now that George Moore requires actors, then actors shall and will be found for George Moore.

V

John Synge, having cycled down from Crosthwaite Park, Kingstown, sits in the fastness of Castle Kevin, near Annamoe in his beloved glens of Wicklow. It is not really a castle, despite the grand name. This smallish country mansion is in fact a boycotted house. Built near the site of Castle Kevin proper (the old pile that had been destroyed by Oliver Cromwell's cannons), it is the property of the Frizelle family who have been forced by hostile neighbours to vacate it.

The large-scale evictions of the early 1880s had provoked action by the tenants of the area; led by Michael Davitt's Land Leaguers, they had successfully ostracized the Frizelles. The landlord is gone, but the house remains unscathed. It suits Synge's mother to take it during the summer months; it being a boycotted house, the rent is low, and she and her family can enjoy the countryside they love best. Cousin Emily lives just down the way, and Aunt Editha and 'The Major' of Glanmore Castle are within easy visiting distance.

The view from the front porch is astonishingly beautiful; it is a vista of which neither Synge nor his mother ever tire. Unlike Aran, there are trees here in abundance; they hide the plateau on the eastern side. North and west lies the valley where the Vartry and Avonmore have their confluence; beyond are the heather-mantled slopes of Tomriland Hill, and on a clear day the farther peaks of Djouce Mountain and Kippure stand out starkly. The vista, like the rivers, is in a constant state of flux; of an evening, Synge can watch the stars come out, and sometimes observe a nightjar flying among the furze.

By day, Synge strolls the long avenue flanked by oaks and beeches, chestnuts, birches and countless rhododendrons. The estate has lain untended and derelict for years. Exploring the ruins of someone else's property gives Synge an uneasy feeling. It is almost trespass, or like going through the intimate letters of a dead stranger. Synge is smitten by a sense of decay and mortality; it brings home to him the reality not quite seen by his mother: that the class to which the Synges belong is a dying one.

There is a garden at Castle Kevin, or, better said, the sad remains of what once had been the work of cultivating hands:

> Above the wall on the three windy sides there were rows of finely grown lime trees, the place of meeting in the summer for ten thousand bees. Under the east wall there was the roof of a greenhouse, where one could sit, when it was wet or dry, and watch the birds and butterflies, many of which were not common. The seasons were always late in this place—it was high above the sea—and redpolls often used to nest not far off late in the summer; siskins did the same once or twice, and greenfinches, till the beginning of August, used to cackle endlessly in the lime trees.
>
> Everyone is used in Ireland to the tragedy that is bound up with the lives of farmers and fishing people; but in the garden one seemed to feel the tragedy of the land-lord class also, and of the innumerable old families that are quickly dwindling away. These owners of the land are not much pitied at the present day, or much deserving of pity; and yet one cannot quite forget that they are the descendants of what was at one time, in the eighteenth century, a high-spirited and highly-cultivated aristocracy. Still, this class, with its many genuine qualities, had little

patriotism, in the right sense, few ideas, and no seed for future life, so it has gone to the wall.

It is well that Synge adds that last sentence; otherwise we may think that he has lost sight of a universal truth: history is written by the victors. If Synge's class remembers the 'high-spirited' bucks and rakes of the eighteenth century as a highly cultivated aristocracy, then the Catholic 'native' Irish may beg to differ. They may remember, as Buck Whaley's editor, Edward Sullivan, tells us, that 'the character of Ireland was then [in the late eighteenth century] an anomaly in the moral world . . . . Lawlessness of every kind was rampant in the metropolis [of Dublin]'. Guardians of law and order were hopelessly few and could do little against the misdemeanours of the bucks. These 'miserable watchmen', says Sullivan, 'looked in terror at the many conflicts which were perpetually waged by day and night in the streets'. Numerous crimes went unpunished because the eighteenth-century aristocracy that Synge admires was almost a law unto itself in his great-grandfather's time. So it had been since Cromwellian times.

VI

The pile of rubble that marks the site of the old Castle Kevin lies a little to the north of the road that skirts the present house. During the English Civil War, Catholic Ireland had remained loyal to Charles I. Cromwell came to the country in 1649 to settle accounts, leaving, in his wake, a frightful trail of destruction and slaughter. Catholic landowners were now dispossessed. Their lands were confiscated by the Roundheads; in this manner the Castle Kevin estate—and, indeed, most of County Wicklow—came into English Protestant hands. The descendants of these colonists were to form the Anglo-Irish Ascendancy.

The ascent of the Catholic James II to the English throne in 1685 promised a revival for his Irish co-religionists. Instead, he was deposed in the 'Glorious Revolution' of 1688, in favour of the

Dutchman William of Orange, who assumed the crown in the Protestant interest. In 1690 William defeated James at the battle of the Boyne. The following year, the decisive battle of Aughrim brought a Jacobite rout. The Treaty of Limerick was signed by victor and vanquished on 3 October 1691, bringing Ireland well and truly under Protestant control, and subject to the crown of England.

The Treaty of Limerick was, given the times, a document unusually generous to the defeated party. In fact, many Protestants thought its terms dangerously lenient towards the Catholics. So great were the fears of the Irish parliament—a body dominated by Protestant landowners—that certain clauses were never ratified, thus leaving the way open for the repressive body of legislation known as the Penal Laws.

To pre-empt further conflict, no Catholic was allowed to possess a firearm or a horse worth more than £5; for similar reasons, Catholics were excluded from parliament, the army, the navy, and the legal professions. They could not own a school, buy land or lease it for more than a short period. The traditional inheritance system, by which an estate fell to the eldest son on the father's death, was dismantled by the 1704 Act, whereby property was divided equally among the heirs, reducing effectively the extent of individual land ownership. If, however, the eldest son chose to convert to Anglicanism, he inherited all. Many young men did just that. Among the measures adopted was the banishment of Catholic bishops, in an attempt to reduce the number of priests they could ordain. The Penal Laws were, in effect, designed to secure the secular power of the Ascendancy. The denomination which benefited most, as R. F. Foster comments, was the Church of Ireland. It had

> survived the great crisis, and reaped its reward. Although
> Presbyterians retained their *regium donum* and even had it
> doubled, their position at law was not much more enviable
> than that of the Catholics; the Established Church remain-
> ed the fountain of privilege in Ireland, more closely linked
> than ever to the Church of England and the possessors of

land. In return, membership gave exclusive rights to political power.

And so there arose, by a series of conquests, a hyphenated class: the Anglo-Irish, whose lands and wealth were the loot of war. They were a people who enjoyed a world of exploitation and luxury to the detriment of the dispossessed Catholics, whose lives, as tenant farmers, were often rendered brutal and degrading. Ireland remained a poor country and the condition of its poorest tenants and labourers was often lamentable. The next century and a half brought first a long peace, then revolution, constitutional change, Catholic emancipation, and the cataclysmic Famine of the 1840s. Still, the central relationship of Irish social life—that of the Ascendancy and its tenants—remained fundamentally the same.

Synge remembers something of the injustice that endured into his own boyhood and involved his own immediate family. In 1885, when he was fourteen, problems arose with the tenants on the Synge properties whose rents were in arrears. Synge's brother Edward, who was land agent and manager of properties in Cavan and Mayo, began a campaign of eviction. John was horrified and protested to his mother. Her reply was brief and contained the pragmatism of a parent who knew where her loyalties lay. 'What would become of us', she asked her son, 'if our tenants in Galway stopped paying their rents?'

Two years later, Edward again shocked John by his brutal handling of an eviction on the Glanmore estate. Having expelled the occupants—they included an imbecile—in the early morning, Edward installed a company of 'emergency men', who would hold the cottage in order to discourage boycotting by neighbours or friends. It was then burned to the ground. By this act, Edward made mud of the Synge name in County Wicklow.

———

Synge sees the ruined garden at Castle Kevin as a metaphor of the decline of the landlord class: the roots and rude weeds of the native soil are choking the cultivated flowerbeds and finely grown lime trees. He is reminded of the previous summer, when Mrs Synge had taken a house on Avondale, the estate of Charles Stewart Parnell. The house itself was empty and the trees, collected by Parnell from all corners of the world, lay felled and rotting. Perhaps Synge, more than most, understands why the landlord class is dying. He is correct in thinking that there is no true patriotism here. How could there be, when the real roots of the Anglo-Irish lie on the other side of the Irish Sea? Though more than two centuries separate the colonists from their ancestral homeland, the majority of the landlord class owes its first allegiance to England. And yet, as Oscar Wilde and George Bernard Shaw have discovered, the Anglo-Irish are themselves a dispossessed race: they have no country; they are neither Irish in Ireland nor English in England, no matter how hard they try.

Their wealth is dwindling too, a consequence of the economic recession which followed the Napoleonic Wars. Land that once supported profligate living is being sold off so that standards can be maintained. The decline, Declan Kiberd observes wryly, 'came from within and owed more to a combination of fast women and slow horses'.

With nowhere to go, no room for growth, the landlord class is looking to itself. In some cases it is discovering that it does, after all, have an identity—and that identity is an Irish one. Augusta Gregory is learning about the love-songs of Connacht, the rhymes of the blind poet Raftery and the stories told by the cottagers. Yeats is moving towards the dramatization of the Celtic epics. And Synge? Synge is still convinced that his energies are best channelled into the writing of narrative. Aran notebook at hand, he sets out the first draft of 'A Story from Inishmaan', the tale told to him by Pat Dirane, the one 'so full of European associations'. It will be published by *The New Ireland Review* in November 1898.

Synge is getting the feel of Aran dialogue. There are no 'ayes' or 'nays' in this brand of English, for the good reason that the Irish language has no equivalents. *Is ea* and *ní hea,* the closest approximations, translate as 'it is' and 'it is not'. Among the many thousands of words of drama Synge will pen, 'aye' will appear on only nine occasions—eight times in *The Playboy of the Western World,* once in *The Well of the Saints*—and the abrupt Anglo-Saxon 'nay' not at all.

But theatre is still some time in the future. John Synge is back in the countryside he knows best: the hills and glens of Wicklow. He delights in walking and bicycling the twisting highways and lanes. 'The engineers who began the improvement of the roads towards the end of the 18th century', writes Edward Stephens, 'were working in the days of the stage coach and the well equipped private four-in-hand. They chose the easiest gradients and followed the courses of rivers, leaving the old roads to degenerate into lanes and byways narrowed by encroaching overgrowth, and used by few but the local farmers, and the tinkers who camped on the wide grass margins.' These last are Synge's favourite haunts. His note-book a constant companion on his solitary rambles, he strikes up conversation with the country people. Those with permanent homes on the estates are interesting enough; their talk pales, how-ever, alongside that of the itinerant folk, the vagrants. There is one very old man he has spoken to before: Honest Jack Tar, a well-known figure in the county:

> I have met an old [vagrant] who . . . believes he was a hun-dred years old last Michaelmas . . . . Though now alone . . . he has been married several times and reared children of whom he knows no more than a swallow knows of broods that have flown to the south. Like most tramps he has the humour of talk and ideas of a certain distinction . . . and this old marauder who [has] lived twice as long and per-haps ten times more fully than the men around him [is] aware of his distinction . . . . If you do not follow his some-times mumbled phrases he will call a blight from heaven on your head, though your silver is only warming in his pouch.
>
> Man is naturally a nomad . . . and all wanderers have finer intellectual and physical perceptions than men who are condemned to local habitations.

Man is naturally a nomad. What a belief to be held by a man of

Synge's background, a man brought up to believe in the primacy of property and a stable hearth! This is anarchy. The wonder is where such ideas spring from. Could Synge have chanced upon the old Moorish proverb which asserts that: 'He who does not travel does not know the value of men'? Perhaps he is remembering lines from *The Anatomy of Melancholy*, written in 1621 by Robert Burton:

> The heavens themselves run continually round, the sun riseth and sets, the moon increaseth and decreaseth, stars and planets keep their constant motions, the air is still tossed by the winds, the waters ebb and flow to their conservation no doubt, to teach us that we should ever be in action.

Whatever his inspiration, Synge considers the life of the nomad preferable to that of the peasants of the glens. While the outdoor life engenders 'good humour and fine bodily health', the existence of the cottagers is, by and large, depressed and lonely. He blames the place and the climate—and there is no gainsaying that the Wicklow weather is more changeable than most in Ireland. Brilliant sunshine can give way to black rain within minutes, and within more minutes change again. 'This peculiar climate, acting on a population that is already lonely and dwindling, has', Synge believes, 'caused or increased a tendency to nervous depression among the people, and every degree of sadness . . . is common among the hills.'

The vagrant, on the other hand, 'has preserved the dignity of motion'. He too can be affected by the vagaries of Wicklow's weather, but he is not confined to one lonely cabin, the 'last cottage at the head of a long glen'. He is a man of the roads, and his life is enriched by those he meets on the roads. Moreover, he can move effortlessly from one community to another, take—or give—where he wishes, without commitment or allegiance. John Synge, torn at this time between love of his family and a growing devotion to his ancient country and its native people, is establishing a bond, as yet tentative, with the vagrants of Wicklow. It is only a matter of time before he will realize their true significance for his art.

But there is another emotion at work here, an emotion far stronger than family ties or patriotism. It is no accident that Synge's poetry to date has been over-romantic and introspective. If it speaks too often of love unrequited, then that is because it is autobiographical:

> And my soul was sick where you went your ways
> And dead if you never find it again.

Love is the passion that drives John Synge's work. The more it eludes him, the more he will seek to capture it, to quantify and qualify it, to take it apart and inspect it; then put it together again, dressed in the finery of art. The theatre of Yeats and Lady Gregory owes its inception to 'the stirring of the bones'; Synge's art springs from the stirring in the loins.

The Young Lady Says 'No'

I

Little Florence Ross was Synge's first love. She was a first cousin, a daughter of Mrs Synge's sister Agnes, whose family often stayed at Mrs Traill's home in Orwell Park, Rathgar. Following the death of John's father in 1872, Mrs Synge leased the house next door to her mother's, and Mrs Traill's help and counsel were invaluable in the rearing of the five fatherless children.

During his childhood at Orwell Park—before he began school at the age of ten—Synge was very often in the company of his oldest brothers, Robert and Edward; he accompanied them on walks or when they fished the Dodder. Yet he had, not unnaturally, a closer bond with his brother Samuel, who was not quite four years his senior. They shared the usual boyhood adventures: wandering and playing in the woods of the demesne of Rathfarnham Castle; sailing toy boats on the river; living in the child's world of imagination and make-believe.

Florence Ross and her older siblings often joined John and Samuel in their play. Mixing with 'unsuitable' children of the neighbourhood was discouraged by Mrs Synge and her mother, and John's nannies were given strict instructions to ensure that he and his brother did not associate with playmates other than those of their own evangelical persuasion.

Mrs Synge's sister Agnes had married an Ulster clergyman called William Steward Ross, and the family had settled in Orwell Park. It was inevitable that John Synge and Florence Ross, who were about the same age—nine or ten—became close friends. He was delighted that his cousin shared his passion for nature and small animals:

We had a large establishment of pets—rabbits, pigeons, guinea pigs, canaries, dogs—which we looked after together. I was now going to school, but I had many holidays from ill health—six months about this time especially which were recommended on account of continual headaches that I suffered from which gave us a great deal of time to wander about among the fields near our houses. We were left in complete liberty and never abused it . . . .

He and Florence were, Synge recalls, 'always primitive. We both understood all the facts of life and spoke of them without much hesitation . . . . We talked of sexual matters with an indifferent and sometimes amused frankness . . . .' The two children went on field trips to observe wildlife in the woods near their homes. A calf-love blossomed; Synge remembers how he used to kiss the chair on which Florence had sat. This period was, as he recalls in his *Autobiography*, 'probably the happiest of my life. It was admirable in every way.'

This was, in short, a childish love affair which did not differ markedly from those of other children in similar circumstances. In time, he and Florence outgrew the friendship and drifted apart. Florence devoted her leisure hours to water-colouring; Synge continued his enquiries into the natural world.

Until he was fourteen, Synge's principal passion was birds and their behaviour; he learned to identify scores of them by their plumage, and spent happy days observing many species in their habitats. By the spring of 1885, his interest had shifted to butterflies, moths and beetles. This absorption brought him into intimate contact with the night: its ever-changing shapes and shadows. Edward Stephens sees this period as an important one in his uncle's development. Gradually, he notes, Synge was 'finding by experience that out of doors there was always variety . . . and that in his home there was uninteresting routine. He was beginning to see the world he knew out of doors as a symbol of inspired life, and the house as a symbol of dull method'. Synge was taking the first steps which would lead him beyond the confines of the garrison.

II

In 1892, when Synge was twenty-one, Cherrie Matheson came to live three doors from the Synge home in Crosthwaite Park. They had met before. For several families of the Protestant enclave of Kingstown, Greystones, a centre of evangelical fervour, was a popular summer destination; the Synges holidayed there, as did the Matheson family. Florence Ross was also a regular visitor, and it was she who introduced John Synge to her friend Cherrie. She was the same age as he, a short, plump girl, 'quick of gesture and remarkable for a brightness of manner' which Synge found attractive.

Greystones in those times was little more than a scattering of small houses lining the littoral, so it was inevitable that the Synges and Mathesons should meet frequently. They had much in common: Cherrie's father was a leader of the Plymouth Brethren, whose fundamentalism and strict codes of conduct, though extreme, were close to Mrs Synge's own beliefs and practices. Like Synge's mother and grandmother, the Plymouth Brethren had hidebound ideas on salvation. The Day of Judgement would separate the sheep from the goats; the sect, needless to say, believed that the delights of Paradise would be the Brethren's happy lot; Roman Catholics, Anglicans and even Nonconformists were all, alas, doomed to the fires of hell. The Brethren knew no church building proper; worship took the form of a gathering in a meeting house, or sometimes members would congregate in the home of a Brother.

The sect was an exclusive one; while relations with non-members were not actively discouraged, they were none the less frowned upon. Mrs Synge and her Low Church family were exceptions to the rule. But John Synge was now a convinced agnostic, and he must surely have felt that a match between him and Cherrie was next to impossible. She accepted without question the teachings and ascetic codes of her father's sect. With the missionary zeal of a pious twenty-one-year-old, she regarded Synge's apostasy as a challenge to her own unswerving faith: the errant lamb could be enticed back into the fold.

But the trouble with an agnostic or atheist youth is his immense difficulty in keeping quiet about his unbelief; just as the convert will exploit every opportunity to defend his new-found faith, so too does the unbeliever turn the slightest allusion to religion into an all-out discourse. John Synge was no exception. Moreover, he was developing an awareness of the injustices perpetrated by the social system of which he was part, and needed no encouragement to make his political feelings known. This, too, was unfortunate; the Brethren eschewed all politics, believing that no man has the right to wield more power than another. So, instead of terms of endearment, Cherrie Matheson heard Darwinism and socialism. Instead of sweet nothings being exchanged, theological argument and social comment were hurled back and forth between her and Synge. To be sure, passions were aroused, but romance, more often than not, took a back seat to dissension. What should have been a battle of the heart became instead a battle of wits—and one where there could be no victor.

Yet, despite these apparently insurmountable obstacles, Synge's devotion to Cherrie grew, and there seems no reason to doubt that it was reciprocated. Unlike his childhood infatuation with Florence Ross, this was a mature relationship; both parties were of age. Nor is there any reason to doubt that he and Cherrie were good companions. She was an intelligent girl and widely read—even if much of her reading had a distinctly religious bias— and could acquit herself well in conversation. She had a deep love of painting, a love that she shared with her father, who brought her often to galleries and museums. But she knew little about music, and even less about musicians. Secular music, dance and theatre belonged to the realm of 'entertainment', a term which had sinful connotations in the Matheson household. If John Synge's agnosticism was not formidable enough a barrier to a union with Cherrie Matheson, then his chosen career must surely have filled the girl with grave misgivings: Synge had set his heart on becoming a professional musician.

III

Mary Synge, an English cousin of John's father, spent some weeks in Crosthwaite Park in the spring of 1893. The event seems, in itself, a minor one— 'Cousin Mary' was only one of many near and distant relatives who enjoyed Mrs Synge's hospitality from time to time—but her visit was to have far-reaching consequences. It was to lead Synge to Germany.

Mitteleuropa, Central Europe—here lay the *Heimat* of European music: of Bach, Händel, Beethoven, Mozart, Haydn, Liszt, Schubert . . . . The lands between the Rhine and the mouth of the Danube had brought forth the Titans of symphony and sonata. When mastering his trade, a journeyman of letters chose Britain or France; the serious student of music looked to Germany and its neighbours for guidance and inspiration. Mary Synge knew this: a professional musician, she herself had polished up her skill at the piano in Germany. The living she made from her concert work was a meagre one, but to Synge it was enough: here was proof that his own musical aspirations were not idle dreams.

During Mary's stay in Kingstown, Synge helped her organize a concert, which proved highly successful. In return, she promised to speak to his mother on his behalf; for money was needed, if Synge was to pursue a serious study in music. His own income from his tiny portion of the family estate, together with a modest inheritance, amounted to about £40 a year; funding would have to be found in another quarter.

Mrs Synge was very chary of her youngest son's proposed career. By this time, John's oldest brothers—Robert and Edward— were well established in their chosen professions, men of independent means, each successful in his own field. Samuel was nearing graduation in medicine, and ordination in the ministry would soon follow; he had set his sights on becoming a medical missionary. Thinking of 'poor Johnnie', Mrs Synge shook her head sadly. Music! She saw disappointment—if not downright disaster—

55

looming. She had already tried to point out to him the folly of his choice, going so far as to enlist the help of her son-in-law, Harry Stephens, who had warned Synge that professional musicians gravitated towards drinking and other vices. Edward Synge offered to train him to be a land agent; but, remembering his brother's brutal eviction methods, John had declined.

Now he had found a new ally in Cousin Mary, a woman possessed of an iron will and great powers of persuasion. She was small 'and full of violence,' Edward Stephens remembers, 'and she used to set her teeth rather aggressively when she laughed. If anyone spoke when she was playing, she used to hit the notes and wrench herself round from the keyboard.'

It was not long before Mrs Synge succumbed to Mary's forceful arguments. Reluctantly, she gave Johnnie her blessing. He could accompany his English cousin to Germany; Mrs Synge would pay his expenses. Johnnie would not be alone in a foreign province, which was (heaven help us!) largely Roman Catholic. If he succeeded, well and good: he would have his wish granted, and perhaps earn the means to make his own way in the world. If not, well then he would surely learn by his error; thereafter, there would still be ample time for the twenty-two-year-old to choose a more suitable profession. She would continue to pray for him.

The date of departure was set for the end of July. Synge was to meet Cousin Mary in London, and they would journey to Oberwerth, a small island-town in the Rhine, near Koblenz. He prepared himself by dusting off his German textbooks and engaging a tutor, Herr Wespendorf. Synge already had some knowledge of the language: he had remained alone in the Synge home in the summer of 1891 while the family were on holiday, and had thrown himself into the study of music and German. German, he had reasoned then, might open the doors to new artistic inspiration. He had no way of knowing how right, how uncannily right, this decision had been. In *Synge and Anglo-Irish Literature*, Daniel Corkery expresses the conviction that Germany affected Synge in a way that England could not:

The love affair [with Cherrie Matheson] apart, one thinks that it was music and not literature hastened Synge's feet from his native Dublin. It cannot have been literature. That would surely have landed him in London, and even if, landed there, he did unconventionally still hanker after Europe, he would have received such instruction as to what was right and proper in Continental literary circles, and who were and who were not to be consorted with there, and what salons and theatres and studios were significant, that the free spirit which did actually set out for Europe would have been bewitched and bewinkered before it got to the Continent at all. His subsequent experience then would have been of European literary circles, and not of European life. That misfortune he escaped, and we may thank his love of music for it. In the years to come, nothing else would befall him so significant as this skipping over London.

Here is wisdom. Corkery cites Oliver Goldsmith as an example of an Irish writer who, to the advantage of literature, 'skipped over' London (he chose Edinburgh instead). The English capital ensnared later members of the Ascendancy Irish and, 'from Sheridan to Shaw, they either fell back on intellectual brilliancy or perished in the void'. Corkery's argument is valid even near the close of the twentieth century. So powerful is the continued dominance of London over Irish society that few aspects of everyday life—of arts, letters, of commercial, legislative and political forms—can in truth be considered native. Despite more than seven decades of independence, John Bull's Other Island relies, as much as ever, on its larger neighbour to vet and filter developments and advancements in the outside world. Ireland shares with Britain more than a common language: the two, though distinctly sovereign nations, remain to all intents and purposes a single, cohesive community, a community that is unusually eccentric to European thought.

Dublin in 1893 was a provincial British city (the cynical insist that it still is). It was an intellectual backwater where change came slowly. A decade later, George Bernard Shaw was to joke bitterly that the returning emigrant found the same old flies on the same old cakes in the same old shop-windows; the Abbey Theatre and Hugh Lane's Museum of Modern Art were, he said, the city's only saving graces. Small wonder that the brightest intellects of Dublin plumped for the literary and artistic circles of London where, like Shaw and Wilde, they could shine in the company of kindred and appreciative souls. The price of admission was truly a nominal one: it required only the dropping of the 'Irish' from their Anglo-Irish nationality. Most were only too happy to do so. Thus did England bleed Ireland of her intelligentsia, for scholarship and distinction were still, to a great extent, the prerogatives of the 'hyphenated' class.

But Synge bypassed London because there was not much melody of distinction there. He travelled to the home-waters of the Lorelei and was captivated, on another island, by six modern Rhine-maidens: the von Eicken sisters.

IV

July 30 1893, 'the day of Valeska'. A single entry, written in Gaelic in Synge's diary, sets a laconic, but excited, tone for his first stay in Germany. The von Eicken sisters ran a boarding-house whose garden sloped gently down to the western bank of the Rhine. The women were delightful companions; on warm evenings they would sit under the trees in the garden, drinking coffee and engaging Mary Synge and their young Irish guest in lively conversation, as the wide river glided lazily by. Valeska, at thirty the youngest of the six (Emma, the oldest, was forty-six), took Synge's fancy from the outset. 'Gorse' he nicknamed her, because of her yellow hair and sunny, open disposition. She and her sisters were Synge's passport to a society very much at variance with the garrison-within-the-garrison he had left behind in Crosthwaite Park. In Oberwerth, music was more than a drawing-room accomplishment. It was an intrinsic part of life, a continuation of a tradition tied up with the history and legends of the Rhineland. Here, the professional musician was no work-shy layabout, but a practitioner of a *métier* as noble and time-honoured as the so-called higher callings of commerce, government, letters and science.

Synge's mornings were occupied with practising the violin. Mary Synge accompanied him on the piano; sometimes he played in quartets with the von Eickens and visiting friends. He performed with the local orchestral society, and attended concerts in Koblenz. It was a stimulating period in Synge's life. He was finding his way in a society that was at once plain and genteel. The openness of the sisters impressed him: he could speak to Valeska of matters too 'improper' to discuss at home. He poured out his heart to her, attempting to explain Cherrie Matheson's religious convictions and the barrier they formed against his happiness. Valeska called Synge 'Holy Moses' because of his frequent use of that expletive; Cherrie she nicknamed, for obvious reasons, the 'Holy One'. Valeska listened as Synge spoke of his upbringing, so much in contrast to her own.

The von Eickens were Protestants of reasonably high social standing: their father had been an officer in the German army. On his death, the daughters had fallen on leaner times; hence the boarding-house they were obliged to run. Their clientele—women, mostly—were both Protestant and Catholic. There was little, Synge noted, to distinguish between the adherents of the two religions in speech, in dress, in manner.

Here was food for thought. John Synge, accustomed from youth to the subservient position of most Catholics in rural Ireland, saw how their European co-religionists enjoyed a social status on a par with that of his own class. It was the Church of Rome, and not those of Luther, Calvin or Zwingli, that was in the majority. Germany's Catholics were a far cry from those of his homeland, most of whom were poor and uneducated peasants. Moreover, the religious outlook and observances of Rhineland Catholics differed from the priest-ridden, superstitious puritanism of the native Irish.

Carnival, the period of feasting and merrymaking just before Lent, was a time, Synge learned, of Dionysian exuberance and revelry; Christmas was a happy *mélange* of Christian devotion and pagan solar worship.

All this impressed Synge. This is not to say that he was drifting back to God. On the contrary, it allowed him to look objectively and from a distance at his upbringing and its dependent narrow morality. His belief that all was not right in Ireland was being vindicated; more than ever, he was aware of the terrible divide between his class and the common people. If Catholicism could give rise to a society so urbane as that of Germany, could not the same be possible in Ireland? Was there not a corresponding richness of history and pre-history? Was there not a mode that could bring it to life?

But his present mode was music and, between relaxing picnics and forest walks in the company of the von Eicken sisters, he considered how best to achieve his goal. Although he had planned to accompany Mary Synge back to London—*en route* for Dublin—at the end of summer, he decided to prolong his stay and his music lessons until December. January 1894 found him still at Oberwerth, contemplating his next step. It had been suggested to him that Cologne might provide the proper training; in the end he chose Würzburg, a city on the river Main in north-west Bavaria.

Once again his mother sent him money. One cannot help but admire the woman; here was her youngest son, alone in a foreign, largely 'papist' country, pursuing a course of study of which she disapproved strongly. At the same time, his letters to her were full of praise of German life, and highly critical of his home and upbringing. Yet she continued to help him in every way she could.

On arrival in Würzburg on 22 January, Synge began taking piano lessons, and renewed his studies of music theory and composition. He read, too, in German. His increasing fluency in the language was indeed achieving what he had hoped: it was opening up to him one of the richest literatures in the world. His reading was eclectic, but discerning, and this discernment led him to the writer who was to exercise a pivotal influence on his future: the dramatist and poet Johann Wolfgang von Goethe.

V

Young men need heroes. When young men are uncertain of their future, they will look for inspiration to figures with whom they can identify; they will project their own aspirations on to a hero—if the fit is not quite perfect, no matter: the one can bend to accommodate the other. Synge read Goethe and found, in the autobiographical account of the great dramatist's early life, parallels with his own. Here is Stephens:

> Their environments had differed greatly in detail, but in basic pattern showed similar features. Goethe, as a boy, had, like John, been greatly influenced by his mother. He had been brought up a Protestant on scriptural teaching and, as a student, had learnt enough Hebrew to give him a deep interest in the Old Testament. The study of nature and the beauty of the country had, from his earliest days, been his constant inspiration. In his time [1749–1832], the power of Greek tradition had flowed into German literature just as the power of Celtic tradition was beginning to flow in the literature of John's home country . . . .

The comparison holds water to some extent: the maternal influence, the Protestant faith, the love of nature. Stephens could also have mentioned the similarities of Goethe's frequent bouts of illness, and his infatuation, at the age of twelve, with the 'Frankfurt Gretchen'. But compared with Goethe's, Synge's relationships with women were far fewer and less intense, both in their carnality and in their consequence for his work. H. G. Atkins writes:

> The mystery of the 'eternal feminine' was a possession that haunted [Goethe], bringing sorrow as well as joy in its train. For good or ill the society of women was necessary to him, acting as an inspiration and a spur, and to the various women who had influence upon his life we owe directly

61

and indirectly a considerable part of his works. The list is a long one, and would include many beside those whom he temporarily enshrined in his heart; the love for mother and sister, and some true friendships, as well as the many actual love affairs of his life.

Moreover, though it is true that Synge had taken Hebrew (together with Greek and Latin) at Trinity College, his scant knowledge of the language could hardly have enabled him to read the Old Testament in the original, even had he felt so inclined—which is doubtful, given his antipathy towards his family's blind acceptance of the literal truth of the Scriptures and the thinking that such acceptance engenders. Furthermore, Goethe 'answered intellectual perplexity out of the rich experience of his life'; Synge's secluded life could scarcely compare.

Be that as it may, Synge read his hero avidly. His sojourn in Würzburg was a relatively solitary one, and he took Goethe's works with him when he went for long walks in the surrounding countryside. Synge was in Goethe country . . . Synge read Goethe . . . Synge identified with Goethe . . . Synge tried his hand at *being* Goethe:

Act IV

Room of the hero, who is chatting with the poet, to him the scoundrel; as he is leaving, the ladies meet him at the door and are frightened. Hero and his wife off and the poet declares his love in vain.

Act V

A wild area near the house, the poet, who has just received the news of his brother's death, sits in the foreground. Behind him comes his love and listens to him for a time without being observed. Then she comes to him and consoles him with a promise of love. Soon the hero and his wife come to them and rejoice in the union. The hero declares that what he had been lacking was a broader view of mankind and that he had learnt so much from the two brothers that from now on he can live striving for higher things.

Thus reads a portion of Synge's 'Plan for a Play' which he outlined on 23 April 1894. It is rather Goetheian. Or, rather, it *strives* to be Goetheian, having, as it does, certain elements of the German dramatist's first play, *Die Laune der Verliebten*, wherein two pairs of lovers are contrasted. Goethe wrote this one-acter when he was seventeen. Like his other Leipzig drama, *Die Mitschuldigen*, it deals with a common weakness of humanity. Synge did not develop his 'Plan' further and, indeed, it shows little promise. Goetheian though it may be in its roughly autobiographical construction and characterization, it is no more than a crude morality play. Synge set it in Ireland, but he wrote the plan in German—a habit he was to continue when learning a foreign language. 'He studied languages', comments Ann Saddlemyer, 'by attempting to write creatively in them (sometimes with disastrous literary results).'

There is also a thinly disguised Cherrie Matheson—which was to be expected. The hero's love for the heroine is, happily, requited; marriage takes place. Synge was already attempting to realize his hopes through writing. His notebook contains poems he wrote in this period, and it is reasonable to suppose that Cherrie was the muse who inspired them. Synge was lonely; Cherrie was very much on his mind. On arrival in Würzburg he had met a girl who had just moved from Oberwerth, but Emma von Eicken cautioned him about the impropriety of calling on her: 'Now, as long as she is staying with [people], you cannot visit her, as the customs here are just the same as in England.' His mind was filled with doubts: doubts about Cherrie—and doubts about his future as a musician. He was a vain young man, seeking to excel in all things. Confronted in Germany by musicianship of a very high calibre, his ego took a drubbing. Not for J. M. Synge the second fiddle . . . .

Goethe may have been instrumental in luring Synge away from music. We shall never know; his letters, diary and notebook are strangely silent on the matter. Certainly he must have experienced some embarrassment about his changing horses in mid-stream, knowing that his mother was footing the bill. But change he did, and a future world would be grateful for his decision. Synge had made his first stabs at playwriting, yet he knew that he was far from ready for this, the most sonant of literary forms. His command of English was unusually stunted; he blamed this on his upbringing, on his mother's insistence that exaggeration and prolixity should be avoided. Exaggeration, she held, was tantamount to lying. As a result, Synge was constrained in his verbalization and ill at ease in light conversation. There is no doubt that the von Eicken sisters drew him out to a large extent, and he had written to his mother, chiding her on her restrictive views: 'I had a long letter from poor Johnnie,' she had noted in her diary on 29 December 1893; a 'curious letter attributing his unsociableness to his narrow upbringing and warning me!'

So literature it was to be. Before leaving Germany in June 1894, Synge made a 'pilgrimage' to Frankfurt, where Goethe had lived as a child. He holidayed for twelve days at the von Eickens', where he and Valeska discussed his decision to abandon music. The mill-wheel of his mind was turning on thoughts of literature. In this, as in music, he was aware of his inadequacy: the German students he had met seemed so much better educated and articulate than he. When he arrived home in Crosthwaite Park, he was a chastened, if not to say a disillusioned, man. To add insult to injury, he learned that Cherrie Matheson, his 'Holy One', was spending a month abroad. The summer of 1894 did not bode well.

VI

'Liebes Frln Valewska, . . . Jetzt sind wir, wie Sie oben lesen können, auf dem Lande und genoßen [*sic*] wir die Herrlichkeiten dieser Gegenden von morgens früh bis tief in der [*sic*] Nacht. Ich will nicht leugnen daß ich ein bißchen ängstlich war ob ich die irische Schönheit wieder so wundervoll finden würde wie ich sie so oft beschrieben habe und auf Ehre versichere ich daß ich *überrascht* und *erstaunt* mit ihrem [*sic*] erhabenen Pracht [bin].'*

In excellent German (his letters in foreign languages were drafted and revised, as he would later draft his plays), Synge kept up a lively correspondence with the von Eicken sisters. The above is the first version of a letter that he wrote to Valeska towards the end of July 1894, when he was staying with the Synges and the Stephenses at Castle Kevin. The date is uncertain, but it could not have been before 28 July, because on this day Mrs Synge recorded in her diary: 'Very fine lovely day . . . . Cherry Matheson came.'

She came at Florence Ross's invitation. Upon the death of her mother in December 1891, Florence had joined the Synge household. Her childhood talent for water-colouring had developed and she had become a very skilful painter. Mrs Synge had suggested to her that she should bring a sketching companion to Castle Kevin. She had chosen Cherrie Matheson.

Synge took pains to conceal from the others his growing love for Cherrie. There seems to have been no obvious reason for this: after all, it was hardly a secret that they were fond of one another. He kept mainly to himself by day. Edward Stephens, who was six at the time, remembers that 'John occupied his time as he would have if [Cherrie] had not come, reading, practising, walking and fishing. As the summer was fine, he often read in the wood near the house and he sometimes played the violin there.'

Synge was writing poetry too: finer verses of better construction and intensity. How they contrast with those he had written two short years earlier! This was Synge in 1892:

> A mountain flower once I spied,
> A lonely height its dwelling,
> Where winds around it wailed and sighed
> Sad stories sadly telling.

---

* *Dear Miss Valewska, We are now, as you can read from the above, in the country, and enjoying the delights of this region from early morning till late at night. I shall not deny that I was a little concerned as to whether I would find the beauty of Ireland so wonderful as I had often described it and I give you my word of honour that [I am] surprised and astounded by its sublime splendour.*

> 'Fair flower,' said I, 'thou art alone
> 'Thy days up here art spending,
> 'Now listening to the sad winds' moan
> 'And now before them bending . . . .'

There is little of John Synge here; it is not even an Irish poem. William Wordsworth springs to mind, but this is a pale imitation of Wordsworth. The alliteration is juvenile and often unnecessary: how else but sadly does one tell sad stories?

The suspicion awakes that Synge in 1892 was not completely at home in the English language; the will was there, but the vocabulary and mastery were missing. So also was the *music*. The contrast with the following verses, composed in the summer of 1894, is striking:

> Wind and stream and leaves and lake,
>> Still sweeter make
>> The songs they wake
> A thrill my throes would prisoner take.

> Birds and flies and fish that glide,
>> Why would ye hide
>> Or slip aside
> From one who loves your lonely pride? . . .

Germany had had an unusual effect on Synge's poetry. This new language is pared and honed, almost as if the poet is addressing a non-English speaker. It scans well too; the melody sings through. There is purity in these lines; the construction of the verses is near-haiku. Synge was getting into his stride, even if Wordsworth, long his favourite poet, was still looking over his shoulder. Their themes are, understandably enough, similar: Synge's love of nature was as fiery as that of Wordsworth.

So much for birds, flies and fishes; a more immediate manifestation of nature was occupying Synge's mind during that summer at Castle Kevin. Love was growing. But it was an idealized love; he worshipped Cherrie Matheson from afar. Synge avoided her company, preferring solitude to the frustration he felt would follow his amorous advances; the only time he was alone with Cherrie was when he drove her to the railway station in Rathdrum, at the end of her two-week stay.

———————

Autumn found Synge in a deep depression. As he gazed out of the front window of No. 31 Crosthwaite Park, the first yellowed leaves lay on the tennis courts across the way; a servant strolled past with a young charge. How simple life could be when one followed the natural bent. Synge took stock.

His plans for a career in music lay dashed. The verses he had written at Castle Kevin he found far from satisfactory. (In 1908, when he was preparing some of his poems for publication, he instructed W. B. Yeats that 'These boyish verses are not to be printed under any circumstances'.) His loved one lived only three doors away; he could visualize her now, sketching happily in the diffused light from the Matheson's bow window. But he found no opportunity of being alone with her. His brother Samuel, who was studying hard for his ordination, continually tried to win him back to the religion he had rejected. Synge felt himself a stranger in these surroundings he had once loved so well; even the beauty of his beloved Wicklow hills had failed to lessen the hurt. What could he turn his hand to now?

Sifting through the drafts of his letters to his German friends, he was struck by the ease with which he had mastered this foreign tongue. He knew English, Irish, Latin, Greek, Hebrew and German. Language teaching: might that not provide a worthy occupation? One could travel, and earn one's living at the same time. Another modern language was needed: French perhaps.

So Paris beckoned, after all; Synge was to experience the Continental literary circles he had skipped over. He would not be 'bewitched and bewinkered', but would be armed instead with the knowledge of ordinary European life he had amassed in Germany.

The thought of Germany, of his friends in Oberwerth, cheered Synge greatly. He would spend some weeks with the von Eickens. He knew that their company and support would be invaluable, as he prepared himself for his new life.

VII

'Je vous remercie beaucoup de votre aimable invitation pour Jeudi prochain.

Cela me fera un grand plaisir d'aller déjeuner chez vous, et je m'y rendrai au jour indiqué . . . .'

Agréez Madame [Cugnier], l'assurance de mes sentiments les plus distingués, . . .'*

Once again, John Synge was displaying his remarkable aptitude for languages. This letter was written in Paris in early February 1895 and is addressed to the mother of Albert Cugnier, a Breton student he had met in Oberwerth the previous winter. French was almost a new language to him when he returned to the von Eickens in November 1894. He stayed only two months at Oberwerth, where he enlisted the help of Valeska to improve his German.

But his most urgent task was the learning of French, which would prepare him for the courses he wished to take at the Sorbonne and the École Pratique des Hautes-Études. A friend of Valeska's, Mlle Mansaca, gave him lessons. He flung himself energetically into the study of the two languages; he was, at the same time, convinced that he could eke out a living by teaching English in Paris, as many young men had done before him.

Music was not entirely laid aside: Synge hired a grand piano for the von Eicken soirées, and celebrated a delightful Christmas in the company of the sisters and their friends. He left Germany on New Year's Day 1895—in gesture to a new beginning. His confidence had returned.

There were few cities to equal Paris towards the turn of the century. It was a magnet for the young intellectuals of Europe and the

---

* *Thank you very much for your kind invitation for next Thursday. It will give me great pleasure to come and have lunch at your home, and I shall present myself on the appointed day . . . . Believe me, Madame [Cugnier], yours sincerely, . . .'*

United States. By day they were to be found browsing among the bookstalls in the rue des Écoles, or sipping coffee and absinthe in student cafés and restaurants. By night the social whirl of the boulevard Montparnasse beckoned. Had Synge not taken Cherrie Matheson with him in his thoughts, he might have been found there, enjoying the fruits forbidden to his fellow anglophones by the stricter, Victorian codes of their native countries. He was a generation too late to have run into Charles Dickens or Henry James. He was nearly a generation too early for Ezra Pound, James Joyce, and the eclectic band of writers who were to patronize Sylvia Beach's bookshop, Shakespeare and Company. However, during those first months of 1895, he might have chanced upon George Moore on one of that flamboyant writer's Paris trips, perhaps in the company of Edward Martyn. He might even have met W. B. Yeats *before* that fateful day in 1896. He could have shared the freedom of self-expression enjoyed by the Anglo-Irish in a city where they were on an equal footing with the expatriate *Anglais.* Just how free Paris was, compared with the cities of Britain, is evidenced by the Parisians' relaxed attitude to prostitution:

> It was not until 1946 that the brothels of Paris were officially closed. For the better part of a hundred years they had been one of the city's major tourist industries and since the middle of the previous century the facilities on offer, especially in . . . central Paris, had grown increasingly elaborate. The 1880s and 1890s saw the publication of numerous 'bachelor's guides' which tabulated their various attractions. Typical of these helpful reference books was *The Pretty Women of Paris, Being a Complete Directory or Guide to Pleasure for Visitors to the Gay City.*

All this was worlds away from John Synge. Contrary to his expectations, Paris had not welcomed him with open arms; his first January in the 'Gay City' was a dark, lonely and miserable one. His Breton friend had arranged attic lodgings for him at the home of a certain M. Arbeau, a cook who augmented his earnings by the preparation of tooth-powder, and whose wife made ladies' hats. Both activities were pursued in the living-room. Synge helped out, in an effort to be integrated into this new foreign society. He was not altogether successful in this, but he did receive valuable lessons in French from his host, in return for a small fee. His nights were full of brooding as he sat alone in his attic room:

> Wet winds and rain are in the street,
> > Where I must pass alone,
> Where no one wayfarer I meet
> > That I have loved or known.
>
> 'Tis winter in my heart, the air
> > Is wailing, bitter cold,
> While I am wailing with despair,
> > As I have wailed of old.

The pain is almost tangible, the technique now so stripped of excess baggage that the key morphemes 'wet', 'wind' and 'wail' complement both the *w* of 'winter' and the *hw* of 'where' and 'while' to lend a primitive, Saxon feel to the lines. Indeed, with the exception of 'despair', we seek in vain for French. This is very intimate verse, with little sense of place; Synge might have written it anywhere. It is a cry in the darkness.

Once more, however, and through no design of his own, Synge was entering a foreign society through the back door—in this case, the tradesmen's entrance. It was fortunate that a Breton family should have been his *introducteurs* to Paris, because through the Cugniers he acquired an interest in the Celtic peasantry of Brittany whose sea-bound lives so closely resembled the Aran Islanders'.

But first came the Sorbonne, where he enrolled in April in courses on the modern French writers, and Petit de Julleville's lectures on medieval literature. At the same time, he was following a course in general and comparative phonetics at the École Pratique des Hautes-Études.

He changed his lodgings, too, and began to make friends among the students. Synge's plan to give English lessons was having some success. The small income from his mother was supplemented by tuition fees that gave him the freedom to engage in the social activities of his fellow students; the evenings found Synge enjoying coffee and conversation in the cafés of the Latin Quarter.

Indeed, with the coming of spring he began to see the city through different eyes; he passed long hours in the Louvre, the Palais and Jardin du Luxembourg, and Notre-Dame, or in lively discourse with his new-found literary and intellectual friends. It was a happy time, made even happier when, at the end of May, he made the acquaintance of a new English pupil, Thérèse Beydon, a drawing teacher. 'She was a devout Protestant,' writes Edward Stephens, 'but had none of the insular prejudices of the Irish Evangelicals. Besides art, with which her occupation was concerned, she was interested in politics. She sympathised generally with the feminist movement which was then taking shape and, in particular, with the efforts that were being made to organise the nursing profession and gave her passionate support to Zola's efforts on behalf of Dreyfus.'

She had, in fact, with the exception of art, almost nothing in common with Cherrie Matheson. Thérèse Beydon was living proof that devout Protestantism and radicalism were not irreconcilable opposites. On one occasion, she brought Synge to a lecture on anarchism; he was not, however, impressed.

There was no question of genuine romance between Mlle Beydon and John Synge; theirs was a friendship based on mutual advantage. They exchanged languages: he taught her English, she helped him to improve his French. Synge's companionship must have suited Thérèse Beydon admirably. No doubt she, the feminist, felt—as most women did—at ease with Synge the willing listener, this gentle, soft-spoken young man, who was eager to acquaint himself better with every kind of socialist thought and liberal opinion, including hers.

In turn, Thérèse Beydon gave Synge an insight into European life; an insight that was deeper than that which he had gained in Germany. While Oberwerth was the epitome of placid and stable provincialism, the Paris of 1895 was a hotbed of revolutionary thought; there were few students of Synge's acquaintance whose politics were not leftist and who, like he, had not lost their religion. 'It is very amusing to me', he wrote to Cherrie, 'coming back to Ireland to find myself looked upon as a Pariah, because I don't go to church and am not orthodox, while in Paris amongst the students I am looked upon as a saint, simply because I don't do the things they do and many come to me as a sort of Father Confessor . . . .'

Cherrie was far from forgotten, despite Synge's infatuation with Parisian student life and the politics of Thérèse Beydon. He had written long letters to her from the outset of his stay in Paris, some filled with agonized self-pity. He was determined that the summer of 1895 would see progress in their romance.

Synge left Paris on 28 June, and returned to Dublin by way of London. Florence Ross, he discovered, was not there; she had left to join her brother in Tonga where he had been appointed doctor and, in consequence, Cherrie did not vacation that year with Mrs Synge in Wicklow. Frustrated beyond measure, Synge devised means of seeing his 'Holy One' on his return to Crosthwaite Park in September. He succeeded. They went to art exhibitions together, took regular walks, visited one of Synge's cherished retreats, St Patrick's Cathedral. Cherrie's parents showed no objection to their meeting, unchaperoned. Romance and marriage seemed a real possibility. Synge went back to Paris the following January with a light heart.

But he had made a grave miscalculation. Cherrie was still the devout young Christian she had always been, unwilling to share the nuptial bed with an apostate. When Synge wrote to her on 3 June 1896 with a proposal of marriage, the young lady reluctantly, but firmly, answered 'no'.

He was devastated. So much so, in fact, that he imagined a conspiracy, involving Cherrie, his upbringing, and the earth. Synge set out his sorrow in a palpably autobiographical piece called *Vita Vecchia*, Old Life, which he had begun writing in 1895. It is a concatenation of narrative and verse. One poem, entitled 'My Lady left me and I said', appears to embody his belief that his love of Cherrie Matheson would amount to nothing; that he saw his future as a lonely, unmarried man, a prisoner of his art and his past:

I curse my bearing, childhood, youth
I curse the sea, sun, mountains, moon,
I curse my learning, search for truth,
I curse the dawning, night, and noon.

Cold, joyless I will live, though clean,
Nor, by my marriage, mould to earth
Young lives to see what I have seen,
To curse—as I have cursed—their birth.

It leaves little *uncursed*. The vehemence with which Synge castigates his mother for his 'bearing, childhood, youth' takes us a little by surprise. We may have been prepared for self-pity and criticism, remembering that while in Germany he had already written to his mother complaining about his upbringing; but clearly these lines spring from a very troubled mind. We cannot call 'poetic licence' to Synge's defence: the poem is much too personal for that; it is the poet baring his tormented soul.

VIII

In the spring of 1898, John Synge at last relinquished his hold on the chimera of marriage to Cherrie Matheson. He had proposed to her a second time, but her rejection had remained firm. There is something very poignant in the fact that it was his mother who finally persuaded him that further perseverance was useless. The chasm that separated him from Cherrie was, by then, too wide to span. Europe had spoiled Synge forever.

He had lived among the godless youth of Paris; Cherrie's place was among the Plymouth Brethren. He talked of socialism; she talked of salvation. He talked of patriotism and a love of Ireland; Cherrie only sketched the Irish landscape. He talked . . . the list of differences could go on; they were too many. In 1902, Cherrie married Kenneth Houghton, a mathematics teacher, ten years her junior, a devout Protestant—and a man with prospects. Soon after the marriage, she moved with her husband to South Africa, and out of Synge's life forever.

Cherrie was gone, though the memory of his passion for her was to colour Synge's prentice work. The mystery of the 'eternal feminine' that had haunted Goethe would also dog Synge's tracks, 'bringing sorrow as well as joy in its train'. There would always be women in his life; he seemed to gravitate naturally towards them, and they to him. It is just possible that he understood women more than men; the women of his plays usually hold centre-stage. Synge listened to women, ever willing to heed their good advice. When Cherrie Matheson suggested, at the end of 1895, that he go to Italy, he agreed readily. Her painters' circle provided Synge with letters of introduction, and so, after spending January 1896 in Paris, he left for the ancient haunt of his spiritual guide Goethe, and arrived in Rome in early February, enrolling at once in courses in literature at the Collegio Romano.

Like Goethe's extended tours of the country, Italy brought Synge into contact with its art and letters, and, as with Goethe, introduced him to some fascinating young women: an American girl called Lily Capps, Maria Antonia Zdanowska, and Hope Rea.

Lily Capps was a fellow-boarder at Synge's *pensione* in Rome, near the Pincio and the Borghese Gardens. At this time, Synge's diverse reading included the works of Ernest Renan, a French historian and essayist who had once studied for the priesthood. It is easy to see why Synge discovered an affinity with Renan, a man whose faith had been shattered by a sudden revelation, obtained during his seminary days, that science had more to offer humanity than religion could. His most important work is the *Histoire des origines du christianisme*, wherein he looks at the Christian faith from a rationalistic—even an aesthetic—vantage. He was, together with Hippolyte Taine and, to a certain extent, Emile Zola, one of the most important protagonists of positivism, an anti-metaphysical movement which recognized only the evidence of facts. Renan's intent was to demysticize Christianity; there was no God, he claimed, but there was a 'power'. Oscar Wilde hailed *Vie de Jésus* (with which Renan's history opens) as a fifth Gospel.

It seems certain that Synge, too, was greatly taken with the study, for he lent a copy to Lily Capps. During the three months which he spent in Rome, he and the young American became quite intimate, if platonically so. She was, Stephens writes,

> conventional, but friendly, and had a much wider knowledge of the world than the members of the family group at Crosthwaite Park. Though naturally reserved [Synge] felt free, in foreign countries, to discuss his life with friends, who would never meet the people of his own home circle. Miss Capps and he discussed art, religion, and the ways of life of the people they knew. He talked to her about the questions of faith that had overshadowed his mind from boyhood . . . .

It is perhaps this American friend, more than anybody else (including Synge himself), who gives us a clue to the nature of his beliefs—or, rather, unbelief. In the course of a letter she wrote to him when he had returned to Ireland, she states: 'You say, "there is no God", but admit there is a power. It is one and the same thing called by a different name. We do agree on many points but you go too far for me.'

Synge, like Renan, had become an agnostic, not an atheist. Once again, by wearing his irreligion on his sleeve, he had turned away the heart of a woman; Lily Capps passed from John Synge's life.

Rome fed the philologist in Synge. Having taken Italian lessons from Dr Eustachio Meli in Paris, he gained a good command of the language remarkably quickly, and immersed himself in Dante and other classical Italians writers, as well as reading Petrarch. By 15 March 1896, Synge was so accomplished that he could write the following to Francesco Morosoni, who had given him Italian lessons in Dublin the previous autumn:

Egregio Signore,
La settimana scorsa le ho mandato alcuni giornali Italiani,
perche sono sicuro ch' ella sara contenta di poter leggere

più dettagliate notizie sulla crise politica di cui parlano i giornali di Dublino. Io sono a Roma da sei settimane e ho molto lavorato non senza qualche buon esito; ma non so ancora se potro imparare abbastanza durante i tre mesi che passero in Italia secondo la mia prima intenzione.*

Synge was referring to the demonstrations against the prime minister, Francesco Crispi, whose disastrous handling of the war in Abyssinia had led to his resignation. The Italians had been defeated, with heavy losses, and stories circulated of the Abyssinians' mutilating wounded men. The letter shows that not only had Synge's Italian acquired virtuosity, but his interest in politics had quickened too; sufficiently so for him to write an 'eye-witness' account of the Rome demonstrations for *The Irish Times*. It was never published.

He was painfully unsure of himself during this period, spreading his talents thinly. All the while, Goethe's writings pulled him towards the literary life. He attempted more poetry, drafted ideas for plays, tried some journalism, literary criticism. All proved mediocre.

———————

Synge went to Florence in May and spent a month there, before returning to Paris. It was in Florence that he met Maria Zdanowska and Hope Rea, fellow-boarders at his *pensione*. They presented a unusual contrast. Zdanowska was Polish, a devout Catholic, who had come to Tuscany to study sculpture. Rea was an Englishwoman, an art student, who was working on a book, *Tuscan Artists: Their Thought and Work*, which was published in 1898.

Maria Zdanowska's beliefs were as hidebound as those of Cherrie Matheson. She found Synge's agnosticism disconcerting

———————

* *Esteemed Sir, Last week I sent you several Italian newspapers, because I am sure that you should like to be able to read more detailed reports on the political crisis that the Dublin newspapers are talking about. I have been in Rome for six weeks and have worked hard with some good results; but I do not know yet if I will be able to learn enough in the three months that I had originally intended spending in Italy.*

and, like Cherrie, gave him religious books to read, that he might yet return to Christianity. Hope Rea, on the other hand, was a sceptic and a rationalist, who took Synge's side in the frequent discussions that the three had, and was contemptuous of Zdanowska's attempts to foist Catholic dogma on him.

It is difficult to ignore the feeling that Rea, despite her rationalistic outlook, was closer than most to Synge in her search for truth; a number of years later, she joined the Theosophical Society in London. Synge remained friends with the two women; they corresponded for the rest of his life. He met Maria Zdanowska often in Paris; Hope Rea he saw on several occasions in London, and they wrote often to one another.

All things considered, Europe and her women had been kind to Synge. But he yearned for more than kindness and companionship; he desired marriage above all else. Like his art, it became an obsession.

IX

Almost a decade was to pass before Synge met the young woman who would finally banish the spectre of his frustrated courtship of Cherrie Matheson. Mrs Synge, in the meantime, made several attempts at matchmaking. Her summer homes in the Wicklow hills played host to a number of marriageable women: Synge cousins and their companions. They were, almost without exception, girls of evangelical stock, in whose company Synge felt somewhat uneasy. Small wonder, then, that he grew resentful of his mother's efforts to find him a 'suitable' spouse.

The exception was Edie Harmar, whom Synge met on 6 June 1899, a year after his break with Cherrie Matheson. His brother Samuel had been ordained on 21 May 1896. He received a posting in China, and there he married a fellow-missionary, Mary Harmar. Her sister Edie arrived at Castle Kevin in the company of her friend Madeline Kerr, a neighbour from Edie's native Norwood, a small town in Middlesex. As it happened, John was the only member of her family who could accompany Mrs Synge to her County Wicklow retreat that year.

Edie Harmar was no less imbued than her missionary sister with a zeal for proselytizing. Yet she had qualities which attracted Synge: she painted, and had a lively interest in occult phenomena. She also understood John Synge's need for proof of the supernatural. She may, indeed, have supplied some when, one morning, she told him of a dream she had had, in which she saw him riding his bicycle, and sitting outside a cottage, smoking a pipe. On questioning her further, he was convinced that she had somehow 'seen' him at the MacDonagh house on Inishmaan.

Synge was quite taken with Edie Harmar, and theirs was to be a lasting friendship. His romantic thoughts, however, were elsewhere that summer. His twin pursuits, the quest for the numinous and his striving to find a literary voice, had led to his tentative courtship of Margaret Hardon, a Bostonian, whom he had met in Paris in April 1898. She was an etcher and a student of architecture; she also shared Synge's burgeoning interest in Celtic studies and mysticism. By autumn, Synge had fallen in love with her; by the spring of 1899, he had proposed marriage, and the young lady had very politely declined. She would—like Cherrie Matheson, Valeska von Eicken, Thérèse Beydon, Hope Rea and Edie Harmar—remain a good friend, nothing more. Europe was not to provide a wife for Synge; his years there were to have another purpose. His travels, his reading, his friends and—not least—his women friends, were to provide the subtle material which one day would coalesce to form the building-blocks of great art. What a shame, then, that our knowledge of Synge's formative period—1895–1903—is so sketchy. Ann Saddlemyer deplores this 'great gap in our understanding of Synge's artistic and emotional development':

> What do we have on record for those important years? A few of his letters to friends—mainly women confidantes such as Valeska von Eicken; Thérèse Beydon . . . and her mother; Albert Cugnier . . . and *his* mother; Mrs Synge's quotations from his letters and conversation in her diaries;

a . . . memoir by Stephen MacKenna which confirms Synge's detailed and technical knowledge of the visual arts and the austerity of his Paris life; a few memories by W. B. Yeats; his own daily diary records of visits to the Louvre, his extraordinary sweeping reading habits, appointments with friends; *Vita Vecchia* . . . ; *Étude Morbide*, which . . . explores . . . some of his sexual urges and fears for emotional and mental stability of the same time.

There are diaries with missing pages, scraps of notes and jottings, some written seemingly at random. Even those who were closest to him have not explained to our satisfaction how it came that Synge made the leap from obscurity to acclaim, from *Vita Vecchia* to *Riders to the Sea*. 'We are depending', says Saddlemyer,

> upon memorialists looking back through the years of Synge's maturity; even MacKenna, his closest male friend during the Paris years, is afflicted with the lamentable hero-worship of the dead. Will we ever come any closer to divining what happened to Synge during that period to give him the substance of the mature playwright . . . ? Until we are able to reconstruct this missing chapter in the life of John Millington Synge, the clue to this enigmatic, very private person whose self-confidence so astonished those who knew him, and whose craftsmanship resulted in such dazzlingly complete works of art, continues to elude us. We do not yet, alas, have all the notes.

There is, moreover, no truly adult memoir from Synge's own hand; all we have is an autobiography which ends with the words: 'I threw aside all reasonable counsel and declared myself a professional musician.' Synge was probably twenty-one when he wrote this. Full artistic—and, possibly, emotional—maturity was still some years distant.

And yet, considering the prodigious amount of reading that Synge did during his 'European' years—in English, Irish, Latin, French, German and Italian, not to mention the more obscure tongues such as Breton—and taking into account the wealth and variety of people and places he encountered during this time, can we not wonder, as Goldsmith wondered of another, that 'one small head could carry all he knew'? That knowledge had to out. Can we not also consider the very privateness of Synge as a clue to the intellectual processes that were shaping the man?

Synge the dramatist was self-confident, yes. Did this self-confidence not rest in the knowledge that the bodies were buried, that the evidence of his trials and errors had disappeared along with those pages he tore from his notebooks, and the discarded plays such as *Sir John and Scherma*, which he worked on in 1895 (no trace of it remains); there was even the beginning of a novel. John Synge was a vain man who wished to excel at everything he touched. He was vain enough not to have wished his failures to see the light of day. When Synge's genius erupted suddenly on the world with 'dazzlingly complete works of art', the notes were indeed missing. Synge had destroyed them. He alone would remember the sweat and labour of his apprenticeship.

First Blood

I

Synge is angry. Synge is seething. Yet his expression does not alter as he stares across at the dumpy little woman seated at her desk in the drawing-room at Coole Park. Two mirrors in elaborate, gilt frames flank the window directly behind her. The sunlight of autumn 1901 slants past the nude, marble shoulders of a statue of Andromeda set before the window, and throws a corona of silver round the woman's head. Synge blinks.

'I'm s-sorry,' he stammers, 'but what did you say?'

'I am afraid, Mr Synge,' repeats Lady Gregory, 'that this is not a good play.'

Synge looks across at Yeats. For once, Ireland's foremost poet is silent, chewing his lip in nervous embarrassment. If Synge expected support from that quarter, then clearly it will not be forthcoming.

With great tact and sensitivity, Augusta Gregory explains why *When the Moon Has Set* does not measure up to the standards of the Irish Literary Theatre. It is not a good play, it seems 'of slight merit', because it contains too much of John Millington Synge, and not enough universality. A successful play, she goes on to say, may be autobiographical, yet it should lend itself to the translation to other climes, other languages, while retaining its import. In her opinion, Synge's two-act work fails in this respect.

John Synge swallows his anger, and his pride. He has made a grave error of judgement, this he knows. But he was so sure of the play, his finest effort to date. He sees Lady Gregory now with new eyes. There sits the woman whose great energy made possible the Irish Literary Theatre. Like W. B. Yeats, Lady Gregory was, at the inception of the grand scheme, a tyro, feeling her way in the theatre business. Yet, from the very outset—the productions of *The Countess Cathleen* and *The Heather Field* in May 1899—it seemed that Lady Gregory could do no wrong. With an unerring eye for quality and originality, she has given her blessing to a succession of pieces whose titles will live long in the national memory: George Moore's *The Bending of the Bough*, Alice Milligan's *The Last Feast of the Fianna*, Edward Martyn's *Maeve*. These are Irish plays, distinctly Irish plays. Synge's play is Irish too. Where lies the difference?

The difference, Lady Gregory tells him, lies in the subject-matter. Synge's play deals with aesthetics, the poet's dilemma. The dilemma is Synge's own, because the play, as Nicholas Grene concludes, 'smoulders dismally round the uninflammable clinker of Synge's personal feelings and ideas'. The first act opens to one of the characters—a nun—reading from a manuscript written by the hero of the play:

> Every life is a symphony and the translation of this sequence into music and from music again, for those who are not musicians, into literature, or painting or sculpture, is the real effort of the artist.
>
> The emotions which pass through us have neither end nor beginning, are a part of eternal sensations, and it is this almost cosmic element in the person which gives all personal art a share in the dignity of the world.

The hero quotes lines from the same source towards the close of Act II:

> Every life is a symphony . . . . If art is the expression of the abstract beauty of the person there are times when the person is the expression of the beauty that is beyond the world . . . .

The credo is Synge's own, and Lady Gregory is correct in deciding that matter such as this has no place on the stage. It is philosophy, not drama; it is the creed of the aesthetes of Paris,

running riot in an Irish country drawing-room. Columb, the protagonist of the play, is a poet-musician who is determined to win
his distant cousin, Sister Eileen, from the celibate life of the nun-
nery. He attempts to convert her, as Mary C. King puts it, 'from the
asceticism of religious dogma to a dogmatic, if confused aestheti-
cism, which is expounded in the play's aesthetic manuscript'.

If the persona of J. M. Synge looms hugely behind the relationship of the protagonist to the nun, then there is worse to come.
The hero's uncle, who dies just before the play begins, has had an
affair with a local woman: Biddy, the aunt of the young maid Bride.
Aunt Biddy, we learn, died many years ago. A marriage between
her and Columb's uncle was ruled out: he was a confirmed agnostic, she a devout Catholic. He was master of the Big House in which
the action takes place, she was poor. So great were these impedi-
ments, in fact, that the woman became insane. This off-stage
tragedy, posits King, 'has as its theme the way in which love when
denied leads to despair, insanity, violence and death.'

These are fears which have haunted Synge from the time of
Cherrie Matheson's first rejection of marriage. They pervade *Étude
Morbide*, a curious account of a musician's love of two women—the
Chouska and the Celliniani—which Synge wrote in 1889. He struc-
tured it in the form of a diary. It is highly autobiographical; he
regards it as 'a morbid thing about a mad fiddler in Paris which I
hate'. Synge's hatred notwithstanding, elements of *Étude Morbide*
have crept into *When the Moon Has Set*.

So, too, have motifs from Synge's earlier prentice work. In his
'Plan for a Play' he investigated the relationships of two couples;
When the Moon Has Set considers two unlikely matches. In this
instance, the couples represent two generations. But they are interchangeable; Synge's characterization is almost non-existent. Robin
Skelton points out that Columb 'is too obviously a vehicle for the
author's opinions and Sister Eileen is little more than cardboard'.
By the same token, the liaison of Columb's uncle and Aunt Biddy
belongs not to a dramaturgical past, but to Synge's own. Cherrie is
to the fore.

The play, moreover, has dangerous tendencies. Towards the

end of the second, and final, act, Columb persuades Sister Eileen to put on a green wedding dress. The dress belongs to Bride, who is pregnant with the child of a servant of the Big House. The poet, in a pointedly blasphemous, priestless ceremony, 'marries' Sister Eileen with the words: 'In the name of the Summer and the Sun, and the whole World, I wed you as my wife.'

Yeats's and Lady Gregory's reluctance to take the play is understandable. Synge is expressing ideas that surely would be repugnant to their audiences. While it is perfectly all right for Edward Martyn's fairy hero—in *Maeve*—to espouse Christian values, it is unthinkable that Columb's ascendancy Protestantism and Sister Eileen's Catholic faith should be reconciled by a pagan nature religion.

That this heathen religion is alluded to elsewhere in the play is evidenced in an early scene when Bride attempts to rekindle the hearth with damp turf. None of the Big House's occupants is able to light a fire; for them it is a forgotten art. The symbolism of the dying hearth and the dead master is obvious—but there is more. Synge knows the importance of the hearth-fire. It is no accident that he has called the maid Bride; she is the only bride in the house, and to her—a latter-day Vestal Virgin—is entrusted the guardianship of the sacred fire of Vesta, the Roman goddess of the hearth. Like that of Sister Eileen, her 'marriage' is, in the first act, a celibate one. Synge has seen the distress caused to the Aran Islanders by eviction, the expulsion from hearth and home. 'The outrage to a tomb in China', he has written, 'probably gives no greater shock to the Chinese than the outrage to a hearth in Inishmaan gives to the people.'

The heathen elements are not lost on Yeats, but he makes no direct allusions to them in his criticism of Synge's first dramatic work:

> I wish to be emphatic about this play. It is just the kind of work which some theatrical experimenter with no literary judgment or indifferent to literature would be glad to get. It is quite complete. It might have a slight stage success

with a certain kind of very modern audience . . . . It is morbid and conventional though with an air of originality. The only thing interesting about it is that it shows his pre-occupation with the thought of death.

The preoccupation is not unjustified. The swelling on Synge's neck, which was removed in 1897, had returned. At the time of its excision, Synge had been told by the doctors at the hospital, the Elpis Nursing Home in Dublin, that they considered him to be completely cured. But in the autumn of last year, 1900, the lymph glands had swollen again. Instead of having to undergo another operation, he was given a number of ointments by doctors. The swelling subsided.

Oddly enough, neither Lady Gregory nor Yeats has commented on the language of *When the Moon Has Set*. Now it must be said that there is little remarkable about the dialogue that Synge has arranged for his principal characters; it is, in the main, common to contemporary British drama. No, it is the talk of the young maid which deserves a closer scrutiny:

> BRIDE. My uncle is a bit queer too, one time and another.
> I'm thinking it was him your honour seen this night
> upon the roads, for he does be always walking round
> like yourself, God bless you, a fine handsome man, and
> it's two years now since we seen him, though we've
> heard tell this last while it wasn't far off from us he was
> at all.

or, to present this little speech in another format:

> My uncle is a bit queer too,
> One time and another.
> I'm thinking it was him your honour
> Seen this night upon the roads,
> For he does be always walking
> Round like yourself, God bless you,
> A fine handsome man,
> And it's two years now since we seen him,

> Though we've heard tell this last while
> It wasn't far off from us
> [That] he was at all.

It cannot have escaped Yeats's notice that almost every line that Bride utters is written in blank verse. Likewise, Mrs Byrne—an old servant—is given monologues which read at times like the words of a lyrical Irish benediction, or, indeed, a song:

> It is true for you,
> And isn't it a grand thing
> To see the like of it
> In the month of June,
> And isn't it a grand thing
> Your honour's getting his health for
> The fine time of year.

The poetry-watcher will have caught the first, infant cries of the 'Synge-song': 'In the <u>month</u> | <u>of</u> | <u>June</u>'; '<u>The</u> <u>fine</u> <u>time</u> | <u>of</u> | <u>year</u>'— the 'thudding three-stress termination' that will become a hallmark of Synge's dialogue.

In contrast, the lines Synge affords Columb and Sister Eileen are written in prose. It could not be otherwise, for this is the mode of speech of their class; it is the language that Synge has heard spoken at his mother's knee. To allow Columb and the nun to talk in the linguistic register of the peasantry would be to deny the status quo. And so we are treated to bland exchanges such as:

SISTER EILEEN. I have heard from the Superior. She is short of nurses, so she wrote to Dr Burke to know when I would be free. He answered that you were nearly well, so I am to go to-morrow. It would have been better if you had let me go last week.

COLUMB [*walking to the window*]. Cannot you wait a few days longer?

SISTER EILEEN. I am afraid not possibly. - - [*looking at her watch*] - - I must soon go and pack.

The problem with this play, however, is that we do not get such dialogue throughout. Columb's prose is not consistent; it waxes lyrical when we least expect it, interpolating lines like 'It is natural for old men to die. This pageant of blossom that fades in a few hours is far more terrible.' We are aware from the outset that Columb is an aesthete, and we *expect* poetic language from him. We do not always hear it, and sometimes it can sit uneasily within the context. It is only towards the end of the second act that the young man's lyricism takes full flight, with imagery such as '. . . your soul has been growing like a germinating seed, and your mind like a moth within the mask of the chrysalis', and 'Every leaf and flower and insect is full of deeper wonder than any signs the cabbalists have invented'.

When the Moon Has Set is 'not a good play' because Synge has mixed his idioms. The characters are compatible within the action, but their speech is not. T. S. Eliot cautions that

> a mixture of prose and verse in the same play is generally to be avoided: each transition makes the auditor aware, with a jolt, of the medium. It is, we may say, justifiable when the author wishes to produce this jolt: when, that is, he wishes to transport the audience violently from one plane of reality to another. I suspect that this kind of transition was easily acceptable to an Elizabethan audience, to whose ears both prose and verse came naturally . . . and to whom it seemed perhaps proper that the more humble and rustic characters should speak in a homely language, and that those of more exalted rank should rant in verse.

Is this perhaps where Synge's problem lies? Has he not created an inverted world where the servant has usurped the exalted rant of the master? And yet Synge has experienced such a world: a place where poet and peasant are one; where storytellers are judged as much by their lyrical verbosity as by the content of their tales. Is wild Aran not so noble in deed and spirit as was the court of Queen Elizabeth; are the fishermen of Inishmaan who hunt the herring any less brave than the well-born sailors of Queen Bess, who fought off the Spanish Armada in 1588? Is their language not equally rich?

Synge takes the train at Gort. On the journey to Galway city, he browses in his Aran notebooks. There are three of them now, one for each of his visits to the islands: 1898, 1899, 1900. They have done good duty in the compilation of his book, *The Aran Islands*, now nearing completion.

There are other notebooks, too. They are full of snatches of speech recorded in the Wicklow hills: the speech of the peasants. Compared with the richness of this language, what Synge calls the 'joyless and pallid words' of Emile Zola and Henrik Ibsen pale even more.

Chastened and thoughtful, John Synge boards the steamer in Galway, for his fourth visit to Inishmaan.

II

The God of Aran knows no appeasement. This year he has visited two plagues on the islanders: death by typhus and death by drowning. Inishmaan is steeped in gloom and mourning. 'No two journeys to these islands', Synge writes laconically, 'are alike.'

Pat Dirane is dead; his stories are not. The islanders seem unwilling to accept the natural causes of the frightful epidemic that has carried off young and old. No, the fairies are at work again; spells fly like guillemots above the rocky fields.

The fever has visited the MacDonagh home too. 'Norah,' Synge notes, 'the girl who was spinning in this house last year, is very ill and some of the people say she is dying.' There are no priests or doctors on Inishmaan, so a fast curagh is dispatched to Inishmore, the Big Island. Synge is appalled by the presence of death so close to him. He has not lived long enough among the islanders; it takes more than a few summer weeks to apprehend fully their precarious existence.

It is fortunate that Synge has brought his fiddle. In the midst of mourning, the islanders dance reels and jigs so fast that Synge can hardly keep up with their flying, pampootied feet. Music may hold the harsh deity at bay, soothe the beast. If this music fails, they can fall back on the keen.

The keen rises in the throats of the men and women as they forgather in the graveyard to lay to rest 'a young man who had died in his first manhood, instead of an old woman of eighty'. It is hard to clear a decent resting place in Aran; too many bones compete for the shallow burial ground. A woman finds the skull of her mother, thrown up by the gravediggers, and her keen turns to a heart-rending shrieking. The scene could have been torn from Dante or Bosch:

> This last moment of grief was the most terrible of all. The young women were nearly lying among the stones, worn out with their passion of grief, yet raising themselves every few moments to beat with magnificent gestures on the boards of the coffin. The young men were worn out also, and their voices cracked continually in the wail of the keen.

Fevers may come and go, but the first blood is always to the sea. When the Atlantic storms rage, the hookers and curaghs that ply between the islands risk destruction on the rocks. Synge hears of a recent drowning.

Some men from Inisheer, South Island, had bought horses on Inishmaan, and wished to transport them in their hooker. They engaged a young man—a good horse-handler—to accompany them home, so that he might tow the beasts ashore with his curagh. No sooner were they in the sound than a storm blew up. Because the curagh was being towed by the hooker, the young man could not turn it into the high waves, and his boat began to take on water. The men of Inisheer yelled to him to let go the rope. It was too late; the curagh had sunk. The young man was seen swimming frantically in circles, but he disappeared before help could reach him.

Anticipating a ghost story, Synge asks whether the young man has been sighted since the drowning. He is not disappointed.

There were 'queer things in it', he is told. Before the young man went to sea that day, his dog began to howl. Some days after the tragedy, when a group of islanders were bringing horses down to the sea, an old woman saw the drowned man riding one of them. No one else saw him. Another young man led the horse which the ghost was riding and he, too, was drowned that day.

Synge lies in the rough grass and sees the spume and foam that crest the black Atlantic waves. In this wild place, thoughts turn back to a time when the race was young. Other gods ruled then: the Dagda, the Morrigan, Manannan . . . .

Manannan Mac Lir, the god of the sea. When Manannan moves across his domain, his horses are white, and their riders are the ghosts of those he has taken. This the islanders know and accept: 'We must be satisfied because nobody can be living forever.'

III

See Synge the dramatist sitting at his typewriter in the summer of 1902. What a cumbersome little contraption this Blickensderfer is! 'A rattletrap metal Sphinx,' Hugh Kenner calls it; 'an absurdity with serried levers like the knees of iron grasshoppers and interchangeable typewheels.' The keys do not follow the QWERTY configuration; T and E are where they should be: at the writer's index fingertips. The QWERTY system was designed to slow down the typist; Synge's Blickensderfer requires no further slowness. Each letter must be chosen with deliberation; the machine is useful only when thoughts and ideas are concrete enough to merit committal to paper.

The machine is portable, though, built for the nomadic writer; it goes where Synge goes. It has seen three European capitals, and has braved many a sea passage, stowed in Synge's old portmanteau. Its working parts smell of oil and brine. There is another odour too; it may be that of burnt peat . . . .

Cottage kitchen, with nets, oil-skins, spinning wheel, some new boards standing by the wall, etc. CATHLEEN, *a girl of about twenty, finishes kneading cake, and puts it down in the pot-oven by the fire; then wipes her hands, and begins to spin at the wheel.* NORA, *a young girl, puts her head in at the door.*

Let us watch carefully those 'new boards standing by the wall'; they may prove significant.

Synge pauses. He rolls a cigarette and looks out of the open window of his study. Swallows scythe the summer air in the rear garden of Tomriland House, Annamoe. A rook complains from its perch in the top branches of one of the horse chestnuts. A young boy and girl, accompanied by two dogs, scamper up Tomriland Hill, whose slopes rise gently from the bottom of the garden. In the kitchen, directly below Synge's workroom, Ellen the cook makes a rude, though witty, remark. Her voice carries up clearly through the wide chinks in the floorboards. Synge smiles.

Cigarette in left hand, he types one-fingeredly:

NORA

Square brackets now, for the opening line will set the mood:

[*in a low voice*].

First line: a question, just as Yeats opened *The Countess Cathleen* with a question; a question invites questions of the audience:

Where is she?

Synge draws slowly on his cigarette. There is still time to choose between verse and prose. The answering line will decide . . . .

A sheaf of paper rests in his old portmanteau; it has lain there unread since his return from Paris at the beginning of the summer. *A Vernal Play* announces the title sheet, typewritten on the Blickensderfer. There is another 'play'; it is no more than two dozen scrawled pages of a notebook. The title, *Luasnad, Capa and Laine*, is just about legible.

At this stage, they are not, by any stretch of the imagination, good plays; they need much revision. But at least Synge has made the attempt at dramatic verse. In *A Vernal Play*, we look in vain for the tragic message of *When the Moon Has Set*. 'The whole piece', Robin Skelton suggests, 'appears to be simply an attempt to express a lyrical mood and show how it is possible to accept and revere both youth and age, death and love', an acceptance and reverence Synge has learned from the people of Inishmaan. There is even a keen, but it is a far cry from that which Synge heard in the cemetery.

Luasnad, Capa and Laine comes closer to the Aran experience: the sense of approaching doom and the futility of human existence. All men are in the hands of the gods; moreover, the gods 'are jesting with them'. The play is based on the story of three antediluvian sailors who discovered Ireland. When the Deluge came they, their wives and their children, were drowned. Synge took the idea from Geoffrey Keating's *History of Ireland*; his review of an English translation of Keating's poems had appeared in *The Speaker* magazine on 8 December 1900. The theme is an epic one, and Synge felt that it could best be expressed in verse. He still does.

Verse will not work, however, for the new play he is scripting. But Synge does not need verse for *Riders to the Sea*; the language he has learned from the islanders is lyrical enough. His notebooks contain sufficient examples of dialogue tailor-made for his theme—a theme that recurs in Aran with horrendous regularity, as the sea claims its blood.

Riders to the Sea. The title is redolent of Scripture, the Book of Revelations. We are all riders to the sea, dust to dust. Synge remembers his Darwin, too: how the amphibian ancestors of mankind crawled up onto the shores of the ancient landmass of Pangaea. The omnipresent sea of Aran is the islanders' constant reminder that they all shall return to the ancestral home.

Synge is scripting a small masterpiece. *Riders to the Sea* is, in more than one sense of the word, a *universal* play. At its centre stands Maurya, an aged woman who has lost 'six fine men' to the sea: four sons, their father and their grandfather. Now it is the turn of Bartley, the youngest. Maurya sees his death by drowning as a grim inevitability. She has had those new boards imported from Connemara; they will go to fashion a coffin for her son Michael, whose drowned body may or not be found. It is nine days since his disappearance.

Maurya is unaware that her daughters, Cathleen and Nora, have been handed a small bundle of clothing taken from a corpse which the men have fished from the sea. The girls deduce that the shirt and 'plain stocking' are Michael's.

A storm is brewing, but Bartley defies the sea and goes to sell a horse in Galway. He drowns. Maurya has lost all her men. She accepts their fate.

Riders to the Sea is little more than a cameo, a slice of life in Aran. Synge is condensing the generations of the islands' past into a one-act piece that captures the quiet horror of an existence pervaded by the presence of the monstrous ocean. No sound effects are necessary to indicate its proximity just beyond the cottage door. The principals tell us that there is 'a great roaring in the west'; the 'wind is raising the sea' and the 'black hags [are] flying on the sea'.

Colour is absent from the world of Maurya and her daughters; they exist in a place where bones and coffin boards are white; some rocks are white too, thanks to the murderous surf. Blackness and darkness are all around them: 'the black night is falling' over the 'black cliffs of the north'; two sons and a husband 'were lost in a dark night', similiar to the 'dark nights after Samhain'. Michael's pitiful bundle of clothing has 'a black knot on it you wouldn't loosen in a week', a testament to the evil power of the sea. Evil even stalks the interior of the cottage: 'the pig with the black feet' has been caught eating the halter that Bartley will use on the mare he rides to his doom.

Synge's monochromy is relieved by three minor colours. A great deal of the off-stage action pivots around the 'green head'; the colours red and grey are suggestively sinister. Red is the colour of Bartley's mare; she is followed down to the sea by a grey pony,

on whose back Michael's ghost is seen riding. Mary C. King, in con-
currence with other commentators, suggests that this horse is 'typologically related to the apocalytic "pale horse; and his name that sat
on him was death"'. Perhaps; but white, not grey, has been tradi-
tionally the colour of death in the Mediterranean countries
whence the Revelations of St John came, as opposed to the mourn-
ing-black of the West. Michael may have been taken by death, but
his soul resides uneasily in a grey, limbo world until he can be
assured of 'a clean burial in the far north'.

Red, the vibrant hue of the petticoats of the women Synge
admires so much, is transmogrified into an emblem of death.
There is the red of Bartley's mare, and there is the 'half of a red
sail' that was used to carry his brother Patch's drowned body.
Maurya remembers that there was 'water dripping out of it—it was
a dry day, Nora—and leaving a track to the door'; now water drips
from a red sail bearing Bartley's corpse. The imagery is that of
blood spilling, staining the path to the cottage.

The cottage is the node—or, equally, the nave or navel: there
are a great many references to the points of the compass—of a
tiny, introspective universe of blacks, whites and greys, relieved
only by a headland where a little greenery grows, and by the blood-
red of death. Indeed, *relieved* is exactly how Maurya feels when her
last son is taken:

> They're all gone now, and there isn't anything more the sea
> can do to me . . . . I'll have no call now to be up crying and
> praying when the wind breaks from the south, and you can
> hear the surf is in the east, and the surf is in the west, mak-
> ing a great stir with the two noises, and they hitting one on
> the other. I'll have no call now to be going down and get-
> ting Holy Water in the dark nights after Samhain, and I
> won't care what way the sea is when the other women will be
> keening . . . but it's a great rest I'll have now, and it's time
> surely. It's a great rest I'll have now, and great sleeping in
> the long nights after Samhain, if it's only a bit of wet flour
> we do have to eat, and maybe a fish that would be stinking.

There is no room in the play for sentimentality, just as the island life that Synge portrays with such unnerving veracity leaves no room for genteel considerations. He has created that which Yeats and Lady Gregory urged him to create: a work which so transcends the author that he becomes the invisible hand behind it, godlike.

For there is nothing of the old Synge in *Riders to the Sea*, except, perhaps, his preoccupation with mortality. If Cherrie Matheson is here, then she, too, is invisible. The sequestered morality of the Syngeian drawing-room does not for a moment intrude on what Yeats calls 'the peasant mind as I know it, a mind that delights in strong sensations whether of beauty or of ugliness, in bare facts, and it is quite without sentimentality'.

No, this is not the old Synge, but a cold Synge. Seldom has a more chilling piece been written; possibly Danilo Kiš's *Hourglass* will, in the future, come close to the calm exposition of the horror of the human condition as it is presented in *Riders to the Sea*. Synge has met the God of Aran, and the injustice of this deity distresses him. He shares with Alfred de Vigny the perception that human life is nothing more than a divine diversion, a

> manteau de misère
> Qui l'entoure à grands plis, drap lugubre et fatal,
> Que d'un bout tient le Doute et de l'autre le Mal.[*]

As the shadows lengthen in the narrow oaked and chestnutted avenue that leads to Tomriland House, Synge applies the last full stop to his play. Already another shadow is forming in his mind, and his muse is still insistent enough to give it substance.

---

[*] . . . *mantle of misery/That He hems with mighty pleat; a garment baleful and fatal,/ Bearing at one end Doubt, and at the other Hurt.*

IV

There is a spectre that haunts County Wicklow—as, indeed, it haunts the whole of Ireland. This shade goes by various names; lunacy, insanity and mental illness being the most commonly used.

There is nothing congenital about the Irish form of insanity (unless we consider inbreeding, though it must be said that the Christian churches strictly forbid the marriage of first cousins, a constraint that close-knit communities like Aran's are careful of heeding). How then do we account for the inordinate number of inmates confined to Ireland's asylums and 'county homes' at the turn of the century? The statistics show that more than 21,000 lunatics and idiots are incarcerated; to be sure, a distressingly high proportion of the population. And yet, as Synge knows by direct observation, many of Ireland's mentally deficient are at large on the streets and country roads.

In the Wicklow hills, a fit of madness can strike at any time, without warning. Synge has heard, for example, of the case of Mary Kinsella, 'a fine woman with two children . . . and a year and a half ago she went wrong in her head, and they had to send her away. And then up there in the Richmond asylum maybe they thought the sooner they were shut of her the better, for she died two days ago this morning.' He has heard, too, of the poor farm labourer who had been

> ' . . . reaping in the glen, and in the evening he had two glasses of whisky with some other lads. Then some excitement took him, and he threw off his clothes and ran away into the hills. There was great rain that night, and I suppose the poor creature lost his way, and was the whole night perishing in the rain and darkness. In the morning they found his naked foot-marks on some mud half a mile above the road, and again where you go up by a big stone. Then there was nothing known of him till last night, when they found his body on the mountain, and it near eaten by the crows.'

Future practitioners of medicine may identify such an attack with manic depression, a mental condition known to cause mood swings that oscillate between extremes of melancholia and elation. Synge has already noted the 'influence of a particular locality' on the minds of many people, which 'has caused or increased a tendency to nervous depression among the people'. There may be others; poor nutrition from the time of birth can stunt the growth of both the body and healthy brain cells. Another cause is enforced celibacy.

'There are so few girls left in these neighbourhoods,' Synge writes in his essay 'The Oppression of the Hills'; emigration to England and the United States has robbed Wicklow of her young women. Marriage into other communities, too, has taken them from native parishes.

And what of the young men? If they are fortunate to be the first born, then the family property will fall to them on their father's death. Should the father die early, when the eldest son is in the flush of youth, then marriage will be a matter of choice, and love the deciding factor. But men often live to a ripe old age among the Wicklow hills, and the eldest boy can watch helplessly his youth and vigour fade, as he waits, decade after decade, for the inheritance to fall to him. Hence the incidence in those parts of May–September marriages, wherein the husband's age is often more than twice that of his spouse. Such unions are not always bonded in love.

So much for the eldest son; what of the others? Their fates are sealed from birth. No marriage for them: they have nothing to offer a bride—no money or property—and the parental home is rarely big enough to accommodate a daughter-in-law, let alone grandchildren. The younger sons must, like the unfortunate fellow who died mad and naked on the mountain, take to the fields of others, sowing and reaping another man's grain for a pittance. Should they have romantic notions, they can best forget them. They are doomed to a life of sexual abstinence. The lucky ones choose the roads, joining, in some instances, a band of tinkers, whose morals do not stand in the way of a man's taking a common law woman. They are dirt-poor, but they are free. The unlucky ones must endure a dismal life of drudgery and ill-paid labour, with no prospects of love, home, wife and family. No wonder they become insane.

V

There will be five characters in the play. One of them—conceivably the second most important figure—will remain unseen. Patch Darcy is dead, but his shadow lies darkly over the glen.

He was, by all accounts, a superman, a shepherd 'who would walk through five hundred sheep and not miss one of them, and he not reckoning them at all', and 'there was never a lamb from his own ewes he wouldn't know before it was marked'. He was 'a great man', a Wicklovian Paul Bunyan, who could run from Glenmalure 'to the city of Dublin [a distance of some forty kilometres], and never catch for his breath'.

So Patch was an astonishingly powerful athlete, apart from being the prosperous owner of five hundred sheep. Well, not quite: the animals were not his own; Patch was a mere herd, a lonely bachelor of the glens. The solitude and the oppression of the hills grew too much for him: 'in the year that's gone', Patch went insane and ran 'up into the back hills with nothing on [him] but an old shirt' and was 'eaten with crows'. The incident has shocked the inhabitants of Glenmalure; the more because the ghost of Darcy still haunts its dark slopes.

Synge sits at his typewriter in his bedroom in Crosthwaite Park as he completes the penultimate draft of *In the Shadow of the Glen*. It is September 1902; he has been writing as he has never written before. He is achieving the literary success that has eluded him for so long. In March, *L'Européen* took an article entitled 'La Vieille Littérature irlandaise', which paid tribute to the great Celtic scholar Marie Henri d'Arbois de Jubainville, whose lectures Synge had attended at the Sorbonne in 1898, and again in the spring of 1902. In June, he paid a glowing tribute to Lady Gregory's *Cuchulain of*

Muirthemne, praising the manner in which she had put the Cuchulain saga into 'a wonderfully simple and powerful language that resembles a good deal the peasant dialect of the West of Ireland'. His review, though, is not without criticism:

> The peasant note alone, however, does not explain all the passages of this book. The peasants of the west of Ireland speak an almost Elizabethan dialect, and in the lyrical episodes it is often hard to say when Lady Gregory is thinking of the talk of the peasants and when she is thinking of some passage in the Old Testament. In several chapters, again, there are pages where battles and chariot-fights are described with a nearly Eastern prolixity, in a rich tone that has the cadence of the palace, and not the cadence of men who are poor.

Synge is on home turf here. None of his peers is more familiar than he with the cadences of the poor, as Lady Gregory will appreciate when he submits his first 'peasant' plays to her and Yeats. There will be talk about Synge's having borrowed some of this language from Augusta Gregory, but Synge has his Aran and Wicklow notebooks which prove otherwise. None the less, he recognizes the debt he owes to her pioneering work.

This month—on 6 September 1902—Synge's review of a reprint of Geoffrey Keating's *Forás Feasa Ar Éirinn: History of Ireland* has appeared in *The Speaker*. The piece is intelligent and informed— even though its objectivity could be called into question:

> A comparison of the general expression of Keating's work with that of the annalists of his time recalls, in a curiously remote way, the difference that can be felt between the work of Irish writers of the present day who have spent part of their life in London or Paris, and the work of men who have not left Ireland . . . . Apart from his natural talent [Keating] owes a good deal to his foreign studies . . . the intercourse he must have had with men who had been in touch with the first scholarship in Europe was of great

use in correcting the narrowing influence of a simply Irish tradition.

Do the readers of *The Speaker* know that the reviewer himself passes several months each year in Paris? The foreign influence in Synge's work will become, for the Irish nationalists, a stick with which to beat him.

But these frictions are still in the future. Nineteen hundred and two sees the sudden flowering of Synge's literary production. Reviews published, plays completed, notebooks full of ideas and drafts. Only one shadow mars this literary success. At the close of 1901, Synge had finished *The Aran Islands.* Richard Best, a friend he had made in Paris who is now living in Dublin, helped to read and check the finished typescript. It was submitted to the London publishing houses of Grant Richards and George Unwin. Both have rejected it; urbane society is not yet ready to read about the trials of the fishing community of Aran, whose life is perhaps the most primitive that is left in Europe.

Be that as it may, the book is the treasure trove from which Synge took the golden pieces that went to make *Riders to the Sea.* There are many more to plunder. The dramatist is discovering the peculiar homogeneousness of the peasant tales of Aran and Wicklow, how effortlessly the creative writer can lift a story from a western setting and insert it seamlessly into the patchwork of the Leinster tradition. And why not, when its provenance lies anyway in the Rome of the first century AD?

Or does it? Synge has long suspected the existence of universal commonalities; he has paid close attention to James G. Frazer, author of *The Golden Bough,* and seen how certain archetypal myths have their echoes in many communities. Synge has written a tragedy that must surely resonate around the world—Maurya and Bartley have existed since the flood, in many guises, in many lands. God, and life and death, bind mankind together as one. So does superstition:

One evening when I was collecting [insects] on the brow of
a long valley in County Wicklow wreaths of white mist

began to rise from the narrow bogs beside the river. Before it was quite dark I looked round the edge of the field and saw two immense luminous eyes looking at me from the base of the valley. I dropped my net and caught hold of a gate in front of me. Behind the eyes there rose a black sinister forehead. I was fascinated. For a moment the eyes seemed to consume my personality, then the whole valley became filled with a pageant of movement and colour, and the opposite hillside covered itself with ancient doorways and spires and high turrets. I did not know where or when I was existing. At last someone spoke in the lane behind me—it was a man going home—and I came back to myself. The night had become quite dark and the eyes were no longer visible, yet I recognized in a moment what had caused the apparition—two clearings in a wood lined with white mist divided again by a few trees which formed the eye-balls. For many days afterwards I could not look on these fields even in daylight without terror. It would not be easy to find a better instance of the origin of local superstitions, which have their origin not in some trivial accident of colour but in the fearful and genuine hypnotic influence such things possess upon the prepared personality.

The question we ought to ask is: *whose* personality was prepared? Certainly the Wicklow glens are rife with local superstitions. Weird tales are told in hushed voices of the Pooka, a malevolent spirit that haunts the dark lakes, notably that known as Poulaphouca, the Lair of the Pooka. Synge has heard stories of Lough Nahanagan, of men who were foolhardy enough to fish its shadowy waters by night, never to return. The glens of Wicklow, wild and beautiful by day, are forbidding after nightfall, when spirits are abroad. To ward off their baleful influence, one might do well to have a sharp steel needle about one's person. Personalities prepared for the dark shadows of the glen can better be left with only a corpse for company 'than to be sitting alone, and hearing the winds crying, and you not knowing on what thing your mind would stay'.

Synge's own prepared imagination has seen the hills and trees arrange themselves into 'ancient doorways and spires and high turrets'. Incredibly, he has seen Hy Brasil where it had no right to be: it is a mythical island said to lie to the west of Aran. When weather conditions are right, Hy Brasil rises from the sea. The historian T. J. Westropp saw it, 'more than once, between 1872 and 1896'. Hy Brasil

> appeared immediately after sunset, like a dark island far out to sea, but not on the horizon. On the last occasion I made a rough, coloured sketch next day which shows the appearance as having two mountains, one wooded, in the low central tract; between rose buildings, towers and curls of smoke, rising against the golden sky westward.

It is natural that children who stare into the glowing coals of a fire will see wonders there. It is rather disturbing when an adult frightens himself with visions of a fairy city guarded by immense luminous eyes—the more because Synge was very much aware of the tricks of light and shade that had caused the phenomenon. What possessed a well-educated man to behave like a superstitious peasant? One explanation is that Synge, like Yeats, has been looking for wonders. When he finds that they do not exist, he invents them. But there is more to it than that.

It is not easy to lose one's belief in God, especially when one's family has distinguished itself in His service for many generations. When John Synge turned to nature for answers, he may have felt as the scryer who looks into a dark pool of water expecting images to form there; or like the saints who went into the desert for forty days, deprived their brains of nourishment, and waited for a sign from the Lord. The myriad faces of nature are indeed glorious to behold, and who in these times can deny that a divine hand is behind their beauty? Certainly not Synge.

Synge is not an unsociable creature; when the mood takes him, he can shine in company with the best of the talkers of his age. But, like as not, you will find him alone, brooding on a lonely rock above the sea, or lying motionless in the ling on a mountain slope: looking, listening and thinking. For Synge is uncertain; he senses the mood of a locality; he listens to the talk of the Pooka and the *sidhe,* and he wonders if there is not *some* universal truth behind them; that the supernatural—and, by extension, God—does exist after all, Darwin or no Darwin. As a serious literary critic and dramatist *in spe,* he cannot compromise his future by confessing openly his belief in such superstition. Yeats can have his fairies, and good luck to him; Yeats's reputation is already assured.

So Synge writes a ghost story.

VI

Nora Burke does not exist; the existence of the ghost of Patch Darcy is surely more palatable for the people of County Wicklow.

Nora is an amalgam of the strong women in whose company Synge has found himself in recent years. She has the feminism and socialism of Thérèse Beydon, and the practicality of Cherrie Matheson; there is also the mysticism of Margaret Hardon, and the fire and rebellion of Maud Gonne. But certainly the Nora of *In the Shadow of the Glen* does not exist in Wicklow. However, her circumstances do.

Nora Burke, still young and attractive, is the wife of an old farmer. Their home, a tiny cottage, occupies the most lonely and isolated part of dark Glenmalure. Nora's plight is pitiful. Trapped in a loveless marriage, she sees her youth fading as she spends her days 'looking out from a door . . . and seeing nothing but the mists rolling down the bog, and the mists again, and they rolling up the bog, and hearing nothing but the wind crying out in the bits of broken trees were left from the great storm, and the streams roaring with the rain.'

Nora's plight differs from that of the people of *Riders to the Sea,* in that her death, when it comes, will probably not be sudden. But her sublunary fate is perhaps more horrible, 'sitting here in the winter, and the summer, and the fine spring, with the young growing behind me and the old passing', sharing a bed with a husband who was 'always cold, every day since I knew him'.

It is the spectre, though, that holds the greatest horror of all. Nora remembers a neighbour, Peggy Cavanagh,

> who had the lightest hand at milking a cow that wouldn't be easy, or turning a cake, and there she is now walking round on the roads, or sitting in a dirty old house, with no teeth in her mouth, and no sense . . . .

Peggy Cavanagh has fallen victim to the shadow of the glen. The young woman with the light hand is now reduced to the itinerant life, 'begging money at the cross roads, or selling songs to the men'. She has lost her youth; but she has also lost her reason, just as the stalwart Patch Darcy lost his. This is what the glen does to human beings. At least the fishermen of Aran die with some dignity, in combat against the sea.

There seems to be no way out for Nora, as she waits for her old husband Dan to die. Synge intimates that she has kept an eye out for a worthy second spouse, and that 'it's a power of men' Nora has known. Dan Burke is convinced that his young wife is conducting an affair with Michael Dara, a shepherd, and he feigns death in order to catch the young couple red-handed. It is on this very night that a tramp appears at the cottage, seeking shelter from the rain.

The Tramp deserves our close attention, because his ilk will appear again in Synge's work. He epitomizes the freedom of the roads, as opposed to the shacklement of the cottage-dwellers. He is a child of nature, revelling in its beauty and accepting its vagaries with a disarming philosophy. There was little or no J. M. Synge in *Riders to the Sea*; in *The Shadow*, Synge is back in the action with a vengeance. It is hard *not* to see the Tramp as a mouthpiece for Synge. His disdain of arranged marriages, of the Church, of the repression of women, of crass materialism (as when Michael Dara shows more interest in Nora's 'dowry' than in Nora herself), of the sheer waste of life and youth for no good reason, pervades his speeches. Synge's message is clear, and it will enrage the nationalists: far better the freedom—and, by implication, the concomitant fornication—of the vagrant life, than cold celibacy in a loveless, Church-blessed marriage. Synge knows that in the latter lies madness, possibly a fate worse than death. The Tramp is the apotheosis of the former. 'Synge,' Alan Price argues, 'in depicting the Tramp as a superior being to Dan, is clearly building upon his own experience and observation; and his perception of strong links and resemblances between the position of the writer or artist in middle-class society and the position of the vagrant in a peasant community is seminal in the creation of a character who possesses notable imaginative qualities.' The *pícaro* may die of exposure, but he will have truly lived first.

As it is, there is only one death in the play: the off-stage demise of Patch Darcy. The violence of Pat Dirane's story, which ended with the cuckolded husband's striking his wife's lover 'a blow with the stick so that the blood out of him leapt up and hit the gallery', is absent in Synge's comedy. Michael Dara, the young herd, is left drinking whiskey with Dan Burke; he has been spared the curse that the old man had intended placing on him: the shadow that 'will follow you on the back mountains when the wind is high'. Michael's fate is to share the lingering death-in-life of the glen, to become like Dan Burke. Nora escapes with the Tramp from the valley of the shadow of death. It will not be an easy life, she well knows, but anything is preferable to the madness that has overtaken Patch Darcy and Peggy Cavanagh. Moreover, she will have the Tramp's marvellous talk for company—and the experience of other natural wonders:

> Come along with me now, lady of the house, and it's not my blather you'll be hearing only, but you'll be hearing the herons crying out over the black lakes, and you'll be hearing the grouse, and the owls with them, and the larks and the big thrushes when the days are warm, and it's not from the like of them you'll be hearing a talk of getting old like Peggy Cavanagh, and losing the hair off you, and the light of your eyes, but it's fine songs you'll be hearing

when the sun goes up, and there'll be no old fellow wheez-
ing the like of a sick sheep close to your ear.

These are sentiments that intoxicate Synge. When Nora and the
Tramp depart the darkness of the glen with the prospect of living
'with the sunshine and the moon's delight', John Synge goes with
them in spirit. It is a laughing, carefree muse that whispers at his
ear. From the black tragedy of *Riders to the Sea*, via the bleak *mise en
scène* of *In the Shadow of the Glen*, he emerges with Nora and her
picaresque companion in a world that is the very antithesis of her
husband's.

This is the world of Ireland's travelling folk, the tinkers.
Synge, as we have seen, has long been an admirer of this mode of
living. Yet he is now old and wise enough to know that true happiness is an ephemeral thing. Michael Dara may plead that 'it's a fine
life you'll have now with a young man, a fine life surely', but Old
Maurya of Aran has weathered enough misfortune to appreciate
that 'we must be satisfied' with whatever life throws at us. The life
of the tinker may appear to some an attractive one, but Synge
knows that there lurks a serpent in every garden.

VII

See Synge sitting near a bridge at the end of the green in
the village of Aughrim. It is the day of the August fair,
when the small farmers and tenants of south County
Wicklow come with their droves of 'bullocks and sheep, in
charge of two or three dogs and a herd, or with whole families of
mountain people, driving nothing but a single donkey or kid'. On
such days, the air of Aughrim is filled with the cries of humans and
animals, and is high with the excrement of the latter. Farmers and
their families jostle tramps and beggars who have come in search
of odd jobs, charity, and the prospect of free drink.

The bargaining is all but done; now the men congregate outside the public houses, taking their fill of cheap whiskey and brag-
ging about the shrewd deals they have made. Synge falls into easy

conversation with a shepherd who speaks 'with some pride of his skill in dipping sheep to keep them from the fly, and other matters connected with his work'.

There sits a tinker next to Synge, mending a can; he is joined by a woman, and together they prepare to return to the village.

'That man is a great villain,' whispers the herd.

'Oh?' says Synge. He proffers his tobacco pouch.

The tinker and his companion are now out of earshot. The herd confides. 'One time he and his woman went up to a priest in the hills and asked him would he wed them for half a sovereign, I think it was.'

Synge raises his eyebrows; ten shillings is certainly not the going rate for nuptials. The herd agrees.

'The priest said it was a poor price, but he'd wed them surely if they'd make him a tin can along with it. "I will, faith," said the tinker, "and I'll come back when it's done".'

An unruly bull has broken loose from its owner; it thunders, snorting, past Synge and the herd, heading for the open green, four or five fellows in hot pursuit. The herd pays no attention, but puffs slowly on his cigarette.

'They went off then,' he continues, 'and in three weeks they came back, and they asked the priest a second time would he wed them. "Have you the tin can?" said the priest. "We have not," said the tinker; "we had it made at the fall of night, but the ass gave it a kick this morning the way it isn't fit for you at all." "Go on now," says the priest. "It's a pair of rogues and schemers you are, and I won't wed you at all."'

The herd turns to Synge and shakes his head. 'They went off then,' he tells him, 'and they were never married to this day.'

Synge leaves Aughrim with the refrain of a street ballad and the drunken shouts of a bellicose tinker ringing in his head.

VIII

I t is difficult to write about a people in whose company one is uneasy. The tinkers are such a folk. John Synge thinks them interesting and picturesque, and—let us be honest—they are as intrinsic to Wicklow life as the herds and cottagers. His young nephew Edward Stephens regards them as 'useless parasites living on the work of other people'. This is debatable, and the nomadic life of the tinkers is close to Synge's heart. Nevertheless, their manners and mores come to him from a distance or from second hand. No, the writing of this play will not be easy.

The heroine of the piece is Nora Casey. Another Nora? Ah, but this Nora is a tinker and the mother of a tinker's two children. Perhaps it is Nora Burke, now well settled in a life that knows no settling. Synge is not telling. He is giving us the other side of the coin, showing us what can happen when a woman enjoys too much liberty. Nora Casey . . . No, Synge decides to call her Sarah instead. Well then . . . *Sarah* Casey, having lived with a tinker for some years in a common law marriage, now wants to see the union blessed. The other tinkers are dumbfounded; why reject the traditions of the roads and espouse the mores of the bourgeoisie? Has the moon got to her?

No, but the sun has. *The Tinker's Wedding* is Synge's bawdier version of *A Vernal Play*. It is a Mayday folly. Spring is come and the sap is rising; Sarah Casey is not left unaffected:

MICHAEL [*angrily*]. Can't you speak a word when I'm asking what is it ails you since the moon did change?

SARAH [*musingly*]. I'm thinking there isn't anything ails me, Michael Byrne; but the spring-time is a queer time, and it's queer thoughts maybe I do think at whiles.

She is indeed thinking queer thoughts, for there appears to be (as far as the tinkers are concerned) no good reason why Sarah should consider it necessary to approach the Priest and ask him to marry her and Michael Byrne; it will not change her life in any practical sense. Certainly Michael's widowed mother, Mary, opposes the plan, arguing that Sarah's putting a ring on her finger will not keep her 'from getting an aged woman and losing the fine face you have, or be easing your pains, when it's the grand ladies do be married in silk dresses, with rings of gold, that do pass any woman with their share of torment in the hour of birth, and do be paying the doctors in the city of Dublin a great price at that time, the like of what you'd pay for a good ass and a cart.'

But Sarah is adamant, for reasons which Michael finds hard to fathom. Nevertheless, he fears that his refusal may lead to Sarah's departure—and his loss of her as a saleable chattel. He grudgingly consents to the match.

An action ensues, whose like appears more in place in a Boccaccio romp than in rural Ireland. The Priest—a worldly individual, fond of drink and creature comforts—bargains with the tinkers about his price. They cheat him and he threatens to go to the authorities. Realizing that it will be his word against theirs (and knowing full well who will be believed), the tinkers bind the Priest in a sack, releasing him only when he swears an oath that he will not betray them to the authorities. Sarah places the ring that Michael has made for her wedding on the Priest's finger, 'to keep you minding of your oath until the end of time'.

Synge knows that, with *The Tinker's Wedding*, he is playing with fire. It will not meet with Lady Gregory's approval; there are too many overt criticisms of the religious life, and to attack the Catholic clergy in Ireland is begging for trouble. Synge's Priest is a caricature of a man whose Christianity is wanting; he seems to spend over-much time at the doctor's house, 'playing cards, or drinking a sup, or singing songs, until the dawn of day'.

Songs play an important role in this play, and we may well ask ourselves the reason; songs are not typical of Synge. Mary Byrne is heard to sing a ballad called 'The Night Before Larry Was Stretched'. Larry seems to be, according to Alan Price,

> some kind of hero to the tinkers, he has the qualities they
> admire; passion and courage; a resolve to enjoy life to the

last; loyalty to his kind and affection for his doxy; and a refusal to compromise his pagan principles. Larry is a symbol of those pagan forces which are directly opposed to the civil and religious powers which put him to death and which harry the tinkers.

We can equate Larry with Patch Darcy of *In the Shadow of the Glen.* Larry's memory haunts the tinkers too. But he died by another's hand, game to the last; his haunting is a proud and joyous one, not bitter like the memory of what befell Patch.

But Larry aside, the presence of songs in *The Tinker's Wedding* is reminiscent of that odd remark of Dan Burke's in *The Shadow*, when he suggests that Nora should 'walk round the like of Peggy Cavanagh below, and be begging money at the cross roads, or selling songs to the men'. Now, euphemisms for the sexual act abound in English literature; this being the case, I am tempted to construe Synge's selling of songs as a veiled reference to prostitution, the more because the selling of her favours is surely a pragmatic— though intensely demeaning—option for a woman doomed to a miserable and destitute life on the roads.

There is, furthermore, the unusual relationship between Mary Byrne and the Priest in *The Tinker's Wedding.* It is a tense one, a meeting of paganism and Christianity. Once more, the promise of sexual intercourse is couched in terms of song. The Priest's (reluctant) celibacy is first explored:

> MARY [*pensively*]. It's destroyed you must be hearing the sins of the rural people on a fine spring.

> PRIEST [*with despondency*]. It's a hard life I'm telling you, a hard life, Mary Byrne; and there's the bishop coming in the morning, and he an old bitter man, would have you destroyed if he seen a thing at all.

Then Mary makes her play:

> MARY [*with great sympathy*]. It'd break my heart to hear you talking and sighing the like of that, your reverence. [*She*

pats him on the knee.] Let you rouse up, now, if it's a poor, single man you are itself, and I'll be singing you songs unto the dawn of day.

Enough, Mr Synge, enough! This will not do. But Synge knows that he has overstepped the boundaries of propriety. He lays the play aside; it will be reworked by and by. At this moment, Synge is heady with the thought that he has great things to show to Yeats and Lady Gregory. He is more than satisfied with *Riders to the Sea* and *In the Shadow of the Glen*. He repairs to Coole Park, *en route* for a holiday on Inisheer, the smallest of the Aran Islands.

The mistress of Coole assumes her seat in front of the nude Andromeda. Yeats hovers in the background. Synge waits, his celluloid collar suddenly grown uncomfortably tight-fitting. Augusta Gregory pronounces on *Riders* and *The Shadow*. Now it is her turn to stammer.

"I–I do not know what to say, Mr Synge,' she confesses. 'The plays are, well . . . masterpieces!'

Synge sits bolt upright. 'Do you mean that, Lady Gregory?'

'How should I put it, Mr Synge?' she says with a smile. 'They are both perfect in their way. You have gathered emotion, the driving force you needed, from your life amongst the people. It is, I feel, the working in dialect that has set free your style.'

Synge colours, his shyness to the fore. He has proved himself! The troika of the Irish Literary Theatre is sound. *The Tinker's Wedding* shall remain, for the time being, among his personal papers.

The boards beckon.

On Trial

I

'Where will you get your actors?' Yeats was asked. 'I will go into some crowded room,' he replied mischievously, 'put the name of everybody in it on a different piece of paper, put all those pieces of paper into a hat and draw the first twelve.'

Well, not quite, but, as far as John Synge is concerned, this might well be the case. The players simply do not know how to speak the lines of *In the Shadow of the Glen*; that girl in particular: Maire Nic Shiubhlaigh—let us call her by her off-stage name: Mary Walker—the one who is to play Nora Burke. She is very pretty, but she lacks experience. Yet this is the very reason why Willie Fay has chosen her.

Fay's name was not drawn out of a hat. At thirty-one, he already has a considerable amount of acting experience to his credit. He and his older brother Frank formed the Ormonde Dramatic Society in 1898; it was an amateur company, touring Dublin halls and nearby towns with light comedies and sketches. In a series of articles in the *United Irishman*, Frank expressed his own wish for a national theatre: he also reviewed several plays performed by the Irish Literary Theatre, which led to an exchange of correspondence with Yeats. The Fays' troupe were engaged to present AE's *Deirdre* last year, on 2 January 1902: they have now become the backbone of the Irish National Theatre Society. It is no longer necessary to go to London to recruit players; Willie Fay is moulding native ones—the like of young Mary Walker.

'When you *read* a book or a play you supply your own characters,' he tells her. 'The author just makes suggestions which you, the reader, enlarge upon.' Mary nods in agreement.

'Now,' Fay continues, 'if you were a more experienced actress, you might read into this part something which, perhaps, was never intended.' He looks across to Synge, who sits in the front row of the little rented rehearsal hall in Dublin's Camden Street, rolling a cigarette of light tobacco. Synge will not be drawn into the conversation. Fay grasps Miss Walker by the shoulders. She blushes.

'Be the *mouthpiece* of Nora Burke, rather than Nora Burke,' he tells the young woman. 'You will be corrected only if you are inaudible or if your movements are wrong.'

Not for the first time, Miss Walker has misgivings about this play. She had liked it when she had heard it read by Lady Gregory in June: 'The plot, strictly speaking, was not original,' Miss Walker said, 'but the treatment was.' It is the treatment, she knows, that is going to create difficulties. And not only with the speaking of the lines. Synge's comments on the morality of Irish womanhood have already caused a minor exodus of players. Dudley Digges and his wife-to-be, Maire Quinn—two prominent members of the former Ormonde Dramatic Society—have resigned from the company, taking some others with them. Indeed, the part of Nora had been rehearsed by Miss Quinn, to great effect. Now Miss Walker is attempting to fill that experienced actress's shoes. It is not easy.

'The speech is much too long, Mr Fay,' she tells him. 'I could never hope to speak all those words correctly.'

Fay groans and accepts a cigarette from Synge, who promptly begins the rolling of another. Fay is very much aware of the problem; he too, while wrestling with the monologues of the Tramp, has had difficulty with the peculiar parataxis of the extended Syngeian speeches.

'Perhaps if you were to break it up, Miss Walker . . .'

Miss Walker tries.

'I do be thinking in the long nights . . . '

'. . . it was a big fool I was that time, Michael Dara . . . '

'. . . for what good is a bit of a farm with cows on it . . . '

'. . . and sheep on the back hills . . . '

Mary Walker pauses now. Synge has stopped his interminable rolling of cigarettes, and is staring at her with an expression more animated than his usual look of polite reserve. W. B. Yeats, dressed in black cloak, black suit and black floppy tie, raven-black lock of hair falling on his forehead, is whispering excitedly to Frank Fay. Frank smiles. Miss Walker has found the 'lilt', the music, in the lines.

They are not lines Synge himself can speak in the heightened manner of the stage; he knows *only* when they sound right. They are neither verse nor prose; they have not a little of the speech of the peasants of Aran, Wicklow and Kerry, lifted whole from the Gaelic.

Kerry? Yes, Synge had been to Kerry in this summer of 1903. His eldest brother Robert had returned from an enjoyable fishing trip on the Iveragh peninsula. Such was his enthusiasm for the place and his host, Philly Harris, that Synge was persuaded to go there too, at the end of August.

Mountain Stage, where the Harris cottage stands, overlooks the deep water of Dingle Bay. The beauty of this isolated locality differs from that of Aran, as do the people. They are bilingual, Synge discovered; English has all but supplanted the ancient tongue. Now the Gaelic League is trying to turn the tide. Synge had given ear to an old man's predicament:

> 'A few years ago,' he said, 'they were all for stopping [Irish] off; and when I was a boy they tied a gobban* into my mouth for the whole afternoon because I was heard speaking Irish. Wasn't that great cruelty? And now when I hear the same busybodies coming around and telling us for the love of God to speak nothing but Irish, I've a good mind to tell them to go to hell.'

But the people's loss is Synge's gain, for now he has heard the authentic note of the Hiberno-English that will elevate his plays above those of Dion Boucicault. More, he has been where that comic playwright has not. He has seen the people at work and at leisure, been welcomed into their poor homes. Synge has,

---

* *Gag; an anglicization of the Gaelic* gobán.

Mrs Synge and family: Samuel, Annie, Robert, Edward; John
is seated in the foreground.

Fish-market in Galway city.

A vagrant of
Wicklow.

Potato pickers at
Tomriland House.

Carrying a curagh.

A curagh by the beach of Inishmaan.

A race meeting on a strand in County Wicklow.

Fairday at Leenane, Co. Mayo.

The MacDonagh Cottage on Inishmaan. The post office window is on the right.

Cherrie Matheson (right).

'Cousin Mary' Synge.

FOUR DRAWINGS BY JACK B. YEATS

Chief Problem.

A Four-oared Curagh.

Near Castelloe.

A Man of
the Glens.

Lady Gregory at her desk in the drawing-room of Coole Park.

Coole Park,
front entrance.

William Butler
Yeats, 1896.

moreover, studied the layout of those homes, how items are arranged in a three-dimensional area. He has acquired a knowledge of spatial dynamics, essential to the dramatist.

Both Yeats and Moore have the painter's eye; Synge has the eye of the photographer. See his wallet of photographs. See how he manipulates his subjects to vitalize the landscape, the men and women of Aran animating its aridity. He has travelled in Tuscany, seen the mountain villages of fiery red roofs; architecture that, far from despoiling its environs, actually enhances the beauty of its natural setting. There are no virgin fields and rocks on Synge's quarter-plates; everywhere the hand of man is visible. Synge is aware of man's place in the scheme of things. 'I cannot say it too often,' he has written in an Aran notebook, 'the supreme interest of the island lies in the strong concord that exists between the people and the impersonal limited but powerful impulses of the nature that is round them.'

The stage is Synge's canvas. No, it is more than a canvas, for a painting has no real third dimension. What Synge arranges in his cranium, what is pieced together in the solitude of a bare Atlantic rock on Inishmaan or a furzed mountain slope in Wicklow, acquires its macrocosmic counterpart on the boards in Camden Street. The theatre is Synge's true *métier*.

'Was Dan standing where he is on the right, behind the table, when he said these lines?' Willie Fay calls to Synge from the stage.

'No,' Synge replies at once and with confidence, having consulted his interior model, 'he was on the right-hand side of the table with his hand on it.'

Synge's gift is one that Yeats can envy. Yeats builds by trial and error; the actual stage business of *The King's Threshold* and *Kathleen ni Houlihan* reveals time and again the weaknesses of his visualization; Yeats is secure only in his dialogue. Synge, on the other hand, reconstructs with unerring aplomb. Here is no apprentice at work; Synge has come to the theatre a master. His pupils—Willie Fay, Mary Walker, George Roberts and P. J. Kelly—are now being taught to remake language.

II

On 7 October, 'Johnnie', according to Mrs Synge's diary, took long ride on his bicycle, and 'went to town in the evening.' Today, 8 October 1903, 'Johnnie again went to town.'

There is what sounds like a quartet practising in one of the rooms of the Royal Irish Academy of Music on Westland Row. The windows are shut—the evening is a cold one—but Synge hears clearly the notes of a violin played by an unsure hand. Memories return of his own studies at the school, and his dreams of one day becoming a professional musician. Tonight will see his debut performance, but of a different kind. He hurries on down Nassau Street, past the railings of Trinity College, turns left into Kildare Street, and arrives at the back entrance to Molesworth Hall. Yeats meets him in the corridor, brandishing a copy of the morning's edition of the *Irish Daily Independent and Daily Nation*.

'My dear fellow!' he cries. 'Have you read this?' The newspaper is folded open at an editorial. Synge catches sight of his own name:

> Mr. Synge did not derive his inspiration from the Western Isles.
>
> We do not for a moment think that all the members of the Irish National Theatre Society can be held accountable for the eccentricities and extravagances of Mr. Yeats and his friends. But once they are made acquainted with what is being done in their name, we hold that those who ambition [sic] the uprise of a dramatic art that shall be true, pure and National, should make their voices heard against the perversion of the Society's avowed aims by men who, however great their gifts, will never consent to serve save on terms that never could or should be conceded.

Synge has not seen the editorial; his mother takes *The Irish Times*, the newspaper of the Ascendancy. He is understandably nervous.

His first night, and he is under attack even before the curtain has been raised!

His trepidation is shared by the company. The Fay brothers are old theatre hands, who know from bitter experience that theatre-goers need little encouragement to 'make their voices heard'. Marlowe and Shakespeare, they remember, played continually under the threat of rioting by gangs of apprentices.

The evening augurs well, however. Molesworth Hall is small, and the auditorium soon fills. Even the Chief Secretary of Ireland, George Wyndham, greatly interested in social reconstruction, is here. Willie Fay arranges six armchairs for him and his party; he places them before the stage. In the excitement of the first night, Fay does not notice that Wyndham's seat has a red upholstery; red, the colour of the Crown. The Irish nationalists will note this and use it in evidence against the company.

Yeats's offering, *The King's Threshold*, is the play that the audience is here to see. Its author is fast becoming a man of reputation in Dublin dramatic circles. Synge's play is the curtain-raiser, the début of an unknown playwright.

As the lights come up on Nora Burke and her Wicklow cottage, Synge stands immobile and unrecognized at the rear of the auditorium. The audience is captivated by Mary Walker. Her beauty, combined with the loveliness and strangeness of the lines Synge has given her, hold Molesworth Hall hushed until near the close of the short play.

'. . . but you've a fine bit of talk, stranger,' Nora tells the Tramp, 'and it's with yourself I'll go.'

There are murmurs throughout the hall. Did we hear that aright? She is going off with a total stranger? The murmurs turn to hisses, then to loud booing. When the curtain falls on Dan Burke and Michael Dara, the latter's final line is difficult to hear. There are more hisses, and a few cat-calls, but the applause wins.

'Author! Author!' The cry that is music to the playwright's ears. Yeats, dressed more dramatically than ever, beckons impatiently. Synge ascends the makeshift stage. The applause increases, all but drowning out the boos and hisses. Synge, shaking like an aspen, wild moustache seeming to droop more than usual, bows to his first audience.

When *The King's Threshold* rounds off the programme, Yeats and the company chalk up yet another successful night for the Irish National Theatre Society. Synge, on the other hand, has recognized a number of well-known critics in the audience. What, he wonders, will the morning papers bring?

III

'All she [Synge's mother] read in *The Irish Times* about the play perplexed her,' remembers Edward Stephens. 'She had thought of John as being over-persuaded by his literary friends into praising everything Irish, but, now that a play of his had been acted, the newspapers were censuring him for attacking Irish character.'

What is a mother to think? This new 'profession' of poor Johnnie's, this playwriting, was bound to result in great mischief sooner or later. Johnnie lives at home, to be sure, but he is his own man. His plays are his personal affair; it is not a mother's place to pry into their content. Heaven forbid! a play. Plays and actors are a breeding ground of licentious behaviour; theatres are little more than glorified bawdy-houses where unchaperoned young girls are *touched*—even kissed—by strange men, in the name of Art. One should do well to keep away, to remain untainted by the sinfulness that has ensnared poor Johnnie. We shall continue to pray that he will come to his senses soon.

Part of the problem, of course, stems from this highly dangerous patriotism that has taken hold of Johnnie. Love of one's country is all well and good, but one should realize where one's first loyalty lies, and that loyalty ought to lie with the landowning classes. Mr Moore and Mr Martyn are papists, and that fact may excuse them somewhat. But Lady Gregory and Mr Yeats, what of them? There is Mr Douglas Hyde to be considered too. 'An Craoibhín Aoibhinn' indeed! He of the Gaelic League, who would have us all return to a barbarous tongue. Next thing you know, there will be home rule, with all the terrible consequences of such a thing.

Still, Mrs Synge is perplexed and bewildered by the news that her son's play is perceived as an attack on the character of the native Irish. Has he seen the light at last?

The storm breaks. The *Irish Independent* critic calls it 'a farcical libel on the character of the average decently reared Irish peasant woman'. Even *The Irish Times*, organ of the Anglo-Irish, thinks the play 'excessively distasteful'. Only the *Daily Express*, once the mouthpiece of Horace Plunkett, the founder of the Irish co-operative movement, looks upon it favourably. The critic finds that *In the Shadow of the Glen* contains a 'convincing ring of truth'; it had, he says, been 'the gem of the evening'.

A week later, Arthur Griffith, editor of the *United Irishman*, enters the fray. His weekly carries a letter written by W. B. Yeats's father, John Butler Yeats, praising Synge as 'a man of insight and sincerity, that is to say, a man of genius'. Such men, he concludes, 'are the salt of Ireland'.

'Far from it!' Griffith responds angrily. Synge has not written an Irish play at all, but simply a reworking of the Widow of Ephesus. It ennobles adultery; surely Synge must know that 'the fact known to the whole world is that in no country are women so faithful to the marriage bond as in Ireland'. There is more than just a perceived attack on purity at issue here; there is, as Robin Skelton observes, politics as well:

> At the time which Synge wrote his play the shadow of Parnell lay heavily upon Ireland, and it seems not unlikely that Griffith, who was not a stupid man, saw in Synge's play an opportunity to assert that he, though a fervent nationalist, was dissimilar to Parnell in refusing to tolerate adultery and in revering Irish womanhood . . . . He saw this production of the Irish National Theatre Society, if regarded as part of the political nationalist movement, as likely to arouse once again clerical opposition. There is no doubt

of course that sheer puritanism had a hand in the opposition to the play, but so did politics.

Griffith has looked forward to great things from the Irish National Theatre Society; he has envisaged the company playing an important role in the advancement of Gaelic culture. Unfortunately, he has seen this role as a propagandist one, whereas the giving of art has been—and still is—the intention of Yeats and his colleagues.

Arthur Griffith has powerful allies: Maud Gonne was part of that audience on 8 October. She left Molesworth Hall in disgust, and she and Synge are no longer on speaking terms. Gonne pours scorn on Irish writers who allow foreign influences to distort their presentation of their own people. James Connolly, who had founded the Irish Socialist Republican Party in 1896, writes in the *United Irishman* that, in his view, an Irish theatre company should be fighting 'the widespread spirit of decadence' emanating from foreign shores. Now Synge is seen as the personification of such decadence.

From Griffith's viewpoint, Synge is indeed ill-equipped to foster and promote Irish nationalism. He knows Synge's history. Here, he insists, is a man who has all but abandoned his homeland for London and the Parisian Latin Quarter.

These are strong words. Yet there can be no denying that Paris, once that bitter and lonely winter of 1894/95 had ended, began to exercise an unusual fascination for Synge. But Griffith is mistaken. Far from causing Synge to abandon Ireland, Paris has allowed him to see his native country and its peoples within the context of a larger community. Warts there may be; Synge's alchemical studies also speak of the jewel concealed in the forehead of the warty toad . . . .

IV

S ynge is on trial; the courtroom is the Irish press. For the prosecution is Arthur Griffith, representing those whom Éamon de Valera will one day call 'the Plain People of Ireland'. The charge is that Synge is guilty of nothing short of treason, and the mounting of a dramatic version of a foreign story in the guise of an Irish play. W. B. Yeats leads the defence. He can call upon witnesses, men who are intimately acquainted with Synge's past, notably that part of it spent in Paris.

Arthur Griffith: *In the Shadow of the Glen* is no more Irish than *The Decameron*. It is a staging of a corrupt version of that old-world libel on womankind—the 'Widow of Ephesus', which was made current in Ireland by the hedge-school master, and derives its inspiration from the decadent cynicism that passes current in the Latin Quarter and the London salon.

Stephen MacKenna: Synge never belonged to the Latin Quarter or to the cabarets. Sometimes he would go to a café and just look on. The boulevards he didn't know or care about. He hated big avenues and chose those which were narrow and winding.

D. J. O'Donoghue, bookseller and librarian: As was the general custom with students, he furnished his small room (in a house in the rue d'Assas facing the Luxembourg Gardens) by a few purchases in the Montparnasse quarter, and there lived his rather lonely life for several years, broken only by his yearly visits to the Aran Islands.

    I met him in Paris in 1900, and sat for many hours each day with him in his little room or in a small neighbouring café, talking over the possibilities of literary life, and perhaps building castles in the air. When talk lagged, Synge would take down his violin, one of his few consolations, and play over many mournful Irish airs, melodies which appealed to his somewhat sad nature.

    Then as always, though a most charming and kindly

companion, and Irish of the Irish in his sympathies, his outlook
was a little morbid and decidedly cosmopolitan. His natural
taste in literature led him to the decadent writers, and possibly
this may account for certain manifestations in his later work.

John Masefield: I first met Synge at the room of W. B. Yeats, a
mutual friend, in an old house in Bloomsbury, in January
1903. Synge told me he had come to London from Paris, and
that he found Bloomsbury strange after the Latin Quarter. He
was puzzled by the talk of the clever young men from Oxford.
'That's a queer way to talk,' he said. 'They all talk like that. I
wonder what makes them talk like that? I suppose they're
always stewing over dead things.' He believed England to be all
suburb, like Ulster 'overhung with smoke'.

Arthur Griffith: Nevertheless, Synge is as utterly a stranger to the
Irish character as any Englishman who has yet dissected us for
the enlightenment of his countrymen. His Wicklow tramp, who
addresses an Irish peasant-woman as 'lady of the house', and
his Wicklow farmer's wife, who addresses the man who has
craved her hospitality as 'stranger', never existed in the flesh in
Wicklow or in any other of the thirty-two counties.

J. M. Synge: Admittedly, the play is set in Wicklow. However, the
story was told to me in Aran, and the characters speak sometimes in the language of those islands, translated by me into
the English vernacular. In this manner does *bean a' tí* (the customary honorific for a farmer's wife) become 'lady of the
house' and not 'woman of the house' which, you will admit,
has a less polite ring to it. In like manner, the term 'stranger' is
a literal translation of the Gaelic *strainséir,* the form of address
employed by the aforementioned islanders in the case of every
individual who is not a part of their community, a category into
which a tramp will naturally fall.

Arthur Griffith: Semantics, mere semantics. Answer the main
charge: that this play has no more title to be called Irish than a
Chinaman would have if he printed 'Patrick O'Brien' on his

122

visiting card. Your play is no more than a foul echo from degenerate Greece.

W. B. Yeats: A writer is not less national because he shows the influence of other countries and of the great writers of the world. No nation since the beginning of history has ever drawn all its life out of itself. Even the father of English poetry himself, Geoffrey Chaucer, borrowed his metres, and much of his way of looking at the world, from French writers, and it is possible that the influence of Italy was more powerful among the Elizabethan poets than any literary influence out of England herself.

Arthur Griffith: We are willing if need be to sit at the feet of the Frank, the Teuton, the Slav, and learn from them—to accept reproof, to accept praise; we shall accept neither from the Anglo-Saxon. I still maintain that the play is an evil compound of Ibsen and Boucicault.

J. M. Synge: I beg to submit as evidence the story of an unfaithful wife which was told me by an old man on the middle island of Aran in 1898, and which I have since used in a modified form in *In the Shadow of the Glen*. It differs essentially from any version of the story of the Widow of Ephesus with which I am acquainted. As you will see, it was told to me in the first person, as not infrequently happens in folk-tales of this class.

Arthur Griffith: It happens, I am prepared to concede, that some men and women in Ireland marry lacking love, and live mostly on a dull level of amity. Sometimes the woman lives in bitterness—she dies of a broken heart—but she does not go away with a tramp! How do you justify this sex-element of your play?

J. M. Synge: Heaven forbid that we should ever have a morbid sex-obsessed drama in Ireland, not because we have any peculiarly blessed sanctity, which I utterly deny—see the percentage of lunatics in Ireland and causes thereof—but because it is bad drama and is played out.

On the French stage, the sex-element of life is given without the other balancing elements; on the Irish stage, the people you agree with want the other elements without sex. I restored the sex-element to its natural place, and the people were so surprised they saw the sex only.

W. B. Yeats: Certain people have objected to Mr Synge's play because Irish women, being more chaste than those of England and Scotland, are a valuable part of our national argument. Mr Synge should not, it is said by some, have chosen an exception for the subject of his play, for who knows but the English may misunderstand him? Some even deny such a thing could happen at all, while others that know the country better, or remember the statistics, say that it could, but should never have been staged. All these arguments, by their methods, even more than by what they have tried to prove, misunderstand how literature does its work. Men of letters have sometimes said that the characters of a romance or of a play must be typical; I submit that it is no more necessary for the characters created by a romance writer, or a dramatist, to have existed before, than for his own personality to have done so.

For a month long the battle rages. Yeats *père* writes to the *United Irishman*, declaring that 'the outcry against Mr. Synge's play seems to me to be largely dishonest'. The real objection, he says, is not that it 'misrepresents Irishwomen, but that it is a very effective attack on loveless marriages'. His one complaint 'is that it did not go far enough'. Arthur Griffith has the last word, and the discussion, for the time being, ends. John Synge has had his first taste of what it means to be part of a theatre that calls itself 'National'.

V

There is no pleasing the Irish critics. The objection to *In the Shadow of the Glen* was that the play did not portray a real situation. *Riders to the Sea* is performed on 25 February 1904, and now Synge is condemned for giving his audiences a surfeit of fidelity. He has brought the corpse of Bartley onto the stage. *The Irish Times* voices its disapproval:

> The idea underlying the work is good enough: but the treatment of it is to our mind repulsive . . . . The long exposure of the dead body before an audience may be realistic, but it certainly is not artistic. There are some things which are lifelike, and yet are quite unfit for presentation on the stage and we think that *Riders to the Sea* is one of them.

The *Irish Independent* thinks it 'too dreadfully doleful to please the popular taste', but concedes that Synge has given the theme 'a careful treatment'. And Arthur Griffith's comment? The drowned body on the stage is, he thunders, 'the cheap trick of the Transpontine dramatists'. To be fair, though, he concedes that the play's 'tragic beauty powerfully affected the audience'.

It is the beginning of 1904. Synge's winter has been neither a happy nor a healthy one. His work has been attacked; he has been branded a West Briton and a libeller of Irish women. The commotion at the first night of *In the Shadow of the Glen* was not an isolated incident; each subsequent performance met with a similar show of outrage.

Synge is not a well man. His teeth are decaying, he has developed a painful abscess on a molar which causes his face to swell, confines him to his bed and prevents him attending any performance other than the début of *Riders to the Sea*; he suffers from cold after cold—or what he himself calls 'influenza'. Now he fears he may have tuberculosis into the bargain; it is, in any case, 'a nasty attack on my lung'. It seems that those bitter winters spent in Paris have taken their toll of an already frail constitution. A sickly, asthmatic boy throughout most of his childhood, Synge the man will seldom know continuing good health. Granted, the chronic headaches, colds and coughs disappeared at about the time of his enrolment at Trinity College, but his asthma did not, despite a course of treatment. It laid him low in Aran during his first visit in 1898; it was particularly distressing in the summer of 1903. But now the other childhood ailments have returned to make his days miserable.

His illness could not have occurred at a more inopportune time. The Irish Literary Society, based in London, has invited Willie Fay and his company to perform a selection of plays. To Synge's delight, they will give his two plays, despite Dublin's antagonism towards *In the Shadow of the Glen* and the lukewarm reception afforded to *Riders to the Sea*.

VI

Synge is no stranger to London. Since 1893, when he embarked on his first visit to Koblenz, the English capital had been a stopoff *en route* to the Continent—but little more. He likes neither London nor the English. He is aware, though, of London's importance for the Irish literary community. Yeats has spent a considerable part of his life there, and has already established a London reputation. Moreover, Synge's book *The Aran Islands* remains unpublished. London is the publishing capital of the world, a city no aspiring author should shun.

In January 1903, Synge decided to give up the little room in Paris, which he had leased since 1896, and take lodgings at a rooming-house in Handel Street, Russell Square. Arthur Griffith's remarks about Synge's involvement with the 'London salon' are true, up to a point. At the time the allegations were made, Synge had but recently been introduced to Yeats's London circle.

The circle was wide. Lady Gregory was included, as was George Russell. Russell now shares a vice-presidency of the Irish National Theatre Society with Maud Gonne and Douglas Hyde.

There were other poets too, men whom Yeats had known since his time as a member of the Rhymers Club: poets like John Masefield, Arthur Symons and G. K. Chesterton. Synge was a little in awe of them, and ill at ease in such distinguished company. Left to themselves, though, Synge and Masefield became firm friends. The future Poet Laureate has fond memories of their time together:

> [Synge's] talk was best when it was about life or the ways of life . . . . His talk was all about men and women and what they did and what they said when life excited them . . . . After that first day, when I called upon him at his room, we met frequently. We walked long miles together, generally from Bloomsbury to the river, along the river to Vauxhall, and back by Westminster to Soho. We sometimes dined together at a little French restaurant . . . . We spent happy hours there, talking, rolling cigarettes, and watching the life. 'Those were great days,' he used to say. He was the best companion for that kind of day.

John Masefield has observed the ease with which Synge talks with women. Men, Masefield believes, 'usually talk their best to women'. Synge's conversation, he observes, has a 'lightness and charm' when in female company.

Noteworthy among the female company at Yeats's gatherings are Pamela Colman Smith, a hermetist and artist; and Annie Horniman, likewise a hermetist, and heiress to a fortune made in tea trading. She displays an unusually keen interest in the affairs of the Irish National Theatre Society.

Miss Horniman was in Molesworth Hall on the first night of *In the Shadow of the Glen*. The idea of an independent theatre appeals to her. Yeats believes that, with a little coaxing, Miss Horniman may be persuaded to put some of her family's fortune to good use.

Lady Gregory is of the same opinion, but does not approve of these theosophers and hermetists. She likes plain-speaking, forthright people, and her fondness for Synge has grown considerably since his first visit to Coole. Moreover, she was so impressed by

Synge's two plays that she arranged three readings of them in her rooms in London. Arthur Symons offered to publish *Riders to the Sea* in *The Fortnightly*; he changed his mind, however, and returned the typescript the following month, as did the book publisher R. Brimley Johnson. Synge was disappointed, but not deterred. He achieved something: J. L. Hammond of *The Speaker* commissioned him to write occasional articles on current French literature. On 18 April 1903, the magazine published a Synge criticism of Joris Karl Huysmans and Pierre Loti. 'In Huysmans', he declared, 'we have a man sick with monotony trying to escape by any vice or sanctity from the sameness of Parisian life, and in Pierre Loti a man who is tormented by the wonder of the world . . . . till at last his one preoccupation becomes a terrified search for some sign of the persistence of the person.'

Between them, Yeats and Lady Gregory had introduced Synge into London literary society. His plays would now speak for themselves. London's Royalty Theatre is filled to capacity both afternoon and evening on 26 March 1904. Important critics, such as William Archer and Max Beerbohm, have come to sit in judgement on the programme which the Irish touring players will mount: Synge's two plays and Yeats's *The King's Threshold* as matinée; Padraic Colum's *Broken Soil* and Yeats's *The Pot of Broth* in the evening.

Synge has gone to great lengths to ensure that both his little one-acters are staged and costumed correctly. Before *Riders to the Sea* was given in Dublin, he had written to Lady Gregory, asking her

> if I could provide four red petticoats, Aran men's caps, a spinning-wheel, and some Connacht person in Dublin who will teach the players to keen. The last item is the most difficult. All the actors want pampooties . . . though I warned them the smell [of the hide] is rather overpowering.

Lady Gregory had found all these items, including a spinning-wheel, which she had acquired from a woman in whose family it had been for more than a hundred years. She also found a Galway woman in Dublin who taught the actors the art of the keen. So successful were the lessons that at this first London performance 'the pit went away keening down the street'.

How utterly different to play to an audience which is uninterested in the hopes and aspirations of the Irish nationalist movement, and to have one's work judged on its own merits, as art. The auditorium gives voice to its acclaim of both the material and the acting. Synge bows before the theatre patrons who have placed him on an equal footing with Yeats. A year ago, he was a nonentity; now he has achieved recognition from London's most discerning critics.

The Shadow of the Glen (the *In* was dropped after the first season) receives good notices; Max Beerbohm writes that it 'illustrates a very odd thing about the Irish people—their utter incapacity to be vulgar'. Most praise, however, is lavished on *Riders to the Sea.* One critic calls it 'a singularly beautiful and pathetic piece of hopeless fatalism'; another thinks it 'intensely pathetic and, in a sense, supremely human'.

As is all too often the case, the prophet, without honour in his own land, is finding acclaim in another. 'Some of our local oracles', Frank Fay writes to Synge, 'must feel disturbed when they recollect how they wrote about *Riders to the Sea.*'

Some shall, most shall not. Synge may have shone in London; it will be a long time before either the Irish critics or the Irish public afford him a fair hearing. Be that as it may, the name Synge will be linked inextricably with one of the most successful and celebrated theatres of all time. Its company, led by the Fay brothers, is in place and proven. Its directors and writers stand impatiently in the wings. A building, a home, is the only element lacking.

Willie Fay thinks he has found the very place, in Abbey Street.

VII

In *Hail and Farewell,* George Moore records his first impressions of the building that was to become the new Abbey Theatre. Richard Cave, who edited the book's 1976 edition, explains in a note that Moore 'has transposed this incident back in time [to 1898] . . . and is probably trying to suggest that he took a more active part in the history of the Abbey than he really did'. None the less, Moore's description of the premises is valuable:

> We went along a passage, which opened upon a gallery overlooking a theatre, one that I had no difficulty in recognising as part of the work done in Dublin by the architects that were brought over in the eighteenth century from Italy. The garlands on the ceiling were of Italian workmanship, and the reliefs that remained on the walls. Once the pit was furnished with Chippendale chairs, carved mahogany chairs, perhaps gilded chairs in which ladies in high-bosomed dresses and slippered feet had sat listening to some comedy or tragedy when their lovers were not talking to them . . . .

It is the *new* Abbey Theatre; a house of that name, built in 1820, had burned down. The site was bought by the Dublin Mechanics' Institute and the theatre was reopened to the public as the People's Music Hall, in order to raise funds. Because it failed to comply with safety regulations, the authorities had forced the institute to shut down. Willie Fay convinces Annie Horniman that this building could—with some alterations—be highly suitable for the performances. She dispatches him to examine it more closely, and he does so in the company of Joseph Holloway, an architect and enthusiastic patron of the Irish National Theatre Society. Holloway declares the building sound. It is, however, a tiny theatre. If you were also to lease the adjoining building, he tells Miss Horniman, then you could make a worthwhile theatre of the two.

The adjoining building has been in use as a morgue.

Yeats runs his fingers through his thick, black hair. A morgue! He had resisted the temptation to mount the first plays in a maternity hospital; now the company is to share its future with the ghosts of the dead. But Yeats must lay his superstitions aside and yield to the combined wills of Miss Horniman and Lady Gregory. The latter engages her solicitors to complete the transaction, and the Abbey Theatre is Annie Horniman's for ninety-nine years. She assures the other Dublin theatres that the new house will not give plays which will be in direct competition with their programmes. On 11 May 1904, the Society formally accepts the offer of Miss A. E. F. Horniman to give it the use of the hall in Abbey Street and the adjoining building in Marlborough Street, to turn into a small theatre. All are aware that Annie Horniman has leased the premises for her friend Yeats, for his plays; the work of other dramatists is incidental. Amid the euphoria, this fact is regarded as a minor detail.

And where is Synge while these momentous events are taking place? Synge is cycling:

> I spent last winter with my ten toes in the grave [he writes to Stephen MacKenna], and now I'm riding my 70 miles in the day, with a few mountain ranges thrown in, doing more and doing it more easily than ever before . . . . Breathe, eat, sleep, smoke not too much, and you'll be fine.

This is not to say that Synge has been idle on the literary front. On the contrary, the frantic muse who inspired him in 1902 has overseen the publication, in April 1903, of 'An Autumn Night in the Hills', an anecdote of County Wicklow; he revised *When the Moon Has Set*, reducing it to one act; Yeats published *Riders to the Sea* in the October issue of *Samhain*, an occasional publication of Yeats in which he defends the theatre. Inspired by the performance of *The Shadow of the Glen*, Synge started writing *The Well of the Saints*. In March 1904, the New York monthly, *The Gael*, reprinted 'A Dream on Inishmaan', an excerpt taken from *The Aran Islands*, which a London periodical, *The Green Sheaf*, had published in 1903. Synge's muse, for the time being, is almost spent. His letter to MacKenna continues:

I haven't seen the spring quite so intimately this year as last—I've been too busy at my play—but not the less I've seen many wonders. . . . I have just got my new play off my hands, it was read to the company on Friday and goes into rehearsal at once, it is a much bigger affair than the others and is in three acts. We hope to begin our new season in October in our new Theatre. Everything is settled now I believe *except patent*, an important point, so we are still keeping whole affair *out of papers—no paragraph*! Miss Horniman (entre nous) is coming out heroically and is laying out about £1000 (dit-on) on the premises which in their way will be unique in Dublin. She . . . has been casting my horoscope, it's pretty bizarre as far as it goes—my hour isn't known—so it is avowedly a little vague. It deals with my temperament and tendencies, I am interested, but of course, entirely unconvinced . . . .

Madame Esposito is translating 'Riders to the Sea' into Russian and French, her Russian I can't judge, in French it loses a good deal as she has put it into standard healthy style,—but hasn't managed to give it any atmosphere or charm. She hopes to get it into a Russian review, and we are thinking of trying the *Mercure de France*, they like young movements.

As soon as I get the rehearsals of my play fairly underway I'm off to the South and West, to forget theatres and all that is connected with them for two months or three. That, I think, is essential for one's soul.

Synge obtains temporary solace of the soul by bicycling often from Crosthwaite Park to the Wicklow hills and home again. His long routes take him out beyond the coastal town of Bray, past the eastern range which Stephens calls the 'retaining wall', and through the valley carved by the river Vartry. The natural features on either side have names that ring with folklore: Djouce Mountain, Glen of the Downs, Annamoe, the Devil's Glen. The last is dominated by the castellated towers of Glanmore Castle; Tiglin, Tomriland House and Castle Kevin are in the vicinity. This is, and has for centuries been, Synge country.

On some days Synge will push westwards from Annamoe, through the vale of Glendalough of the 'Seven Churches', to the wilder rifts of Glenmacnass and Glenmalure, 'where after a stormy night's rain the whole valley is filled with a riot of waterfalls. Sometimes these sudden rainfalls are followed by a singularly beautiful morning and then each of these glens can be seen at its moment of most direct and wonderful colour [and] beauty.'

The asthma attacks have returned, however, and Synge is careful not to linger too long in those pollen-rich regions which make his breathing troublesome. One such place is Tomriland, which Mrs Synge has again rented for the summer. Fanny and Lucy Synge, distant cousins from Australia, are visiting. The younger, Lucy, is much taken by her famous relative, John Synge the dramatist; she fails to understand why his mother disapproves of her son's chosen profession. Samuel has returned on a two-year leave from his mission in China. The brothers meet hardly at all this summer. John has business at Coole; his soul, without recourse to Samuel's grave spirituality, is, for the time being, uplifted and fortified.

Lady Gregory is revising her three-act historical play *Kincora*, and has asked Synge to help her. As we have seen, his dramatic dialect was, to some extent, inspired by *Cuchulain of Muirthemne*, a retelling of Irish epics. Synge has never made a secret about this. Now the mistress of Coole House is returning the compliment by seeking his assistance and advice. She has already collaborated with Yeats on many plays, and written several others under her own name. In time, Lady Gregory will become the most prolific and most produced playwright of the Abbey.

It is the new theatre, needless to say, which is the talk of Coole when Synge arrives on 16 July. Yeats is there, and so is AE, the grand master of arbitration, who will manage the new company. Between them, the four are stirring up a witches' cauldron of excitement. Yeats, characteristically, remembers these seminal days in pyrotechnical metaphor:

Their creative thought and excitement charged the atmosphere, so that scholars and tourists are still thick on the ground, trying to get a whiff of the ozone still in the air from the electrical discharges, the squibs, crackers, backarappers, sparklers, torches, dwarf candles, elf fountains, goblin barkers, and thunderclaps that lit up the . . . sky . . . .

In August, the workmen preparing the Abbey Theatre for occupancy are clearing out some rubbish at the spot where the dressing-rooms will stand, when they come across a human skeleton. 'Oh', says the caretaker of the quondam morgue, 'I remember we lost a body about seven years ago. When the time for the inquest came, it couldn't be found.'

If there are members of the company inclined towards superstition, then there will not be much whistling in the dressing-rooms of the Abbey Theatre.

VIII

See Synge taking the September sun on the Atlantic Ocean. He stands at the rail of the little steamer that is bringing him and his bicycle from the town of Sligo to Belmullet, Co. Mayo.

He has given Aran a miss this summer, despite a letter of invitation from Martin MacDonagh. There is a smallpox epidemic in Kilronan, Inishmore. John Synge, concerned about his health even at the best of times, fears smallpox as no other contagious disease: it killed his father. Besides, avoiding Aran affords him the opportunity of visiting a part of Ireland he has not seen before. He has spent a month in west Kerry, returning to Dublin on 1 September. Ten days later, he set off to explore those parts of Sligo which both Yeats and AE have praised for their loveliness and charm.

Mayo is not charming. The northern coast is black and cliff-lined. The Mullet is a ragged, treeless peninsula of bogland and stretches of sand. It has much of the wildness and isolation of Aran and it appeals greatly to Synge. The Mullet is a Congested District, so called because its aridity cannot support its population; the people must have outside help. In contrast with his beloved Aran Islanders, these people seem to lack the fierce independence he associates with the West of Ireland. 'In Mayo', he notes, 'one cannot forget that in spite of the beauty of the scenery the people in it are debased and nearly demoralized by bad housing and lodging and the endless misery of the rain.'

A debased people: surely good subject-matter for a play? In Kerry, Synge mused over some ideas for his next dramatic work. It will be, he believes, another Aran play, this time a comedy, like *The Shadow of the Glen* and *The Well of the Saints*. A farce, perhaps. In Philly Harris's cottage at Mountain Stage, he had leafed through his first Aran notebook. Pat Dirane's story of the father-killer has possibilities. He has scribbled a working title: *The Fool of Farnham*. Maybe simply *The Murderer*?

The title will present itself in time. Synge returns to Kingstown at the beginning of October, to find that Samuel, his wife Mary and their infant daughter, together with his cousin Stewart Ross and his son, are guests. Peace and quiet is what Synge needs if his writing is not to suffer. Moreover, he must devote his hours to the serious business of rehearsing his first three-act play. The cast is large, the material demanding; Kingstown is too distant from the new theatre for daily travel back and forth. He takes rooms at 15 Maxwell Road, Rathgar, fifteen minutes by tram from the Abbey Theatre, a stone's throw from Zion Church and the pastor whose most sterling efforts to rewin Synge for Christ had foundered.

Synge writes to Lady Gregory that Willie Fay 'is in despair at an epidemic of love-making' that has broken out among the players. The dramatist thinks that 'it makes the rehearsals much more amusing than they were, but it is easy to see that the good people are much more taken up with each other than with the plays'. He believes that Frank Fay 'is one of the ones who have not escaped' the epidemic of love-making.

Synge cannot know that he himself is another whom the epidemic will infect.

Other Girls and Men

I

Synge needs a number of walk-on actors and actresses for *The Well of the Saints*. The Irish National Theatre Society is prospering, thanks to the generosity of Annie Horniman. Nevertheless, theatre production remains an expensive business. It is hoped that the takings on the door will be sufficient to cover advertising, set-design, carpentry and other expenditures necessary for the mounting of the Abbey productions. Of course, the future of the enterprise is uncertain; it will be some time before the new Dublin theatre has established itself enough to attract full houses. Some of the players have given up their jobs and thrown in their lot with the Abbey, drawing a tiny salary. They have swopped financial security for the unknown; drudgery for love.

One such is Sara Allgood, whom Willie Fay has cast in an important role in *The Well of the Saints*. Sara has a younger sister, Molly, who works as a sales assistant in Switzers, one of Dublin's most fashionable department stores. It is a fine position for a girl of Molly's working-class background, but she, like her sister, yearns for more than financial security. When the theatre company sends out the call for walk-on players, Molly persuades Sara to secure an audition for her.

Molly Allgood is not quite eighteen years old when John Synge meets her for the first time in January 1905; he is nearly thirty-four. David Greene gives us this description of the girl who is to become Synge's last, and most passionate, love:

> She was slight in build, and large brown eyes gave her face a look of seriousness. She was not beautiful but had an actress's ability to make both her face and body interesting

and expressive. She seems also to have had a special attraction for men, particularly older men, despite the fact that she had had only a grade-school education and no more sophistication than one would expect to find in a girl of her class.

Why Molly's poor education and lack of sophistication should prevent older men being attracted to her Greene does not make clear; nevertheless, the comment is interesting. It raises the question: who is attractive to whom? Certainly both parties are exciting prospects. Synge is a successful playwright whose star is ascending rapidly: *The Shadow of the Glen* has had its second Dublin season; the London critics know and approve of him; Nathalie Esposito's translations of *Riders to the Sea* will procure a European readership. On top of this, he cuts rather a dash. His young (and, we may infer, impressionable) nephew Edward Stephens writes of meeting Synge in Dublin about this time; seventeen-year-old Stephens was returning from football practice with his friend Edward Hatte:

> He was wearing a wide-brimmed hat under which, in the evening light, his moustache and imperial* looked thick and dark. His cape hung to his knees, and he carried one of his heavy walking sticks. He looked like a figure from a foreign city. (I remember his saying that it was the duty of everyone to make himself as picturesque as possible.) Hatte whispered: 'Is that the playwright?' and I realized suddenly that to him John was a public character of importance.

This is the Synge that seventeen-year-old Molly sees. No doubt her sister Sara has regaled her often with gossip about the prominent members of the Theatre Society: Yeats the flamboyant poet-genius, Augusta Gregory the black-clad aristocrat; Synge the darkly brooding autocrat . . . . And now Molly is auditioning for a part in a play by the same Mr Synge, Dublin's most controversial dramatist—a play that must surely lead to further controversy and notoriety.

---

* *A point of tufted beard, cultivated on the lower lip and chin.*

Given Molly's predilection for older men, and her artistic ambitions, Synge must seem to her an almost irresistible object of desire.

We have John B. Yeats's sketch of Synge watching rehearsals at the Abbey. We have, too, Oliver St John Gogarty's reminiscence of Synge at an earlier rehearsal in Camden Street. Picture and words dovetail wonderfully well:

> He sat silent, holding his stick between his knees, his chin resting on his hands. He spoke seldom. When he did, the voice came in a short rush, as if he wished to get the talk over as soon as possible. A dour, but not a forbidding, man. Had he been less competent it might have been said of him on account of his self-absorption that he 'stood aloof from other minds. In impotence of fancied power'. He never relaxed his mind from its burden.

II

The Saint is played by Frank Fay; his brother Willie is both acting in and directing the play. Frank leads the blind beggar, Mary Doul, into the 'church'. Willie beckons to a small knot of young men and women waiting in the shadows beside the stage: the 'Other Girls and Men'. It is their cue to tread the boards and be put through their paces.

'Beginners, please!' Fay calls.

Molly Allgood is appalled. The shame of it! She is at once painfully conscious of her inexperience, not knowing that Fay's summons is nothing more than the customary call for 'extras'. Molly bursts into tears of hurt and indignation. What will the great Mr Synge think of her now?

'You eejit,' hisses a young woman at Molly's elbow, 'that's just what they always say. You don't have to take it personal.'

Happily for Molly, Synge has not noticed her tears; his attention is on the script in his hands. Molly has time to compose herself. Martin Doul, the other blind beggar, played by Willie Fay, 'comes on to the People. The Men are between him and the Girls. He verifies his position with a stick.'

Now most directors agree that actors playing walk-on parts are very difficult to work with. They invariably overact, in an attempt to focus undue attention on themselves. Can Synge fail to notice this pretty, petite girl with large brown eyes and the walk of a queen, whose every gesture and smile seem intended for him? He is a vain man, and such flattery is not lost on him. His script is forgotten. Not that he has real need of it; as with all his plays, he knows intimately, by dint of constant revision, the text of *The Well of the Saints*.

Synge has little need to pay heed to Molly's speaking of her few lines—her part is relatively unimportant: that of one of the village girls—and her voice is lost in the chorus. For all her effort, she could just as well be speaking Hebrew.

That evening, Synge returns to his rented room at Mrs Stewart's house in Rathgar, the beginnings of romance stirring once more. But there are other stirrings—professional ones. Willie Fay is not happy with the play.

Saints are holy men. It follows, then, that a saint is 'a good-natured easy-going man'—and certainly in a play like Synge's, where, as far as Willie Fay can ascertain, *all* the characters are bad-tempered. Synge does not share Fay's opinion.

'Let me put it this way,' Fay says; 'there are certain rules that you cannot break without destroying the sympathy between the stage and auditorium. They are not technical but psychological. If all the characters are bad-tempered throughout, all this bad temper will inevitably infect the audience and make them bad-tempered too.'

A fair point.

'I will not change the Saint's character—or Molly Byrne's either,' Synge replies. 'I have written this play like a monochrome painting, all in shades of one colour.'

Fay tries another tack. He has objections to a speech in the second act, where Timmy the Smith says, 'And she after going by with her head turned the way you'd see a priest going where there'd be a drunken man in the side ditch talking with a girl'. Such a thing, he argues, simply could not happen in Ireland. Furthermore, Mary Garvey, an actress who had a non-speaking part in *Riders to the Sea*, agrees with him.

Synge is disgusted. Is it not enough that Arthur Griffith and the other so-called nationalists should have renewed their attack on *The Shadow of the Glen*, when it was given a second production last year? Now must he endure similar nonsense from some members of the company itself?

'Tell Miss Garvey,' he says, 'or whoever it may be, that what I write of Irish country life I know to be true, and I most emphatically will not change a syllable of it because A, B, or C may think they know better than I do. I am quite ready to avoid hurting people's feelings needlessly, but I will not falsify what I believe to be true for anybody.'

Yet, despite his reservations, Fay thinks the play the best thing Synge has ever written—from an actor's point of view. It is certainly the most ambitious play. Hitherto, he has—with the exception of the ill-starred *When the Moon Has Set*—condensed the action into a short time-span; now he must sustain the attention of an audience throughout three full acts. For the first time, Synge has to take the interval into account: he will have to ensure that, when the curtain falls on the first and second acts, his audience will be left wanting more.

The Well of the Saints is set on the Irish mainland: in some 'lonely mountainous district in the east of Ireland, one or more centuries ago'. There are two sources for its inspiration: first, the presence of the holy well on Inishmore, which Synge visited with his practically blind Irish tutor, Old Mourteen; second, a fifteenth-century farce by Andrieu de la Vigne, *Moralité de l'Aveugle et du Boiteux*. The latter recounts how two beggars, one blind and one crippled, have learned to function as a single, symbiotic, unit. The blind man has borne the cripple on his back; their partnership has been a lucrative, if a pathetic, one. Lo! the pair are cured miraculously of their disabilities when they chance to meet a procession bearing a relic of a saint. The blind man is delighted—being relieved of two burdens. The cripple is less than ecstatic; now he must toil for his living—without his mount. He rails at the saint.

Why Synge should base his new Irish 'peasant drama' on an old French farce is open to conjecture. Is he not playing right into the hands of the nationalist press, who have, two years running, denounced him for palming off a second-hand foreign plot as original Irish art? Perhaps the title of de la Vigne's farce gives the clue: *moralité*, a morality play. Despite his wide European learning, despite the urbanity and secularism of the London salons, Synge the agnostic has been unable to rid himself of the naïve moral teachings and certainties of Protestant fundamentalism. To be sure, the Aran story had a happy ending—'Oh mother,' exclaims the once-blind boy, 'look at the pretty flowers!'—but Synge's new play does not. How could it, when it examines the human condition, whose only outcome inevitably must be death?

The Well of the Saints expands a theme which Synge introduced in *Riders to the Sea*: the tragedy of human existence, a matter very close to Synge's heart. Every individual life is a movement in an unending symphony, as a single wave to the shore. 'The emotions which pass through us', his *Autobiography* insists, 'have neither end nor beginning' but are 'a part of the sequence of existence'. The individual mood, Synge suggests elsewhere, is 'often trivial, perverse, fleeting'; it is the racial, or national, mood that is 'provisionally permanent'. The individual is little more than a carrier of the cosmic information; man bestows intelligence, and, by extension, art, upon nature. This is simple humanism, of course; but Synge goes further by speculating that, 'as the laws of the world are in harmony', it is the 'almost cosmic element in the person which gives great art, as that of Michelangelo or Beethoven, the dignity of nature'.

It will be noted that not once does Synge make mention of God; for him, the 'cosmic' is evidently not a divine entity. He has studied Renan well. Yet he does believe in heaven and hell, and it is just conceivable that he imagines these states to be of mankind's own making, and within our sphere of influence. He has come to the belief in an afterlife through his dabbling in the occult, ably abetted by Stephen MacKenna and W. B. Yeats. Mrs Synge once confided to Edward Stephens that she

> had received a strange assurance of his belief in a life after death. She said that once Cousin Emily had broken her usual silence about all that John discussed at Uplands [her home in the Wicklow hills], and had recounted a story she had heard from him of how he had been on the verge of abandoning all belief in the spirit world when Yeats was sent to him by the spirits to show him his mistake. What Yeats had shown him, Mrs. Synge did not know, but she said it had been enough to remove from his mind all doubt about our survival after death.

It has been suggested that *Riders to the Sea* and *The Shadow of the Glen* can be seen as opposing themes—determinism versus free will. If so, then *The Tinker's Wedding* develops the latter theme, in order to explore its extreme consequences. It might be said that Synge's received morality has led him to conclude that an idea, when taken to its extremity, will (in accordance with Heraclitean philosophy) become its opposite, i.e. untrammelled freedom eventually leads to stricture. Now, in *The Well of the Saints*, Synge explores the dialectic condition at its biblical fundamentals: light versus darkness.

III

Martin and Mary Doul represent darkness, *doul* or *dall* being the Irish word for 'blind'. Throughout Synge's play, 'blind' and 'dark' are interchangeable. The Christian names Martin and Mary also suggest (because of their common initial syllable) that the pair embody the male and female aspects of this darkness. They are old, too, these beggars; the final darkness of death may soon be upon them.

But, rather than being a handicap, the beggars' blindness

enables them to rejoice in a radiant world of fantasy. Mary imagines herself to be young and beautiful, and her husband handsome and virile; indeed, she is convinced that, given their sight for only one hour, Martin and she should 'know surely we were the finest man, and the finest woman, of the seven counties of the east'; Martin is in no doubt that he is 'married with a woman he's heard called the wonder of the western world'.

Synge's exposition contains little subtlety; the beggars' self-image contrasts so starkly with the old and wizened reality on the stage that only farce can ensue. It is a cruel farce, however, for when Martin and Mary are cured of their blindness through the Saint's intercession, the villagers mock them pitilessly. Martin, the first to be cured, mistakes the beautiful young Molly* for his wife, and she takes obvious pleasure in holding him up to ridicule. When both Douls confront one another with eyes no longer sightless, their anguish is pathetic. Like de la Vigne's cripple, the couple resent their restored sight. No longer can they live by the charity of others. Moreover, the world of the seeing holds far less attraction than they had expected:

> MARTIN DOUL [*fiercely*]. Isn't it finer sights ourselves had a while since and we sitting dark smelling the sweet beautiful smells do be rising in the warm nights and hearing the swift flying things racing in the air, . . . till we'd be looking up in our own minds into a grand sky, and seeing lakes, and broadening rivers, and hills are waiting for the spade and plough.

Having experienced sight, the Douls choose to revert to blindness. They have seen the world of the seeing, and confirmed their belief that 'they're a bad lot those that have their sight'. The pure beauty they had beheld in their imagination is lacking in the world of the sighted; Mary and Martin choose fantasy above reality.

It is this choice of darkness above light that renders the play

---

* A village girl, played by Sara Allgood.

Synge's most invidious to date. Not one of the company suspects as much. Willie Fay's worry is the prevailing mood of the play; Lady Gregory reserves judgement. (There is much in Synge's plays of which she disapproves. 'Fundamentally,' says Elizabeth Coxhead, 'she is a moral writer; equally fundamentally, Synge is an amoral one.') Yeats, true to form, is as enthusiastic and hyperbolical as ever. While rehearsals are in progress, he writes, in his preface to the first edition of the play, that

> Mr. Synge has in common with the great theatre of the world, with that of Greece and that of India, with the creator of Falstaff, with Racine, a delight in language, a preoccupation with individual life. He resembles them also by a preoccupation with what is lasting and noble . . . .

Lady Gregory does not share Yeats's enthusiasm. Whether the rest of the world will one day talk of Shakespeare and Synge in one breath remains to be seen, but she is fair-minded enough not to let her personal feelings about Synge's drama cloud her objectivity. She also delights in language, dialect in particular, her so-called 'Kiltartan' Hiberno-English. Her own first play, *Kincora*, a tale of Brian Boru, is almost ready. She has wedded peasant speech with history and nobility.

But what of Yeats's remark about Synge's preoccupation with 'what is lasting and noble'? Lady Gregory has seen little of it, unless by 'preoccupation' Yeats means that Synge is determined to scoff at, hold up to ridicule, or simply attack those institutions she holds dear. To be sure, *The Shadow of the Glen* was a condemnation of hypocrisy and marital cruelty, where adultery was offered as the lesser evil. But *The Well of the Saints* is an assault on goodness, on the very light of the world.

It is the story of the Fall, yet Synge's retelling of it is perhaps the most singular to date. Instead of the pair being cast out of the Garden into outer darkness, they are thrust, instead, into the light. Their safe, dark, prelapsarian world had shielded them from all manner of evil; now they see—literally—that the denizens of the big world of light are villains. The younger and more lovely they are, the more invective, cruelty and treachery Synge places in their mouths. Martin, his sight restored, toils by the sweat of his brow, is cursed for his laziness and ineptitude by his former 'friends', and longs for the comforting world of darkness. Like Adam, he is aware of the mortality—if not imminent death—of his wife, and the ravaging by age of her beauty and health. Light brings discontentment; darkness is perfection. Synge's philosophy is a curious echo of a sentiment which Douglas Hyde has expressed in his *Love Songs of Connacht*:

> Happy 'tis, thou blind, for thee
> That thou seest not our star;
> Couldst thou see but as we now see her,
> Thou wouldst be but as we now are.

The light of the outside world brings conformity to the will of the majority; in blindness, the individual, though impaired, may yet retain his autonomy.

Never before has Synge the dramatist expressed such anarchic views. There is something of the little boy in him, the desire to shock, the delight in outraged sensibilities; especially so when the outraged belong largely to the nationalist press. It comes as no surprise, then, that Arthur Griffith's *United Irishman* leads the adverse criticism. But Synge is no longer an unknown quantity; *The Well of the Saints* attracts large houses and no newspaper can ignore the play. Nor is it ignored: Ireland's literary critics join together in a disparaging chorus.

Synge, however, receives the news he hardly dared hope for: Europe has noticed him. Henri Lebeau, a young Frenchman whom Synge had met in Paris, visits Dublin, together with Anatole le Braz, the Breton folklorist and novelist. Lebeau is so taken with Synge's new play that he calls it

> une oeuvre subtile et gracieuse, l'esquisse d'un drame plutôt peut-être qu'un drame proprement dit, mais le raffinement de l'observation, l'usage discret et adroit qui y est fait du symbolisme, et aussi la langue, une langue à la fois

savante et populaire, adroite utilisation par la plume d'un
artiste du dialecte anglais parlé par les paysans de l'Ouest
de l'Irlande, en font tout l'opposé du banal et du vulgaire.*

Lebeau's article is published simultaneously in Paris and in *Dana*, a
short-lived Irish periodical. The translator Max Meyerfeld writes to
Synge, asking his permission to translate *The Well of the Saints* into
German, with a view to having it performed in his own country.
Synge is overjoyed; Yeats claps his hands when he hears the news:
he has already gone on record publicly to assert that Synge would
soon have a European reputation. If Ireland does not want
J. M. Synge, then J. M. Synge does not need Ireland.

IV

T he truly needy of rural Ireland in the early years of the
century are concentrated in those areas which the
authorities call the Congested Districts. Confined in the
main to the west of the country, they are congested not
through overcrowding (the horrors of the Great Famine of the
1840s have left their populations much diminished), but because
their poor arable land cannot support its inhabitants, most of
whom are holders of very small properties. A new famine is the last
thing the government wants. It has, therefore, under the provisions
of the Land Purchase Act of 1891, called into being a council of
wise men, the Congested Districts Board, whose brief is to prevent
starvation. Their method has been the breaking up of big estates in
order that the smallholdings might be enlarged; they are also

---

* *a subtle and graceful work, what one would perhaps call the outline of a
play rather than a play proper, but the refinement of observation, the dis-
creet and deft use which is made here of symbolism, and also language, a
language at once erudite and homely, is skilled penmanship by an artist
of English dialect as it is spoken by the peasants of the West of Ireland,
whose use of it is the complete opposite of triteness and vulgarity.*

empowered to relocate families, to ensure a fairer distribution of the land's poor resources. These are policies fraught with danger for the politicians; Westminster cannot afford to forget the mistakes it made in its handling of the Famine. The people of Ireland have long memories.

An unseasonable, driving June rain whips in from the ocean as John Synge and his companion tread the Mullet. Synge knows what to do. He leads the way off the rough track and heads for the sandhills.

'Quick,' he urges, 'heap the sand over you. It will keep you dry.'

Jack B. Yeats does as he is bidden. When the rain passes, the men emerge from their shelters with soaked faces, but dry clothing.

The two are the same age. Jack is the young brother of William Butler Yeats, with whom he has always had a curious relationship. This is, in itself, hardly surprising in the sons of a painter father who had uprooted his family many times in the course of his early career, setting up homes, at irregular intervals, in County Sligo, Dublin and London. From a tender age, the Yeats children—Willie, Jack, Lily and Lollie—seemed destined to pursue artistic careers. There are, for example, children's drawings which reveal talent inherited from the father. Oddly enough, Willie's sketches show more promise than Jack's. Could this, we may well wonder, have a bearing on the obvious rivalry shown by the brothers in adult years? It is a fact that Willie, throughout his formidable literary output, rarely refers to his brother by name—if he mentions him at all. Nor is there much praise forthcoming; only when Jack produced an illustration to accompany a poem by Ernest Rhys, a friend and fellow-member of the Rhymers Club, did Willie acknowledge the 'tragic intensity' of his brother's work. There is no doubt that Jack could have benefited from Willie's influential London circle; instead, as Hilary Pyle observes, 'he followed his own inclinations, preferring always to strike a lone path'.

Jack Yeats lives uncomfortably in his older brother's giant

shadow. He himself is a playwright of sorts. He works to a small scale: his plays are children's theatre, miniature Punch and Judy dramas which involve a succession of pirates, smugglers and the like. In a significant way, their plots and their use of temporal space are superior to those of Willie. Jack will go on to write novels too. They will not be great novels, but will none the less enjoy minor success. There is something not quite right here: one—or both brothers—has chosen the wrong path. Perhaps the pathways to art are interchangeable; asked once why he had become a painter, Jack replied that he had had no option, that he was 'the son of a painter.' What might have happened if Willie had developed his childhood painting skills will never be known.

And Jack? In 1905, it is by no means easy to see that Jack B. Yeats will, one day, become a meritorious, if not quite a major, painter. His illustrating is, at best, workmanlike. His faces, drawn mostly from memory, have a repetitive sameness, as though the artist employs tried and trusted technique, rather than feeling for the subjects; he has had a lifelong love of horses, yet his illustrations reveal an abysmal ignorance of equine anatomy. That said, there is a quality about Jack B. Yeats's work that sets him apart from other Irish and British artists of his time; it manages to capture what Synge calls the 'psychic state' of a person or locality. Crude though they may be, Jack's illustrations take the viewer beyond a simple, line description of rural Ireland; there is real statement. Hilary Pyle explains Jack's motivation:

> The problem had been to choose between painting and words as a means of communication, but he opted for painting which he said was greater than writing. Painting was direct vision and direct communication.
>
> The constant comparison [he] was making between words and visual images show how much he was concerned with literature.

He is concerned with literature, yes, but sees his own contribution to the Irish Literary Renaissance in other terms:

Having worked as a black-and-white illustrator accepting
the London tradition he entered the Gaelic Revival movement his brother was engaged in and became the artist of
a cause which had never had an artist before. The Irish tradition rejoiced in a spoken literature. [Jack] now translated the essence of that tradition, and the life from which it
emanated, the love of poetry and the spoken word, of
landscape, of humour, of legend, of idiosyncratic character into his paintings.

How unfortunate for the literary revival, then, that old childhood
rivalries prevent the brothers' working more closely together; until
now, Jack's principal contribution has been the design of stage
sets, a task he shares with one or two of Willie's theosophical
friends. Jack Yeats as Abbey playwright-painter: what wonders of
word and image might have emerged from his hand, given other
circumstances . . . .

They are the best of companions, Jack and John. Edward Stephens
likens their relationship to 'a marriage made in heaven'. They possess, he says, 'highly trained powers of observation' and appreciate
anything that is 'beautiful of land or sea'. Jack senses the rawness
in Synge, a man who cares 'nothing for comfort except perhaps
that of a good turf fire'. He is content to go wherever Synge leads
(at the outset, the two men agreed that the elder would decide
their itinerary; Synge discovered that he was Jack's senior by several
months).

Jack Yeats has always loved the Irish countryside, in particular
a fishing village called Rosses Point, not far from Sligo harbour,
where the Yeats children spent many a summer. Jack delighted in
the seafarers he saw there, men who sailed the tall ships he was so
fond of sketching. Willie Yeats remembers how his brother used to
spend hours leaning over a bridge, looking into a trout-filled pool,
and regretting 'that he did not spend many more hours in that
apparently unprofitable pastime'. We are reminded of Synge's own

penchant for solitary contemplation; truly, he and his companion are well matched for the task in hand. They have been commissioned by the *Manchester Guardian* to report on the relief works initiated by the Congested Districts Board.

Synge is achieving considerable literary success. In January, the *Manchester Guardian* printed 'An Impression of Aran', a short piece taken from the first part of Synge's book. John Quinn, the American friend of the Abbey Theatre, copyrighted the text of *The Well of the Saints* in New York in February, thereby safeguarding the American rights; at the same time, Maunsel and Company in Dublin published the theatre edition of the play. On the strength of the first article, John Masefield urged the *Guardian*'s editor, C. P. Scott, to take further extracts from the Aran book; Synge suggested, instead, that he might prefer to investigate the Congested Districts. Jack Yeats would accompany him as illustrator.

V

The companions began their month-long odyssey in Spiddal, gateway to the Connemara *gaeltacht,* or Gaelic-speaking area. They will travel by open car along the coast, with the Aran Islands to the south.

Synge's articles—there will be twelve—are intended for an English public. They are not his best work, because little of the emotion he would have liked to express is contained in them. Even so, the character sketch, a forte of Synge, is found throughout. We meet the old beggarwoman, who, upon hearing that Synge speaks her language, showers thanks on him with Irish exuberance; there is the horse-breeder who laments 'the dying out of the ponies of Connemara'; the garrulous Dinish ferryman who has seen the shores of America. Synge writes with affection about these, the common people.

There is another class, though, he hardly mentions in his articles. This class is Ireland's rising bourgeoisie, for whom Synge has little sympathy. He alludes to Spiddal shopkeepers 'dressed like the people of Dublin, but a little more grotesquely; then the more well-to-do country folk, dressed in the local clothes . . . but the best and newest kind'.

In reality, of course, these people are Synge's social equals. There is one important difference: they are Roman Catholics. Old prejudices die hard, even in a man as well travelled as Synge. There is something 'grotesque' about these well-to-do native Irish. But are they not the country cousins of those who have reviled his plays? In words reserved for his friend Stephen MacKenna's eyes only, Synge reveals the extent of his contempt for the Catholic middle class:

> There are sides of all that western life the groggy-patriot-publican-general shop-man who is married to the priest's half-sister and is second cousin once-removed of the dispensary doctor that are horrible and awful. This is the type that is running the present United Irish League anti-grazier campaign while they're swindling the people themselves in a dozen ways and then buying out their holdings and packing off whole families to America. The subject is too big to go into here, but at best it's beastly. All that side of the matter of course I left untouched in my stuff. I sometimes wish to God I hadn't a soul and then I could give myself up to putting those lads on the stage. God, wouldn't they hop!

To put them on the stage; now there's a thought. Synge has been toying with an idea for a new play. His visits to County Kerry in 1903 and 1904 had brought him into contact with a language more robust than that of Wicklow or Aran. He has been looking for a suitable vehicle for it, for a people in whose rough mouths it will not seem misplaced. He has been twice to the Mullet. Twice among the honest poor he has come upon a degenerate race, 'an ungodly ruck of fat-faced, sweaty-headed swine', as he calls them. In Ireland, it seems, his dramatic works have been no better received than pearls before swine. What a joke—what a *farce*—it should be, to give the swine fodder befitting their coarse palates!

VI

See Synge sitting at the court of the King of the Blasket Islands. The kingdom is a clustering of stark islets that rise like mountains from the sea, some little distance off the western extremity of Kerry's Dingle peninsula. Pádraig Ó Catháin, the headman of Great Blasket, lords over the twenty-five island families. As usual, Synge has chosen his quarters well; the Ó Catháin cottage is the focal point of Great Blasket. The people, curious about the Irish-speaking stranger among them, troop into the kitchen to welcome Synge, and stare.

Life in Blasket is hard, though perhaps not as dangerous as that of Aran, for Synge hears that there has not been a drowning here in forty years. But fish sales to the Kerry mainland are a diminishing source of livelihood, and many of the young men are leaving for America. There is a general feeling of malaise, that an era is ending. Ó Catháin himself has no illusions that his small kingdom will endure. The race of Blasket, he tells Synge, has been degenerating for some time: 'The young people is no use. I am not as good a man as my father was, and my son is growing up worse than I am.'

It is not the son who has Synge's attention. Ó Catháin has a twenty-year-old married daughter who does the housekeeping. Synge, the incurable lover of peasant beauty, is immediately attracted to her, calling her 'the little hostess'. She is, he writes, 'a small, beautifully-formed woman, with brown hair and eyes—instead of the black hair and blue eyes that are usually found with this type in Ireland—and delicate feet and ankles that are not common to these parts, where the woman's work is hard'. She could well be Molly Allgood; perhaps this young Kerrywoman reminds him of the Dublin girl who has so recently taken his fancy. Synge shows her his photographs of Aran and Wicklow, and an old snapshot of himself taken in the Luxembourg Gardens. There are marble statues in the background. The girl, who has never seen such statues before, takes them for living, nude people.

There is chemistry at work here between John Synge and his 'little hostess'. So convivial are their intimate conversations by the kitchen fire that he fantasizes about their being married and his sharing with her the bucolic life of the Blaskets. He pens a charming little poem:

> You've plucked a curlew, drawn a hen,
> Washed the shirts of seven men,
> You've stuffed my pillow, stretched the sheet,
> And filled the pan to wash your feet,
> You've cooped the pullets, wound the clock,
> And rinsed the young men's drinking crock;
> And now we'll dance to jigs and reels,
> Nailed boots chasing girls' naked heels,
> Until your father'll start to snore,
> And Jude, now you're married, will stretch on the floor.

For all that, life in Kerry is boisterous. Synge hears of drunken brawls and fisticuffs, of men returning from the sports day in Ballyferriter, 'fighting and kicking in the canoes'. He learns that 'sport' has various interpretations in Dingle; he is given an account of a pitched battle fought on the beaches:

> 'There was great sport after you left,' a man said to me in the cottage this evening. 'They were all beating and cutting each other on the shore of the sea. Four men fought together in one place till the tide came up on them, and was like to drown them; but the priest waded out up to his middle and drove them asunder. Another man was left for dead on the road outside the lodges, and some gentleman found him and had him carried into his house, and got the doctor to put plasters on his head. Then there was a red-headed fellow had his finger bitten through, and the postman was destroyed for ever.'

Synge is collecting impressions of a harsh and bellicose society. His new play will draw on violence and brutality, will depict a community whose morality is wanting. On the surface, the people seem civilized; scratch that surface and the savage emerges. Synge makes an entry in his Kerry notebook; an idea for a play called *Smuggler's Island*:

> Island with population of wreckers, smugglers, poteen-makers etc. are startled by the arrival of a stranger and reform for dread of him. He is an escaped criminal and wants them to help him over to America but he thinks that they are so virtuous he is afraid to confess his deeds for fear they should hand him over to the law that they are so apparently in awe of. At last all comes out and he is got off safely.

Of course, the play, by this time, is in a far more advanced form. Last autumn, Synge had prepared the first draft, complete with the names of the principal characters: Christy, his father, Shawn, Widow Quin, Pegeen . . . .

Before he leaves Kerry, Synge has a very clear picture of Pegeen. She is a composite of a Dublin walk-on actress and a young Blasket woman who, to Synge's chagrin, is already wed.

VII

All is not well at the Abbey. John Synge returns to Dublin to find that a most divisive situation has been developing in his absence. On the one hand are those with nationalist sympathies, many of whom are active in the Gaelic League, who see their theatre as a vehicle for the dissemination of propaganda. Plainly put, an Abbey production should advance the cause of Irish independence and be devoid of any criticism of the country and its people. W. B. Yeats and Lady Gregory head the opposing faction: those who see the theatre fulfilling its broader function of producing art without nationalistic restraints.

Things come to a head when Annie Horniman generously agrees to donate up to £500 towards placing the actors on full

salary. The step from amateur actor to professional is not one to be
taken lightly; many members of the company have well-paying day
jobs. In November 1905, the company embarks on a highly successful English tour; successful both in artistic and monetary terms:
receipts are large. Clearly, those who choose to side with Yeats can
be assured of a fine future, together with a good income.
Perversely, the nationalists of the company see success in England
as a failure of their original, political purpose: the furtherance of
the cause of Irish freedom. To entertain the English is to betray
this cause. The alternative is possible Thespian obscurity, but one
in which one's political ideals remain intact. What price idealism?

Mary Walker, arguably the finest actress in the company, is
the most vocal in the dispute with Yeats, accusing him of reneging
on his original promise of a national theatre. The success that the
company is achieving is, oddly enough, proof to her that Yeats is
following his international star to the detriment of the cause of
Irish freedom.

Synge, that most mild-mannered of men, always loath to offer
a politically tinged opinion, bears some of the blame. With the
exception of *Riders to the Sea*, all his drama to date has succeeded in
calling down the wrath of the nationalist movement on the heads
of the company. They have had enough. Mary Walker walks out,
taking six others with her, and establishes a rival company, 'The
Theatre of Ireland'. The playwright Padraic Colum is torn between
the quarrelling factions; he eventually goes over to the dissident
side. George Moore, for other, more personal, reasons, has with-
drawn his friendship and support. The Irish National Theatre
Society is decimated; only the directors and a handful of players
remain.

Now Yeats and Lady Gregory must salvage what they can from
the shambles. They have two formidable allies in the Fay brothers,
whose performances are probably the best on the Irish stage. They
also have John Millington Synge.

Synge's allegiance is to W. B. Yeats and Lady Gregory, the two
people who have helped him most in his career. In the days of
regrouping that follow the secession, the troika reaches the

conclusion that the future of the Abbey Theatre will depend on its leadership. Where before the company was run on democratic lines, it is now decided that the three alone will dictate policy, what plays will be performed, and will be 'absolutely supreme in everything'. Synge, Yeats and Lady Gregory share joint directorship of the Abbey Theatre. The Fays, and those whose work and devotion helped the company to greatness, lose their right of veto. The troika loses many friends. In a letter to Padraic Colum, Augusta Gregory mourns their passing; they have, she tells him,

> lost many helpers by the way. Mr. Lecky, who served us well in getting the law passed that made these dramatic experiments possible, publicly repudiated us because of Mr. Yeats's letter on the Queen's visit. Edward Martyn withdrew when we had to refuse the *Tale of a Town* which did not, as we thought, come up to the required standard. George Moore from a friend became an enemy. Then . . . others were lost for different reasons—[P. J.] Kelly and [Dudley] Digges and Miss [Maire] Quinn and Mrs. [Maud Gonne] MacBride, all of whom have been helpful in their time. Now others are dropping off.

But the nucleus remains. The troika has the invaluable support of George Russell, Fred J. Ryan, the Fay brothers and the Allgood sisters. The last are happy to step into the shoes of the seceding actresses. The Abbey directors make plans for the coming season, due to begin in early December. Lady Gregory has two plays ready—*The White Cockade* and *Hyacinth Halvey*—but there is a shortage of more new material. They decide that next year, 1906, should be ushered in with revivals of past successes. Among these will be *Riders to the Sea.*

VIII

Molly Allgood is talented. The voice which was lost in the crowd in *The Well of the Saints* proves to be rich and strong. Moreover, her working-class manner of speech suits well the lines Synge gave to Bartley's sister Cathleen in *Riders to the Sea*. Molly Allgood responds admirably to the coaching of the Abbey's new stage-director, J. M. Synge. In the reduced company, Synge's tasks are multifarious. He is both company director and theatre manager; he helps the Fay brothers recruit and train new actors; he reads playscripts; he directs rehearsals; he helps balance the books. He has never been happier.

In the winter of 1905, Synge takes to his new duties with a passion that belies the weakness of his constitution. He is chronically unwell; his letters to friends and associates bemoan a succession of colds and other complaints. Most ominous in this respect is his letter to Yeats on 19 November. 'My neck is much better, but I have been . . . unwell in my stomach the last days . . . '. The cancer of Hodgkin's Disease has returned; as yet, no accurate diagnosis has been made. Synge's body is wasting. Long days and nights spent tramping the wet roads of Ireland, poor lodgings and bad food in Paris—all have taken their toll. At thirty-four, Synge looks ten years older. Molly Allgood, dressed in madder-coloured petticoat, shawl and pampooties, could be mistaken for his daughter.

The work brings him and Molly into close, if not to say intimate, contact. At this stage, however, he is careful to conceal his feelings for her from all but Molly. There is his position to think of; it is considered taboo for a director to form liaisons with members of the company; Lady Gregory is especially strict about this. There is, too, the matter of his family. Brought up to believe all theatre to be sinful, reared in protective isolation from the 'evils of popery', Synge could hardly have chosen a companion more unsuitable than Molly Allgood who, in his mother's eyes, must surely embody all she has fought against: the immorality of the theatre, coupled with the superstition of Roman Catholicism.

But a secret romance brings its own difficulties. The Abbey Players—the newest recruits in particular—are an amiable, high-spirited crew whose code of conduct is markedly different from that of bourgeois society. They enjoy an intimacy which appals Synge, who has been reared to treat womankind with respect in the full Victorian sense of the word. Hands are held, lips are kissed in the most casual manner: improprieties grudgingly tolerated by Lady Gregory and Synge, who, of all concerned, are most Victorian in their codes and values.

The love affair begins in earnest when *Riders to the Sea* closes in January 1906, and preparations begin for a revival of *The Shadow of the Glen*. Once again, Synge takes charge of rehearsals. Molly's interpretation of Cathleen has so impressed and delighted him that he has no hesitation in having her read the part of Nora Burke. It is soon clear to the company that the girl's performance will be, at the very least, as good as that given by Mary Walker, who had made the role her own. Molly Allgood, Edward Stephens comments, is quick to appreciate the way Synge wants her to act the part, and uses 'her rich voice wonderfully in the speaking of his rhythmical prose'.

Synge, in order to coach Molly in the role, assumes the character who is probably closest to the Synge persona: the Tramp. The ambience of the theatre and the concentrated intimacy of rehearsing what is essentially a story of love and passion exert their magic on his shyness. He woos Molly with lines like:

Is it go away and leave you, and you having a wake, lady of the house? I will not surely. And it's none of your tea I'm asking either.

So closely does Synge identify with the character that he soon begins signing his letters to Molly Algood with 'Your old Tramp' or 'The Tramp'. She to him is the 'Changeling', or fairy child—a name he invariably misspells 'Changling'.

Synge's taking of the rooms in Rathgar enables him to be closer to the Abbey Theatre. It also brings him nearer to Molly's home in Mary Street, less than a kilometre from the theatre. Synge is actually the only director who lives in Dublin: Yeats spends most of this period in London, Lady Gregory at her home in Coole Park. Although there is now every opportunity to do so, Synge is too much of a gentleman to invite Molly unchaperoned to his rooms. Instead, they meet regularly at Westland Row railway station and travel together to Bray, to take long walks in the Wicklow hills. He delights in showing her the countryside he has loved since childhood.

It is a strange romance. Synge does his best to 'improve' Molly, in order that she should make a good impression when, inevitably, he must introduce her as his fiancée to his mother. But there is more to it. Synge himself is not happy with Molly's inadequate, primary-school education, or her working-class background; he has ambitious plans for her.

Synge's efforts to improve the unrefined former shopgirl call to mind George Bernard Shaw's *Pygmalion*, and Henry Higgins's promise to Eliza Doolittle that 'you shall marry an officer in the Guards, with a beautiful moustache: the son of a marquis, who will disinherit him for marrying you, but will relent when he sees your beauty and goodness'. Synge seems bent on Molly becoming a suitable marriage partner for a man of his background and social standing. This is bewildering: Molly's wilfulness and relative lack of inhibition are the very attributes which attracted Synge to her in the first place. She seemed to personify the independent spirits of Nora Burke and Sarah Casey. But now he attempts to mould the girl into a more fitting companion. He encourages her to read literature and to improve her way of speaking. In time, he will even go so far as to persuade her to try her hand at playwriting.

He is also an unusually jealous and possessive man. 'I heard accidentally of your walking arm in arm with Wright at Longford', he writes to Molly. 'Is that true?' What he does not know is that Udolphus 'Dossie' Wright—one of the new actors—is actually teasing Synge whenever he can by putting his arm around Molly. Jealousy begins to intrude on Synge's writing. 'It is curious', he comments, 'to have a jealousy for that island—the whole island and its people—like the jealousy of men in love.'

This year—1906—more than ever, John Synge is learning how it feels to be closely involved with a repertory company. More, it is a *touring* company, and travel, life on the road, is for him an immensely agreeable pursuit. In February, he accompanies the players to Wexford, where they perform *The Shadow of the Glen*, with Molly in the leading role. They visit Dundalk in March and again in May; the same repertoire is given in Longford in July. It might be expected that provincial audiences—being composed largely of nationally minded theatre-goers—should accord Synge's contentious play a reception much worse than Dublin houses had given it, but this is far from being the case. Synge's reputation has grown to such an extent that ovations greet the performances at every venue. As David Greene puts it: 'Synge had every reason to feel that at last he had arrived.'

Britain, too, proves as satisfying as before. The company tours the north of England in May, playing to appreciative houses in Manchester, Liverpool and Leeds. An extended tour follows from 26 May to 9 July, with performances in cities as far afield as Cardiff, Glasgow, Aberdeen, Edinburgh, Newcastle and Hull. Synge can take at first hand the measure of his popularity. They are exhilarating days; more so when he can spend so much time in Molly's exciting company. Love grows. So too does the embarrassment it causes W. B. Yeats and Lady Gregory. They are both flustered and exasperated; if Synge were a common stage-director or producer, they could—and would—intervene. But John Synge is too powerful; they hope the love affair will peter out and die, as theatrical romances so often do.

Mrs Synge, living now in Glendalough House in Glenageary, Co. Dublin, shares their misgivings. She has hoped and prayed for better than a young actress, whose sole income is her meagre Abbey salary. Once again, however, Mrs Synge proves what a tower of strength she is. In November, Molly expresses a wish to meet John's mother; she visits Glendalough House on the 22nd and stays for a couple of hours. So charming is she that Mrs Synge, while not quite accepting her as a future daughter-in-law, extends a warm welcome.

Yeats, Lady Gregory and Mrs Synge cannot begin to guess at the depth of John's love for Molly. To him, she is life itself: life ablaze with the fire of youth and energy. Now, more than ever, he senses that there is something seriously amiss with his health, that his time may be short. His letters to the young woman are full of his devotion to her; they also paint a depressing picture of his chronic illnesses: 'I get a sort of Hay-fever at night that worries me' (30 August); '. . . I have a sort of asthma . . . ' (1 September); 'I'm a good deal better . . . . I have not even opened my play yet, after all it is far more important for me to be out in the fresh air now, getting a stock of health to carry me through next winter . . .' (4 September); 'I am very unwell—nothing at all serious but an ailment brought on by the damp, and unsuitable food, that causes me intense pain at times, I nearly fainted yesterday I was so bad . . .' (8 September); 'I am much better again now, nearly well in fact. You have no idea how much I have suffered' (18 September); '. . . I will not be well enough I fear to walk tomorrow . . . And with the continual, deadly strain of my writing I haven't much health over . . .' (22 September); 'I'm not at all well, inside . . . If my ailments get *much* worse I'll write tonight to put you off . . . ' (20 October); 'I wasn't well enough to go in [to Dublin] last night . . .' (21 October).

For a short time, all seems well; but less than a month later, the litany of complaints begins anew: 'I've had a bad turn enough, but I'm much better though I'm in bed still . . . it is only a bout of influenza . . .' (16 November); 'I am very unwell, we got the doctor out from Dublin [to Glenageary] to see me last night' (18 November); 'If I am well enough I go in to the doctor on Thursday or Friday afternoon' (20 November).

Molly's visit to Glendalough House comes at a time when Synge's state of health has so deteriorated that his physician, Dr Parsons, advises him to suspend work on his play for a week or two. He suggests that Synge should pay a visit to his cousin Edward Synge at Byfleet, Surrey. 'The doctor says . . . I've a very slight irritation on one lung still, so it is well for me to be careful . . . ' (23 November); 'The doctor says I am going on well, getting better slowly' (24 November).

The fortnight in Surrey will afford Synge the opportunity to consider his damaged health: 'I have had rather a worse attack than I expected . . . One of my lungs . . . has been a little touched . . .' (25 November); 'I am not well . . . . I feel broken down and infinitely wretched . . . ' (29 November).

It is in the last month of the year that Synge conveys to Molly his intimations of mortality: ' . . . if I don't kick the bucket I ought to be able to do good work and plenty of it still' (2 December); '. . . I have got a sort of asthma at night that disturbs me a good deal' (3 December); 'The asthma has left me with a heavy cough...' (6 December); '...I look so thin now and generally unwell' (7 December).

Between the lines is written the story of Synge's Trojan efforts to complete the most difficult of his plays to date, while his body was racked by almost continual illness. He has struggled against bronchitis, asthma, influenza, hay-fever, and a host of other minor demons. He is still unaware of the greater demon that lurks in his body: the lymphatic sarcoma, the demon that will destroy him.

To be sure, he has his angel Molly Allgood, but this is an angel who exasperates and frustrates him at every turn. She is untameable and, as he himself puts it, 'tiffable'. Her erratic letter-writing drives him to distraction; so, too, do what he sees as her loose ways with other members of the company.

Fatal illness, love, jealousy, violence, passion; seldom have these factors conspired together so forcefully as in this, John Synge's most fecund year. Seldom has a dramatist succeeded in bringing together the tortured strands of his experience in one all-encompassing statement. Synge is here; Molly is here. Aran, the Mullet, Kerry, Wicklow, Ireland, more.

'It is all', Synge tells Molly, 'that accursed Playboy'.

A Shadow Upon Her Mirror

I

'**S**hifts,' says Christy Mahon.

'Shame!' cries theatre-going Dublin—and promptly render the players' subsequent lines inaudible, up to the final curtain. They do the same at every performance, a week long; until W. B. Yeats invites the most vociferous critics to the Abbey Theatre and, shrewdly, charges them admission—not to see a play, mind, but to give them an opportunity to articulate their grievances in a more civilized fashion, and in order that he and a handful of others may spring to Synge's defence. Both factions claim a victory, and the play completes its run.

This is a potted account of Dublin's 'Playboy riots'. The full story has been told before in such detail that it hardly seems necessary to repeat it here. Nor can it serve any purpose to open old wounds, because the Playboy riots are a sorry and embarrassing stain on the history of the Irish theatre movement as experienced by the Irish theatre-goer—even if similar scenes will be recorded some four years on, when the play tours the United States.

Part of the problem is that Synge's star is rising on the cusp of modernism, the international movement in art and literature whose exponents transcend realism, departing from an apparently given world to one of conscious human construction. It is a trend that has gained little sympathy among the traditionalists, who find their conventions and assumptions under assault from the avant-gardists. Synge is a modernist, yet Dublin does not recognize him as such. Instead, his new play is received at face value; the perception is that Synge is holding Ireland and the Irish up to ridicule. Is it so surprising, then, that rioting ensues? The riots demarcate the boundary dividing two distinct camps: philistinism is ranged against art;

decency opposes blackguardism. The *Freeman's Journal* rails against 'this unmitigated, protracted libel upon Irish peasant men and, worse still, upon Irish peasant girlhood. The blood boils with indignation [at] this squalid, offensive production . . . .' Arthur Griffith takes up the cudgels, and denounces this 'vile and inhuman story told in the foulest language we have ever listened to from a public platform'. The play, he continues, 'represents the peasant women of Mayo contending in their lusts for the possession of a man who has appealed to their depraved instincts . . . .'

Griffith cannot believe that Synge's play is based on the genuine harbouring of a murderer by a peasant community. If that is the case, he says ominously, 'we shall regret that so vile a race should be permitted to exist'.

And yet, it is not quite so simple and clear-cut—simply because *The Playboy of the Western World* is anything but a simple play.

Take the title. The OED defines 'playboy' as 'an irresponsible pleasure-seeking man, esp. a wealthy one'. This is a comparatively recent listing; a star set against the corresponding entry in Webster's Dictionary indicates that 'playboy' in this sense is of American origin, and refers presumably to the type of individual apotheosized by Hugh Hefner's eponymous organ. This is obviously not the same playboy that Synge is writing about. What kind of man, then, is *Synge's* playboy? If we think we know, then Johannes Kleinstück may destroy our delusion, for the task of the translator leaves him or her little or no room for ambiguity, and demands an interpretation closer and less equivocal than would a casual reading in the original language:

> The difficulty of translating Synge becomes evident as soon as one tries to find an equivalent for the very title *The Playboy of the Western World*. Five suggestions have been made: (1) *Der Held des Westerlands* by G. Sil-Vara, (2) *Der Wunderheld aus dem Westerland* by Werner Wolff, (3) *Der Gaukler von Mayo* by Katrin Janecke and Günter Blöcker, (4) *Ein wahrer Held* by Annemarie and Heinrich Böll, (5) *Der Held der westlichen Welt* by Peter Hacks. The first may be

dismissed as particularly unfortunate, as Westerland is an actual seaside resort on the German island of Sylt, while the second is hardly an improvement. What about the *Gaukler* (juggler) ['charlatan' and 'trickster' are better translations] and the *wahrer Held* (true hero)? Both titles contain an interpretation of the play, the first by open statement, the second by ironic implication, and both mean the same thing: they maintain that Christy is just the opposite of what he seems, that he is nothing but a wind-bag or a sham, and not the daredevil he pretends to be.

All these interpretations, says Kleinstück, for one reason or another, miss or blur the point Synge is trying to make. The clue lies in the fact that 'playboy' is a translation of the Irish *buachaill báire*. *Buachaill* means 'boy' and *báire* is both the game of hurling and a goal scored therein. So a 'playboy' is a hurling-player or goal-scorer, and, by extension, a young man who plays games with those around him and scores points off them. We are getting closer to defining Christy Mahon.

Even the plot of *The Playboy* is deceptively simple. Synge sets the action in a shebeen, or public house, in a remote part of County Mayo. The house is at the hub of a tiny community near Belmullet; it is typical of such communities, as Synge found in the Congested Districts whose plight he reported for the *Manchester Guardian*.

Christy Mahon bursts in upon the lives of the local people as a young fugitive who has murdered his father. He is given sanctuary from the 'peelers', and proceeds to win the admiration of all and sundry (the local girls in particular) because of his 'gallous talk' of how he performed the 'dirty deed'. As the adulation grows, so too does the hyperbole in Christy's version of the event. He becomes a local hero, winning all the prizes at the horse-races, as well as the love of both Pegeen Mike, the publican's daughter, and the Widow Quin, a somewhat older, though seemingly no less attractive, woman.

Christy's talk, however, is exposed as a load of froth when his father appears, very much alive. Christy then 'kills' him a second time—like *Riders to the Sea*, the play relies on much off-stage action—and the villagers turn on him, beating him and burning his leg with a hot sod. His 'resurrected' father returns once more from the dead; he and Christy leave the shebeen, the son now having power over the father he once feared. 'Oh my grief,' wails Pegeen, 'I've lost him surely. I've lost the only playboy of the western world.' Curtain.

II

The play is Synge's *magnum opus*, the last work he will complete in its entirety, and it shows his dramaturgical skills at their most accomplished. The sudden appearance of Christy's father, and the subsequent assault on the Playboy by the villagers (including Pegeen herself) is surely peripeteia at its most effective—if not to say its most comic.

The typescript has gone through an astonishing eleven drafts, and, during rehearsals at the beginning of January 1907, Synge is still revising the dialogue. There is the matter of the language: oaths and curses abound; fifty cuts must be made before the play can be performed by, and for, mixed company.

Synge expects trouble. The programme notes on *The Playboy*, written on 21 January, five days before the first performance, read less like an introduction to the drama than a forestalling of criticism of the language used. 'As in my other plays,' he writes, 'I have used one or two words only, that I have not heard among the country people of Ireland, or spoken in my own nursery before I could read the newspapers.' (That last seems unlikely; it is highly doubtful that Mrs Synge would have approved of her son's nurses' taking the Lord's name in vain—a recurrent feature of *The Playboy*, and the root cause of the fifty cuts.) Driving home his point, Synge goes on to say that 'Anyone who has lived in real intimacy with the Irish peasantry will know that the wildest sayings and ideas in this play are tame indeed compared with the fancies one may hear in any little hillside cabin in Geesala, or Carraroe, or Dingle Bay.'

So Synge is prepared for trouble, as are the company and directors of the Abbey Theatre. In the event, when trouble comes, it comes not in response to robust imprecations such as 'that the Lord God would send a high wave to wash him from the world,' but because of the use of the word 'shifts'—a shift being a woman's underskirt.

But 'shifts' is merely the last straw that breaks the camel's back for this opening night audience: there are more important issues at stake. For instance: would young Irish womanhood give its heart (and, presumably, its favours) to a patricidal stranger? Certainly not! Another instance: are the peasants of Mayo as brutal, vulgar and crude as Synge has painted them? The idea! The play is called, variously, 'dreadful'; an 'offensive production'; and a 'sordid, squalid, and repulsive picture of Irish life and character. It is calumny gone raving mad.'

There lurks a Judas too within the ranks of the Abbey playwrights. William Boyle, two of whose own plays have been hissed at, announces publicly that he is withdrawing his sanction to the performances of his work by the company. 'This', he explains, 'is my protest against the present attempt to set up a standard of National Drama based on the vilification of any section of the Irish people, in a theatre ostensibly founded for the production of plays to represent real Irish life and character.' It is this last remark that brings us back to the matter of philistinism, and it is ironic that it should come from one of the Abbey's most popular dramatists.

Despite his apologia, Synge has never intended to portray real life, any more than Shakespeare's Falstaff was representative of medieval English knighthood, and one might say that *The Playboy* is as true to life as is any other great work of drama. To be sure, art and reality can sometimes interlace, but the fact remains that they occupy different universes. Drama obeys its own laws; it is in no way subject to the rules of the real world. Yet this fairly obvious point is missed in the scuffle, as the two quarrelling factions worry Synge's play between them.

Echoing Arthur Griffith's editorial on *The Shadow of the Glen*, which accused Synge of representing 'adultery as a feature of Irish moral life', Stephen Gwynn, president of the Irish Literary Society in London, writes to the newspaper that he does 'not in the least regret that the play was hissed at its first performance, for the very good reason that if it were played with acceptance, word would immediately go out that parricide is a popular exploit in Ireland'. He is reflecting a general attitude towards the play; one hopes he is not speaking on behalf of the Irish Literary Society. We can only wonder what Euripides would have thought if *his* critics had accused him of fostering the notion that murder and mayhem were popular pastimes in ancient Greece.

What response is forthcoming to such philistinism? W. B. Yeats and his father confront the critics nine days after the opening night. Oddly enough, both men are at pains to stress the verisimilitude of Synge's work. Yeats *père*, having reminded the audience that Ireland is the 'Land of Saints—of plaster saints', tells them that not only are Synge's peasants accurately portrayed, but that they are more true to life than William Carleton's. The wonder is that he does not liken Synge to Samuel Lover, and Christy Mahon to Lover's oafish Andy Rooney . . . .

W. B. Yeats's defence is not recorded, though Mary Colum assures us that she 'never witnessed a human being fight as Yeats fought on that night, nor knew another with so many weapons in his armoury.' We know only what form the defence takes: 'Step by step he interpreted the play, delivering in the process some of his most complex theories of art, one moment cowing his audience, the next shouted down by them . . . . Even on the patriotics Yeats was equal to them.'

Delivering 'complex theories of art' sounds promising, but it is idle to speculate on what these might entail. It is safe to say, however, that one of Yeats's most fiercely held beliefs, and one that he will set down in writing at a later date, is that 'Irish life contains, like all vigorous life, the seeds of good and evil, and a writer must be free here as elsewhere to watch where leek or flower ripens'. In an interview given during the week of rioting, he had stated that all great literature deals with 'exaggerated types, and all tragedy and tragicomedy with types of sin and folly'. A dramatist, he concluded, 'is

not an historian'. It is unfortunate, then, that an announcement
had appeared in the *Freeman's Journal* on opening day, apparently
submitted by the Abbey Theatre:

> No one is better qualified than Mr. Synge to portray truth-
> fully the Irish peasant living away in Western Ireland. He
> has lived with them for months at a stretch, in the Arran
> [*sic*] Islands and Mayo. He has noted their speech, their
> humours, their vices, their virtues. He is one of the best
> Irish speakers in the country, and is thus brought into the
> closest contact with the people. 'The Playboy' is founded
> on an incident that actually occurred.

Mr Synge's own version is not so cut and dried. When the fury is at
its height, he writes a letter to *The Irish Times* in which he describes
The Playboy as not being 'a play with "a purpose" in the modern
sense of the word'. He insists that parts of it were meant to be
'extravagant comedy, still a great deal that is in it, and a great deal
more that is behind it, is perfectly serious, when looked at in a certain light'. He observes that Patrick D. Kenny, in his review of the
previous day, had noticed that there are 'several sides to "The
Playboy"'; sides not immediately apparent to the general public.
'There may be still others,' Synge suggests cryptically, 'if anyone
cares to look for them.'

———————

The search is still on, its vigour hardly dampened by the passage of
almost ninety years since the first production of *The Playboy*, and
there is every reason to believe that it will continue for a long time
to come. Critics may differ on many points regarding the play's
interpretation, but are invariably in agreement that Synge's simple
plot should not be taken at face value.

III

If we are to explore Synge's motives for writing *The Playboy*, it might be useful to examine the contention that it 'is founded on an incident that actually occurred'. If this is so, then there is one likely candidate that springs readily to mind: the story told to Synge on Inishmaan by Pat Dirane in 1898. Yeats had heard it too:

> He often tells me about a Connaught man who killed his father with the blow of a spade when he was in passion, and then fled to this island and threw himself on the mercy of some of the natives with whom he was said to be related. They hid him in a hole—which the old man has shown me—and kept him safe for weeks, though the police came and searched for him, and he could hear their boots grinding on the stones above his head. In spite of a reward which was offered, the island was incorruptible, and after much trouble the man was safely shipped to America.

The notebook that Synge kept at the time of writing *The Playboy* confirms this as the likely source. It is, agrees Seán Ó Súilleabháin, the folklorist and archivist, even if Synge has been somewhat economical with the truth. He regrets that Synge, in *The Aran Islands*, devotes only ten lines to his account of the story. There is more to it, as Ó Súilleabháin learned from the Galway scholar Tomás Ó Máille. The original Playboy was a namesake of Ó Máille who was born in 1838, probably in Connemara:

> His father drank heavily, and young Ó Máille went to sea at an early age; he sent home money with which his father bought some extra land; when his wife died, the father re-married and refused to give the land to his son when he returned home and married; in the course of a quarrel in the potato-field, the father was injured (not killed) by the son; both wives advised him to flee and, after hiding here

170

and there in Connemara, he reached Aran *via* Garumna and was sheltered there by a kinswoman . . . . The local people of Inishmore took pity on the fugitive who was downcast on account of what had happened between himself and his father and provided him with gifts and entertainment to cheer him up; when the search for him became intensified, two Conneely men rowed Ó Máille to Inishmaan, where he was taken in by an old man; the house was surrounded one night by the police, who, in error, allowed Ó Máille to escape in the belief that he was the old man; he hid in a cave near the shore until some time later a boat, which was taking potatoes from Aran to Tralee, took him on board; he finally reached Cork and later arrived in America; a few years later, as a sea-captain, he brought his ship into Galway, making himself known only to a few trusted friends.

A fascinating tale, to be sure. What we are not sure about, is whether Synge heard it in its entirety, though Ó Súilleabháin's friend criticizes the playwright 'for having misinterpreted the kindness of the Inishmore people to the young man and for having misused this part of the story in the play'.

But did he? Could it be that Synge is remembering another story, a Mayo one; and that *The Playboy*, while not being a conflation, borrows, nevertheless, elements of the two. I refer to the remarkable—and well-documented—story of James Lynchehaun. It is not for the squeamish; indeed, it is a far cry from the high comedy of Synge's play. Here is one version, recounted by Lorna Reynolds, who visited Achill Island, Co. Mayo, in 1986, and enquired about the history of a hotel she saw there:

> The new hotel had once been a fine house belonging to a Mr and Mrs MacDonnell who were English and very wealthy. Mr MacDonnell did not like Ireland and was seldom in Achill but Mrs MacDonnell loved the country, and spent most of her time there. She walked and rode about the island, keeping several horses and employing a groom

called Lynchehaun. Mrs MacDonnell was a very beautiful woman and Lynchehaun, it was clear to everyone, soon developed a passion for her and followed her around like a faithful dog . . . . One day Lynchehaun lost control and declared his passion, only to be repulsed and rebuffed in a way that maddened him. Late that night he . . . set fire to the stables and then hammered on the door, calling out to Mrs MacDonnell that the stables were on fire and that her favourite mare, Lady Jane Grey, was in danger. Mrs MacDonnell came down in her night clothes and dressing gown and opened the door. Lynchehaun fell on her, bit off her nose and practically flayed her alive. He then flung her behind some bushes and decamped. The fire naturally brought the villagers around . . . . Mrs MacDonnell was . . . rescued and taken to hospital where she recovered from her terrible injuries. She came back to Achill and lived in the house and used to walk invisible along the roads with her face behind a thick veil.

Lynchehaun was hidden by one of the people who dug a hole in the earthen floor beneath a dresser. There was a warrant out for his arrest. He escaped from Ireland to America, where he joined the police force under an assumed name. After some time he went to England and joined the police force there and under his assumed name was walking around with a warrant for his arrest under his true name of Lynchehaun.

The doctor who examined Mrs MacDonnell reported wounds, including a fracture, to her head, likely to have been caused by a blunt instrument, a boot and a stone. Her nose had indeed been bitten off. Her whole body displayed signs of extreme violence— even her vagina had been torn; he 'thought it was caused by kicks'.

Synge knows the story—he refers to it in his notebooks kept at the time of writing *The Playboy*, and in a newspaper interview admits to having based his play on the incident (though he mistakenly believes that the woman had been murdered). Most of Ireland knows it too; the horrendous events that took place on 6 October 1894 were much publicized. They were to have wide repercussions. James Lynchehaun was arrested in 1895, charged with attempted murder, and committed for life to Marlborough Gaol, Wiltshire. He escaped in 1902 and made his way to Indianapolis. He was re-arrested there and the British government sought to extradite him. The application was refused by the Supreme Court of the United States, and Lynchehaun became a free man—provided he remained in America. James Carney writes that:

> The Achill peasant had come a long way in less than a decade. He had come, though briefly, to be compared with the greatest of Irish patriots, Wolfe Tone and Robert Emmet. The final public accolade, attesting though with questionable justice, to his innocence and patriotism was conferred upon him in January 1906: basking in the heady glory of Irish political exile, but ill from rheumatics as a result of his struggle for liberty in two continents, he was visited at his home . . . by [the] Vice-President of the United States.
>
> The 'Great Extradition Case' of Edward VII *versus* James Lynchehaun has continued to affect the American law on extradition up to the present day.

Was James Lynchehaun Synge's model for his Playboy? It is tempting to think so. Certainly more than one member of the audiences that attended the first production believed he was; cries of 'Lynchehaun! Lynchehaun!' were heard in the auditorium. Carney draws our attention to a reference, at the beginning of Act II of the play, which seems to have gone largely unnoticed, and whose meaning becomes clearer when considered in the light of the incident of 1894. Susan Brady is encouraging Sarah Tansey to follow Christy:

> SUSAN [*going to the window*]. Maybe he's stolen off to Belmullet with the boots of Michael James, and you'd have a right so to follow after him, Sara Tansey, and you the one

yoked the ass cart and drove ten miles to set your eyes on
the man bit the yellow lady's nostril on the northern shore.

The 'northern shore', Carney suggests, is the 'Valley', the name of
the village where Lynchehaun committed the atrocity, and 'yellow'
is Hiberno-English slang for 'English' or 'Protestant'. 'The word',
according to Carney, 'echoes Seán Buidhe, or "Yellow John" which
connotes Englishman . . . . '

Vile would-be murderer or not, James Lynchehaun was the
type of criminal long considered a hero among the peasants of
Ireland. He was on the run from justice—which, inevitably, meant
English justice—and he had succeeded in assaulting a member of
the Protestant Ascendancy without retribution. A common villain is
elevated to the status of political champion. All of which prompts
another question: did Synge intend the play as a political statement?

IV

*T*he *Playboy of the Western World* is more disingenuous than
it appears at first reading. Now, disingenuousness can
appear in a number of guises, one of the most obvious
being verbal wordplay, the Joycean game. Names—
placenames and proper nouns—are important to the game; they
also act as pointers to the fact that there is a game, that things are
not quite what they seem on the surface. Is there evidence of
nameplay in the Synge *oeuvre*? There is, and it seems that Synge (in
common, of course, with a great many Irish writers, past and
present) enjoyed verbal dissembling.

Leaving his drama aside for the moment, we encounter one
of the first instances of Synge's nameplay in the pet-name he gave
to Cherrie Matheson: 'Scherma'. A bit of sleuthing will uncover
the first syllables of his sweetheart's first name and surname:
(S)cher(rie)ma(theson). But why the S? This is Synge's little joke;

ostensibly German, the pronunciation is actually French: by transposing the syllables we get ma-scher, or *ma chère*.

Later, Synge used French again when he had his friend Valeska von Eicken appear in *Étude Morbide* as the Chouska. *Chou*, 'cabbage', is also a term of endearment; the final '-ska' is found in Valeska's name.

Still later, Synge would call his beggars in *The Well of the Saints* Martin and Mary Doul. How many members of the audience that attended the play's first performance on 4 February 1905 understood? Could their numbers have been counted on the fingers of one hand? Stephen MacKenna (who was an Irish speaker, though not a fluent one) remarked that 'Doul is a splendid name'.

In *The Shadow of the Glen* we find Synge again up to his linguistic tricks. Michael Dara is the young herd who woos Nora. Dara is not an Irish surname either, but a forename. In Gaelic it means 'second', and it can be no coincidence that Michael plans to become Nora's second husband.

If we care to look, we shall find many more such examples scattered throughout the Synge canon. But it is in *The Playboy of the Western World* that Synge is at his most playful.

It has been suggested that Christy Mahon is a messianic figure, and a strong case can be made for this theory. The name Christy is cognate with 'Christ'; he is the son of Old Mahon, and Mahon can be elided to sound like 'man': hence Christ, the Son of Man. Stanley Sultan sees many scriptural references and analogies in *The Playboy*. He says that

> what Synge has concretely presented is a mirror-image of the story of Jesus' mission of exhortation to obedience to His Father. And it is this fact which makes the sudden and shocking reversal in the last minutes of the play comprehensible. Like Jesus, when Christy confronts with the true significance of his message those who have followed and praised him, they prepare to have him executed by the standard method used for common criminals. The crucifixion is no less complete and sudden a reversal in a

triumphant short earthly career; and it came about precisely because the people would not risk secular and spiritual trouble when the issue arose.

'Once the notion of Christy as in some way related to Christ enters the picture,' says Robin Skelton, 'it is likely to dominate it.' The notion, though, will never give way to a conviction that Synge meant *The Playboy* as an analogy of the Christian story. There are too many other veiled references and allusions to be considered. For instance, Declan Kiberd presents a signal and erudite hypothesis of Christy Mahon as an evocation of Cuchulain, hero of the Ulster Cycle. While cautioning that it 'would not be wise to seek for one-to-one correspondence between the narrative of *Cuchulain of Muirthemne* and the incidents of *The Playboy*', Kiberd, at the same time, draws up an impressive list of such correspondences. Christy is a parody, though—a mock-hero. Synge, Kiberd argues, has turned the heroism of Cuchulain on its head:

> Cuchulain in early youth was renowned for his athletic ability, his comely face and pleasant speech, all of which made him so attractive to women that the men of Ulster decided to safeguard their wives and daughters by forcing him to wed . . . . Christy Mahon, on the contrary . . . is neither athletic, nor handsome, nor sweet of speech . . . . [He is] so ridiculous to the local girls that they call him 'the laughing joke of every female woman where four baronies meet'. However, attempts are made by his father to marry him off to the Widow Casey . . . . Cuchulain's initiation as a warrior occurs when, attired in King Conchubor's borrowed arms, he defeats the three brave sons of Nechtan and returns with their three heads as trophies. Christy, too, attired in the borrowed wedding-suit of Shawn Keogh, defeats all comers at the local sports, returning also with three trophies.

There is also the matter of those shifts: Christy's line, 'It's Pegeen I'm seeking only, and what'd I care if you brought me a drift of

chosen females, standing in their shifts itself maybe, from this place
to the Eastern World?' may owe its imagery to an episode in the
Celtic narrative, when, to cool Cuchulain's battle-rage, the men of
Emain Macha send out thirty chosen naked females to meet him.
(Synge's original line read, not 'in their shifts' but 'standing
stripped itself'.)

Kiberd's interpretation is a valid one. Certainly, *Cuchulain of
Muirthemne* is a work which Synge greatly admires; it is his 'daily
bread', as he tells Lady Gregory. Unfortunately, the Cuchulain
myth has turned Yeats's head somewhat, and is having a deleteri-
ous effect on the nationalist movement; a pupil at St Enda's,
Padraic Pearse's school, claims that Cuchulain is the invisible member of the teaching staff. Ancient myth, with its attendant bar-
barism, is being held up as a model for present and future conduct. It is a development that is not to Synge's liking. In this
regard, *The Playboy* may be seen in an iconoclastic role; Synge is cautioning against graven images.

It may also be seen, as suggested earlier, as a political statement. Let us go back to that last sentence of Stanley Sultan's: 'The
crucifixion is no less complete and sudden a reversal in a triumphant short earthly career; and it came about precisely because
the people would not risk secular and spiritual trouble when the
issue arose.'

This sounds oddly familiar, when taken in an Irish context. If
we leave aside the Christ analogy, we might substitute another: the
fate of Charles Stewart Parnell.

V

If there has ever been anything resembling a messianic move
ment in Ireland, it surely must have been the push towards
independence taken up by the followers of Parnell. In life,
this brilliant politician came near to achieving home rule for
Ireland; in death, he was mourned as Ireland's uncrowned king.

A member of the Irish Protestant Ascendancy, Parnell became
leader of the Irish Parliamentary Party in the British House of

Commons. He led it with an autocratic brillance that brought it within sight of its goal: home rule. For years he had lived with his mistress, Katharine O'Shea, and she bore him three children. Eventually, Mrs O'Shea's husband—one of the Irish Party's MPs—filed for divorce and named Parnell as co-respondent. The scandal split the party and Parnell was ousted from the leadership. He fought to regain control against an alliance of British Liberal non-conformists, Irish Catholic clergy, and a majority of his former colleagues, who calculated that the home rule cause would be lost if Parnell remained at the helm. His health, never robust, gave out, and he died in October 1891; he was only forty-five. His body was shipped back to Ireland. Parnell's funeral cortège was the largest Ireland had ever seen. As his coffin was lowered into the ground, a shooting star was seen to fall, in daylight—a fitting sign to accompany the burial of a fallen messiah.

Parnell's death hastened the march towards home rule. Herbert Howarth sees it as the source of the creation of the Irish Republic, as well as the inspiration of the Irish Literary Revival:

> The young gradually integrated his memory into their hopes of an ancient, powerfully imaginative, physically powerful and audacious Ireland. A literary movement found symbols and a language for their dream. The literary movement thereby inflamed—half-consciously, for it doubted the value of dynamite—the military movement . . . . What Parnell's death immediately did for the writers and artists, besides raising their passions, was to raise their sense of responsibility, indicate emphatically the necessity for Irish self-criticism; and because there were men and women looking for guidance in the perplexity that followed the 1891 schism, it multiplied their audience.

Synge was among those who 'doubted the value of dynamite'. He was twenty when Parnell died, and already a committed patriot. We learn, too, from a passage in *The Aran Islands*, that he was moved deeply by a train journey he made from Galway to Dublin, eight years after Parnell's death. Synge shared a railway carriage with

Blasket Islanders photographed by J. M. Synge in 1905. (In the foreground is the 'Little Hostess'.)

Synge's Blickensderfer typewriter.

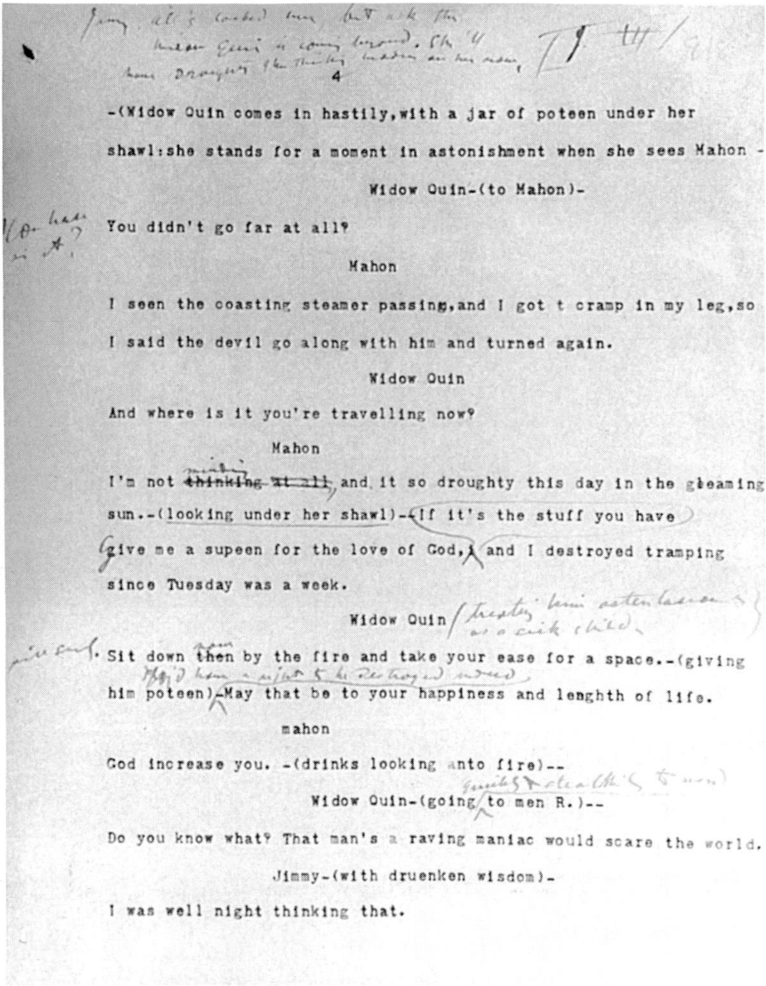

[handwritten at top: Jimmy, all's cooked ... but ask the ... Widow Quin is coming beyond. She'll ... house Drought the Thirsty Maties on his road,]

4

-(Widow Quin comes in hastily,with a jar of poteen under her

shawl:she stands for a moment in astonishment when she sees Mahon -

Widow Quin-(to Mahon)-

[handwritten left margin]

You didn't go far at all?

Mahon

I seen the coasting steamer passing,and I got t cramp in my leg,so

I said the devil go along with him and turned again.

Widow Quin

And where is it you're travelling now?

Mahon

I'm not ~~thinking at all~~ and it so droughty this day in the gleaming

sun.-(looking under her shawl)-(If it's the stuff you have

(give me a supeen for the love of God,) and I destroyed tramping

since Tuesday was a week.

Widow Quin *(treating him ostentatious / as a sick child)*

[handwritten left margin] Sit down then by the fire and take your ease for a space.-(giving

[handwritten: they'd have a ... to be destroyed indeed,]

him poteen)-May that be to your happiness and lengbth of life.

mahon

God increase you. -(drinks looking into fire)--

Widow Quin-(going to men R.)-- *[handwritten above]*

Do you know what? That man's a raving maniac would scare the world.

Jimmy-(with druenken wisdom)-

I was well night thinking that.

Lady Gregory in the title role of W. B. Yeats's play *Kathleen ni Houlihan*.

Arthur Sinclair as Martin Doul, the blind beggar in *The Well of the Saints*.

A scene from an Abbey production of *Riders to the Sea*, with Molly Allgood (standing), her sister Sara and Eileen O'Doherty.

Sketch by Jack B. Yeats of a jockey costume for use in the first production of *The Playboy*.

J. M. Synge at the Abbey Theatre, pencil sketch by
John B. Yeats, 25 January 1907.

J. M. Synge during his final visit to Koblenz, October 1908.

Maire O'Neill (Molly Allgood) in a scene from an Abbey Theatre production of *The Playboy of the Western World.*

Two views of ring fort Dún Conor, Inishmaan.

Gravestone of J. M. Synge, Mount Jerome cemetery, Dublin.

Connacht people, who were travelling to the Irish capital, in order to commemorate their fallen 'Chief':

> The whole spirit of the west of Ireland, with its strange wildness and reserve, seemed moving in this single train to pay a last homage to the dead statesman of the east.

Synge is also singularly adept in raising passions among Irish theatre-goers. The question is, has he used his skills when writing *The Playboy of the Western World* to raise their passions and 'their sense of responsibility' in a messianic play which is actually a parallelism of Parnell's rise and fall? If so, is it because he appreciates that a *comedy* is the ideal vehicle for social and political commentary? There are no comic elements in the story told to him in Aran; Lynchehaun's brutal attempted murder is likewise very far from being amusing.

But *The Playboy* began life, in 1904, as *The Murderer (a Farce)*. One obviously farcical episode in Synge's rough draft has the murderer being elected by those who harbour him to the office of county councillor! This was later dropped. Why? Was Synge concerned that the allusion to Parnell might be too obvious? Then there is the matter of those infamous shifts; they were the very undergarments waved scurrilously in Parnell's face when he visited the villages of Ireland in 1891. But we have already seen that 'shifts' was inserted in a later draft; the original line read 'a drift of chosen females, standing stripped itself', so it is better to assume that Synge decided that semi-nudity was less likely to give offence than total nudity, rather than construe that his use of 'shifts' was a means of cocking a snook at Parnell's vilifiers. We shall have to examine more compelling evidence.

The setting of *The Playboy* may be seen as rural Ireland in microcosm. Enter an outsider: Christy Mahon. Parnell was an 'outsider' to the common people of Ireland: a wealthy Protestant landlord, the son of a beautiful American woman, Delia Tudor Stewart, he was clearly not 'of the people'. His speech, moreover, was that of an Englishman, and he held the mob in contempt. Christy confesses openly his crime and receives no denunciation: Parnell lived openly with Katharine O'Shea and, for a long time, a blind eye was turned to his immorality. Christy 'commits' his crime a second time—not in distant Kerry, the scene of the original 'murder', but almost under the noses of his hosts in Belmullet. In a dramatic volte-face, he is betrayed by the people. Parnell's crime is made public by the divorce proceedings, he is betrayed by his followers, and the Irish people turn against him.

The role of the father-figure in the play is more complex, as are Christy's relations with Pegeen and the Widow Quin. Christy introduces Old Mahon as a tyrant who has 'sons and daughters walking all great states and territories of the world'; he is 'a man never gave peace to any'. Enumerating his father's crimes against his son and others, Christy has no difficulty winning the villagers' sympathy. It is not, I believe, too fanciful to see John Bull in Christy's description of his father: the John Bull whose armies had overrun 'all great states and territories of the world' and who had brought anything but peace—and certainly not to Ireland. When Synge began *The Playboy*, the horrors of the Boer War were a fresh memory; Irish sympathy was with the Dutch settlers and not with the British army. Christy kills the tyrant and oppressor and, in so doing, becomes a hero.

A patricidal element in a play naturally calls to mind the most famous patricide of all: Oedipus. Having killed his father, the king, Oedipus assumes the crown. He then marries the widow queen. From 'widow queen' to 'Widow Quin' is a very small step indeed. But Synge introduces rivalry too: Pegeen Mike and the Widow Quin both vie for Christy's favours. I suggest that the two main female characters personify, respectively, Ireland and England. Pegeen, like Christy, has been under the domination of her father. She seeks freedom and self-identity. She is a romantic girl, but one easily roused to anger and violence when she thinks herself betrayed by a lover; she is the Dark Rosaleen of Irish myth and song. She favours Christy above Shawn Keogh, whom she exhorts to 'go off till you'd find a radiant lady with droves of bullocks on the plains of Meath, and herself bedizened in the diamond jew-elleries of Pharaoh's ma'. Such a woman would be an appropriate match for 'Shaneen'. (It should be remembered that 'Shaneen', while being the diminutive form of Shawn—and, used with reference to a grown man, belittling—is also the term used to denote a West Briton, i.e. a person who prizes English values and conventions above their Irish counterparts. Pegeen's insult is twin-barbed.)

The Widow Quin, on the other hand, has a bad reputation. She is cunning and conniving and appears to be unprincipled, prepared to sacrifice the innocent girls of the village in order to achieve her ends. We need look no further than John Bull's principal island for Synge's model; Britain had been ruled, until 1901, by history's most famous widow queen: Victoria. Christy chooses Pegeen above the Widow Quin; Parnell flew in the face of his Protestant Ascendancy upbringing and rejected the Widow Queen in favour of Ireland. Worse, he cast traditional morality and respectability aside and took up with Katharine O'Shea; he called her his 'queenie'; to her he was a 'king'. His choice of allegiances brought about his downfall.

Augustine Martin examines the choices the Playboy has:

> In the meantime Christy must discover and reject an alternative and different father in Michael James [the publican, father of Pegeen], a different form of female domination in Pegeen Mike. It is significant that Pegeen is the first person to offer him violence when first he enters the Flaherty cabin, and that she behaves towards him with the most surly possessiveness (*seizing his arm and shaking him*) when the Widow Quin makes her play for him towards the end of Act I. Before she leaves, the Widow Quin warns him that 'there's right torment will await you here if you go romancing with her like'.

The situation in which Christy finds himself grows in complexity. Synge was unsure how to resolve the difficulties which the interaction of such strong characters created. His early drafts reveal how he toyed with a variety of possible endings. One such has Christy marrying the Widow Quin; another involves a curious *ménage à trois* involving Christy, his father and Pegeen. A third has Christy marrying Pegeen. Had Synge intended *The Playboy* as a farce, then this last possibility would have been the obvious choice, given the tastes and dramaturgic conventions of the times. He chose instead to have Christy take his leave of both Pegeen and the Widow Quin. Hardly the stuff that farce is made of.

VI

So what, in the end, is *The Playboy of the Western World*? Farce, parody, a modern epic—all three? Perhaps. Synge wants to shock, to provoke. The nationalists have given the dog Synge a bad name; *The Playboy* is Synge's way of living up to it. He is tired of hypocrisy; if Griffith and company wish to shore up their myth of the nobility, inherent decency and chastity of the native Irish *as a race*, then Synge is equally determined that this gloriously offensive broadside will pound that myth into the dust.

The final version of *The Playboy of the Western World* is a reckless, no-holds-barred, satire. Perhaps it had started life as an innocent piece of play—but this has always been Synge's *modus operandi*. His method is to make a rough outline of a story—the sillier the better, it seems. In draft after draft he expands the outline, adding dialogue here, deleting a character there; compounding and inspissating, almost in the same way Joyce will build the fearsome *Finnegans Wake*. And, like Joyce, Synge has peopled *The Playboy* with mirror-images—if grossly distorted mirror-images—of the men and women who shared his life while each successive draft emerged from his Blickensderfer. Unable to vent his true feelings about the unsavoury characters he has met in his travels with Jack B. Yeats, he has instead immortalized their villainy in *The Playboy*. Thus do we find Shawn Keogh (*seanchaí*, perhaps? The pronunciation is remarkably similar), Pegeen's weak and treacherous suitor. Satisfied with the status quo, and living in fear of Father Reilly, Keogh refuses to help a man in need, preferring stories to 'mixing yourself up with the queer dark deeds or the dead men of the world'. Philly O'Cullen, whose only gift is the ability to tell tall tales; Father Reilly whom (significantly) we do not see, but whose authoritarian presence pervades the play; Michael James Flaherty, the publican, who lives by his animal instincts and cares for nobody: they are all grim caricatures of men Synge has met in that lonely part of County Mayo; they embody, as Synge puts it, 'the psychic state of the locality'. Their composite is an uncouth creature, the possessor of 'a rampant double-chinned vulgarity I haven't seen the like of'. It is a creature that is 'horrible and awful'.

There is, however, a character who is not entirely beyond salvation. If Pegeen Mike displays a great many of the traits that Synge sees in Molly Allgood, then this is more than coincidental. He was determined that the role of Pegeen should fall to his beloved. There is little doubt too that Synge has been seeing even more of Molly than Lady Gregory has suspected; the language of *The Playboy* attests to it. The words he puts in the mouths of Christy and Pegeen must have been learned and practised in the hills behind Bray, where John has courted Molly by the light of the summer moon, 'coining funny nicknames for the stars of night'. Gone are the veiled allusions to sexuality of *The Tinker's Wedding*: Sarah's 'I'm thinking there isn't anything ails me, Michael Byrne; but the spring-time is a queer time, and it's queer thoughts maybe I do think at whiles.' The Tramp's talk in *The Shadow of the Glen* of 'the half of a dry bed, and good food in your mouth' pales beside Christy Mahon's unequivocal proposal:

> CHRISTY [*encouraged*]. Let you wait to hear me talking till we're astray in Erris when Good Friday's by, drinking a sup from a well, and making mighty kisses with our mouths, or gaming in a gap of sunshine with yourself stretched back unto your necklace in the flowers of the earth.

and Pegeen Mike's acquiescence:

> PEGEEN [*in a lower voice, moved by his tone*]. It'd be nice so, is it?

It'd be nice so—and it *has been* nice so, as Synge remembers in a letter he writes to Molly in May 1907, reminding her how they are 'so perfectly happy in each other', and wondering if she too looks forward 'to lying up in the heather again and eating purple grapes', the wild bilberries of Wicklow.

Pegeen is possibly the only flesh and blood character in the play. Reading her, we can read Molly Allgood. As Robin Skelton remarks, Pegeen 'differs from the other girls in the energy of her passions, the liveliness of her tongue, and the decisiveness of her temper'. Her treachery in Act III can only be an exaggeration of the infidelity of which Synge continually suspects Molly. He wrote the part with the intention of providing a superb acting vehicle for his 'changeling'; if Pegeen is too wilful, this, then, is a warning (or a supplication) to Molly.

By a different token, it is pointless to look for the personality of J. M. Synge in Christy Mahon; the Playboy is almost Synge's antithesis. All Christy borrows from Synge are the words he speaks. They are not even used as Synge might use them, but instead Christy employs them to bluster, lie and cheat. Synge is otherwise; he is a thoroughly scrupulous and honest man.

The Playboy of the Western World is an elaborate game, conceived by Synge to confound his enemies. If it is seldom what it appears to be, that is because Synge has constructed it as a puzzle containing many ramifications. If one wishes for myth, he will find plenty of it. If another seeks allegory or symbolism, they are here too. Political satire? There is more than enough to inflame the nationalist movement *anno* 1907. But reality? Little more than can be found in Lewis Carroll's *Through the Looking Glass*. Indeed, this last may be our final clue. When Pegeen tells Christy that he 'should have been living the like of a king of Norway or the Eastern world', she is not referring to monarchs of flesh and blood; 'the Eastern world' exists only in Celtic mythology; it is the equivalent of Paradise. Its topsy-turvy mirror-image is Synge's Western World, whose monarch reigns over a people who are 'nothing but a deck of cards'. This royal fool is the Playboy, the brainchild of the playwright.

Also John Millington Synge

I

'I am a poor man,' Synge once said to Cherrie Matheson, 'but I feel if I live I shall be rich; I feel there is that in me which will be of value to the world.'

That was in 1897—before Aran, before the first play. In 1907 John Synge is still a poor man and, as he reflects sadly and bitterly on the fracas caused by his masterpiece, he wonders whether the world is ready for what is in him. For philistinism is once again abroad in Dublin, that much is clear. Padraic Pearse and Arthur Griffith declare the cot-death of the 'Anglo-Irish Theatre'; *The Playboy* has tolled its knell. In a leading article in the Gaelic League paper, *An Claidheamh Soluis*, Pearse underlines 'the absolute necessity for the foundation of an Irish Theatre in the capital of Ireland'. Weren't Pearse and Griffith correct all along? How could anyone in his right mind have expected a gaggle of Ascendancy ladies and gentlemen (aided and abetted, mind you, by a Mazawattee tea-heiress and divers other bluestockings and heathen spiritualists!) to give Ireland an Irish theatre? Synge's latest libel is proof that such a theatre was built on sand.

The call goes out from Dublin to the provinces of Ireland, to England's expatriate Irish communities: boycott and repress *The Playboy* at all costs. In Liverpool, the combined might of the United Irish League, the Irish National Foresters, Cumann na nGaedheal and the Gaelic Athletic Association vows to prevent the play's production in their city. In rural Ireland, district councillors pass resolutions against it; priests denounce it—unread and unseen— from pulpits. W. B. Yeats and Lady Gregory are ostracized in the west of Ireland, where Synge, unfortunately, set the play.

But wait. There are indeed philistines abroad; some are in

England, and they are found not only in the enclaves of the expatriate Irish. When the play is brought to Britain in early May, many of the spoken lines are not those of the printed version. Plays are subject to censorship in England (as Yeats took pains to remind the Irish at the foundation of the Abbey Theatre). Lady Gregory explains in the columns of *The Arrow*—a new theatrical periodical, edited by Yeats—that 'we, the players and I, went through it and struck out any expressions that had given offence'. Now the English censor goes to work, that *The Playboy* might give even less offence. 'I wouldn't be fearing the loosèd kharki [*sic*] cut-throats, or the walking dead' is excised, along with other lines that could upset English sensibilities. 'If, therefore,' Daniel Corkery comments, 'there are motes in the eyes of the Irish people, there are whole beams in the eyes of the English people.'

Nor are the beams confined to England. When the Abbey Players bring *The Playboy* on a United States tour in 1911, it will—despite protests from Irish-Americans—fare marginally better than some drama written by Americans and set in other countries. Lady Gregory: 'A newspaper man . . . said all nationalities here are very sensitive. The Swedes had a play taken off that represented some Swedish women drinking. The French Canadians, he says, are as touchy as the Irish.' And France, *la mère-patrie* itself? Gerard Leblanc describes the Parisian reception of Synge's drama in 1913:

> On the first night of *The Playboy*, the main reaction of the public seems to have been amazement at the paradox of the opening situation, the unchecked flood of language and most of all, the rough-and-tumble action in the third act which shocked the audience much more than any mention of female underwear, not an infrequent property on the Paris stage of the time . . . . It is ironic that whereas the adverse criticism chiefly attacked the play for being alien to French sensibility, the few favourable reviews stressed the essentially French qualities of liveliness and humour. Cultural chauvinism, indeed, does not pertain exclusively to the Dublin rowdies of January 1907.

'If I live I shall be rich,' Synge insists. He has little cause for optimism; health and wealth seem more distant than ever. During the *Playboy* riots in Dublin, Synge had taken to his bed with chronic 'influenza'. Lady Gregory: 'I think the week's rioting helped to break down his health. He was always nervous at a first production, and the unusual excitement of this one upset him and he took a chill and was kept to bed for a while.'

Matters are a good deal more serious than Lady Gregory thinks. The 'chill' is, in fact, a bad attack of bronchitis. It lingers through February; Synge's doctor visits often. 'I am glad I did not ask you to come out [to Glendalough House in Glenageary],' he writes to Molly on 7 February 1907, 'as talking makes me cough, and coughing hurts me as if I had ten scarlet divils twisting a crowbar in the butt of my ribs.' Some days later, his illness is compounded by laryngitis and a concomitant fever. There are stomach upsets, pains in the legs, backache. Worse, the ominous swellings on his neck have returned. Dr Alfred Parsons suspects tuberculosis and has Synge's sputum examined. The tell tale bacilli are not found. As yet, Parsons can make no connection between the swellings and Synge's devil's brew of ailments. It is, surprisingly enough, Willie Fay who suspects that matters are far more critical than John's doctor has diagnosed. He thinks the swellings should be removed without delay and confides as much to Molly Allgood. Synge is unkind in his dismissal of the actor's advice:

> [Fay] is a little ass very fond of talking wisely about things he knows nothing about. It is a very simple operation getting these lumps out. The last time, when they were much bigger than they are, now, I was perfectly well in ten days. So you see you needn't mind him.

187

II

Good news arrives to brighten up Synge's confinement. Annie Horniman writes from London that she loves the play—this despite her hostility towards it last December. *The Playboy of the Western World* is published by Maunsel in Dublin, and two hundred copies are sold in the first week; George Moore writes a letter to Synge on 6 March, in praise of the play but, as Synge grumbles to Frank Fay, Moore 'as usual' wants him 'to rewrite some of it according to an idea of his'.

In time, the influenza, asthma, leg and back pains, stomach complaints, bronchitis, laryngitis and, as John puts it, 'a sort of dis-sentry [*sic*]' run their courses and Synge leaves his bed towards the end of February, in order to prepare some pieces he has promised Joseph Hone for *The Shanachie*, a quarterly journal devoted to Irish writing. There is little new writing necessary: the essays seem to be an amalgam of stories and impressions garnered in the course of many years. One of them is entitled 'The People of the Glens', and is a collection of reminiscences about County Wicklow. It is a piece with few surprises, and attaches itself almost seamlessly to 'The Vagrants of Wicklow', which *The Shanachie* took last autumn. In the context of the *Playboy* row, however, Synge's remarks on the morali-ty of the country people are enlightening:

> The younger people of these glens are not so interesting as the old men and women, and though there are still many fine young men . . . who are extraordinarily gifted and agile, it too often happens, that the men under thirty are badly built, shy and despondent. Even among the old peo-ple, whose singular charm I have tried to interpret, . . . it is possible to find many individuals who are far from admirable either in body or mind. One would hardly stop to assert a fact so obvious if it had not become the fashion in Dublin, quite recently, to reject a fundamental doctrine of theology, and to exalt the Irish peasant into a type of almost absolute virtue, frugal, self-sacrificing, valiant, and I

know not what. There is some truth in this estimate, yet it is safer to hold with the theologians that, even west of the Shannon, the heart of man is not spotless, for though the Irish peasant has many beautiful virtues, it is idle to assert that he is totally unacquainted with the deadly sins, and many minor rogueries.

Coming hard on the heels of *The Playboy of the Western World*, Synge's observations will do little to restore good relations with the nationalists. But Synge is unconcerned; he has decided that he has exhausted the peasant theme, the very medium which has made his reputation.

No, there will be no more plays like *The Playboy*—Synge has made his final satirical comment on the psychic state of the rural Ireland he knows and loves. It is time for other things; there is fresh earth to turn. The legend of Deirdre and the Sons of Usna begins to occupy his thoughts.

III

If Cuchulain is Ireland's pre-eminent Celtic hero, then Deirdre must rank as the most famous tragic heroine. Her story is part of a written tradition extending from the twelfth-century *Book of Leinster*, which incorporates fragments of earlier works, probably set down in the eighth or ninth century. In its oral form, it has many variations, as Synge has learned in his travels in the countryside. It is the epic tale of a girl, at whose birth it is prophesied that she will bring destruction on the world, and the fall of Emain Macha, a hill-fort near Armagh and the seat of the kings of Ulster. Deirdre is betrothed to Conchubor, the reigning king, who keeps her, together with a nurse, Lavarcham, in isolation until she is of age. But shortly before the king—now considered to be too old to take a young bride—can claim the girl, she falls in love with Naisi, one of the three Sons of Usna. Together they flee with Deirdre to Scotland, where they live happily for seven years. Conchubor persuades the four to return and guarantees safe passage. It is a ruse; the king slays the brothers, thereby fulfilling the prophecy. Emain Macha is destroyed by fire. Deirdre commits suicide rather than submit to the murderer of her lover.

Synge has read—and heard, in Aran and Connemara—the story in the original Irish, shunning several written translations which appeared in the nineteenth century. He has reason to shun them: his 1905 review of the latest attempt—contained in A. H. Leahy's *Heroic Romances of Ireland, Vol. I*—left the reader in little doubt that Leahy's translation was far from perfect:

> This is seriously put forward . . . as a translation from the *Book of Leinster*, . . . and yet is hard to imagine a more deplorable misrepresentation of the spirit of these old verses. This kind of facile parody has been written very frequently by writers who have set out to translate Gaelic poetry, and their verse has shown to an extraordinary extent the provinciality which—at least till quite lately—has distinguished a good deal of Anglo-Irish taste. It is hardly too much to say that, while a great part of Gaelic poetry itself is filled with the most curious individuality and charm, there is probably no mass of tawdry commonplace jingle quite so worthless as the verse translations that have been made from it in Ireland during the last century.

So much for the printed word; Deirdre has fared little better in the theatre. 'During the past hundred years', Daniel Corkery laments, 'from the great story of Deirdre has sprung a vast quantity of closet drama, which, of all sorts of literature, is certainly the least readable. Closet drama is bookishness . . . . ' It is a phenomenon closely allied to that of the Stage-Irishman (perhaps one might coin the expression Stage-Irish Heroine?). Synge has seen two recent dramatic versions of the Deirdre epic: that by George Russell, mounted in 1902; and Yeats's production of 1906.

Russell, writing as his mystical *alter ego* AE, treated his Deirdre as a seer; the whole play had magical and supernatural overtones. It was an extraordinary piece of experimental theatre: the players moved behind a gauze screen lit by green lights, which served to render an other-worldly atmosphere to the performance. The lines were in verse, emphasizing the story's epic nature. Russell himself played the part of a druid, and a woman in the audience protested that he, when delivering a speech in a sonorous manner, had sent three waves of blackness over the auditorium. All in all, the press received the play well, although one critic complained that there was 'altogether too much Deirdre, too many visions and dismal forebodings; to come down to arithmetic, the heroine is on the stage for nine-tenths of the action'.

W. B. Yeats's *Deirdre* was first given on 26 November 1906. All the action is compressed into one act. Yeats's version is more robust than Russell's; yet he made little attempt to present the principals as people of flesh and blood. The lines are beautiful, almost elegiac. The critic John Eglinton likened the blank verse to that of Shakespeare. That said, Synge must have smiled on hearing Yeats's Deirdre voice sentiments which Synge had expressed often in his peasant drama:

> *Deirdre.* Were we not born to wander?
> These jewels have been reaped by the innocent sword
> Upon a mountain, and a mountain bred me;
> But who can tell what change can come to love
> Among the valleys? I speak no falsehood now.
> Away to windy summits, and there mock
> The night-jar and the valley-keeping bird!

Or 'Man is naturally a nomad'. The speech rings with Syngeian nature-worship. It may well be that W. B. Yeats is in debt to John Synge for these sentiments, for thoughts and themes are readily exchanged between the leading lights of the Irish Renaissance. Synge, for example, is grateful to Lady Gregory, because it is she who—through her translation of *Cuchulain of Muirthemne*—first intimated that Ireland's heroes of old may well have spoken a language whose alliteration, hyperbolical simile and parataxis were close in flavour to Synge's Hiberno-English dialect. In doing so, she had demonstrated that 'peasant speech' could be bent to accommodate loftier stuff. 'Like the folk storytellers,' Declan Kiberd remarks,

'Synge grasped the relationship between the heroic world of the ancient legend and the peasant Ireland in which the story still lingered.'

True enough; but Synge has his audience to contend with. He must tread carefully. He remembers the thrill that went through the hall when the name Cuchulain was first spoken on the public stage, in the course of Russell's *Deirdre*. Synge tampers at his peril with the icons of Ireland's past; they are too important for the nationalist cause. Deirdre, Conchubor Mac Neasa, Cuchulain and the heroes of the Red Branch Knights are pre-Christian incarnate gods, to be treated with the greatest reverence—and most certainly by a member of the Anglo-Irish Ascendancy.

The nationalists can rest easily; Synge's *Deirdre of the Sorrows* will be no 'libel on Irish womanhood'. Quite the reverse. The play presents a young woman who follows her passion, and rejects the crown of Ulster in favour of her true love. At the same time, she knows that a dire prophecy must be fulfilled. Deirdre does not struggle against this, but goes to meet her destiny with a brave heart. When her lover is slain, she joins him, without hesitation, in death.

Synge's Deirdre is a queen from head to toe. Her queenliness takes us unawares. When she makes her appearance in Act I, she is 'poorly dressed with a little bag and a bundle of twigs in her arms'; even Naisi, her lover-to-be, is unimpressed by this ragged, nondescript girl he has met in the woods. Conchubor is fooled, too, especially when Deirdre refuses to be his queen. It is only towards the close of the first act—when she emerges 'royally dressed and very beautiful' in the finery the High King has sent her—that we see Deirdre as she really is. The contrast is sudden and startling, and thus all the more effective. (Yeats's Deirdre has her hair combed by courtiers, her jewels affixed and her cheeks rouged while the audience looks on.) This is ancient Ireland's most beautiful and most tragic queen. Or, rather, future queen; in no version of the legend does the High King have her for his consort. In Synge's play, it is so taken for granted that she is born to reign, that she is referred to continually as queen. Deirdre's regality is immanent.

How oddly plain, then, is the language she speaks. Context aside, it is language indistinguishable from that of the farmer's young wife in one of Synge's peasant plays:

> DEIRDRE . . . . I'm a long while watching the days getting a great speed passing me by, I'm too long taking my will and it's that way I'll be living always.

> NORA . . . . Isn't it a long while I am sitting here in the winter, and the summer, and the fine spring, with the young growing behind me and the old passing . . . and I a fine girl growing up . . . .

And yet we should be hard put to find a more suitable idiom for the epic. Synge's characters are living, breathing human beings. There is nothing pathetic—or bathetic—about Conchubor; not even when he tells Deirdre that 'it isn't long till a day'll come when you'll begin pitying a man is old and desolate and High King also . . .'. We may—and do—sympathize with him, but Synge never allows us to forget that this lonely old man is indeed the most powerful king in the province. We see no throngs of retainers accompanying him, yet this spareness only enhances Conchubor's strength. When his weakness as a man breaks through, it is right and fitting that his hearers are few, often only Deirdre and her nurse Lavarcham.

But this is detail that should not distract from the pageant that Synge is planning. *Deirdre of the Sorrows* will be the synthesis of his dramatic work. He desires a change from peasant comedy and a return to the tragedy of *Riders to the Sea*. An earlier scenario makes clear that Synge's Aran play is not forgotten. This is how he plans the final act:

> III   At Dawn after the death of the Sons of Usnach. Grave being dug left. Deirdre alone. Conor comes. Final summing up and death of Deirdre (Rider-like)

Synge is convinced that he is writing his masterpiece; *The Playboy* was a mere 'extravaganza'. He is bringing together strands of

genius from many sources, in order to weave a tragedy more pro-
found than *Riders*. Even the heathen wedding ceremony, so incon-
gruous in *When the Moon Has Set*, reappears in an extended version.
As Nicholas Grene puts it, 'What is pretentious and embarrassing
about an Anglo-Irish Protestant marrying a nun seems plausible
enough from the supposedly Druid Ainnle':

> AINNLE [*joining their hands*]. By the sun and moon and the
> whole earth, I wed Deirdre to Naisi. [*He steps back and holds
> up his hands.*] May the air bless you, and water and the
> wind, the sea, and all the hours of the sun and moon.

Synge is parsimonious with his writing, always loath to discard what
may be of use in a future work. Evidently, he considers this ceremony valuable enough to merit a second airing. The union of Naisi
and Deirdre is blessed by the very cosmos; theirs is a *natural* union.
But we know from the outset that this union will bring disaster; we
have read the legend. Indeed, the story of Deirdre is one with
which Dublin theatre audiences are perhaps *over*familiar. Why is
Synge wrecking what is left of his health by writing a play whose
outcome is known even before the curtain rises on the first act?
This is hardly characteristic of the dramatist who allowed a
farmer's wife to go off with a stranger; a priest to be tied in a sack;
a father to become the willing slave of the son who tried to murder
him.

Perhaps Donna Gerstenberger comes closest to divining
Synge's motivation. She observes that the sorrow in the play lies
not in the deaths of Naisi and Deirdre, nor in the slaughter visited
by Ulsterman on Ulsterman, but 'from the knowledge the lovers
come to on the edge of the grave about the nature of human life
and love'. The audience, knowing the legend, will expect the
heroic, and Synge will not disappoint them. Yet his definition of
heroism is not the classical one; it is 'Rider-like'. *Deirdre of the
Sorrows* is not the departure it, at first blush, seems to be, but a natural dramaturgical progression that serves to underline the splendid unity of Synge's work, from *Riders to the Sea* to *The Playboy of the
Western World*.

The way of heroism, according to Synge, lies not in bloodletting. Rather, true courage is revealed by the acceptance of and acquiescence in preordained fate, no matter how horrible this fate may be. Through the tragedy of Deirdre, Robin Skelton concludes, Synge is reiterating the views expressed in his earlier plays, 'that youth's splendour passes, that "the heart's a wonder", and that what matters is not the small circumstances of our lives and deaths, but the way in which our vision can enhance the lives of others, giving them images of strength, courage and beauty.'

This is the heroism of the humanist-pacifist. How it differs from that of the headhunter Cuchulain—and the Kali-like Kathleen ni Houlihan!

IV

Yeats has wooed theatre-goers with his beautiful Kathleen, played to stunning effect by that epitome of fighting Irish womanhood, Maud Gonne. Kathleen, the spirit of Ireland, has called on her sons to fight—nay, to die for her. The martyred dead, it seems, are the truest patriots.

This unusual proposition has not been lost on republican Ireland. Yeats has spotlighted (literally) the blood-sacrifice, the cult of the dead, and Padraic Pearse has listened. In old age, long after Pearse, Maud Gonne's husband John MacBride, and other leaders of the insurgents have been executed for their part in the 1916 Rising, Yeats will ask himself in horror if it was not he who sowed the seeds of death:

> Did that play of mine send out
> Certain men the English shot?

The cults of Kathleen and Cuchulain are taking root among the nationalists; the Abbey is fast becoming what Synge feared it might: a purveyor of potentially lethal dreams. 'I do not believe in the possibility of "a purely fantastic, unmodern, ideal, spring-dayish,

Cuchulainoid National Theatre",' he told Stephen MacKenna in 1904, when Yeats's *The Shadowy Waters* had gone into production, 'because no drama . . . can grow out of anything but the fundamental realities of life . . . .'

Already two Home Rule bills have failed, and Synge wonders if men like Pearse will wait for the failure of a third. 'Home Rule is Rome Rule' is no empty slogan in Mrs Synge's household. The Synges fear the cult of Cuchulain, the blood-sacrifice that could set Ireland ablaze with sectarian warfare. There is a letter which Synge drafted in French in 1895; no correspondent is named:

> Le premier resultat de l'application de Home-Rule en Irlande serait un guer[r]e, ou du moins un grand conflit social entre Catholique et Protestant. Les Irlandais sont maintenant si habitués de vivre dans un état d'agitation politique, que la question de la possession du terrain suffirait de bannir toute paix interieure pendant probablement plusieurs siècles.
>
> Pour pouvoir introduire sans danger un pareil changement if faut attendre un moment plus tranquille.*

Synge recoils from Yeats's cult of sacrifice, as urged by Kathleen ni Houlihan. When Naisi wants to go to help his brothers, Deirdre pleads with him to stay with her; Synge's 'Kathleen' does not wish for a dead son/lover. At the same time, she is aware of the grim prophecy, and knows that fate, like the sea in *Riders*, must win in the end. Conchubor's remark in Act I is Synge making his own, pacifist, plea: 'What we all need is a place is safe and splendid . . . .'

In other hands, Deirdre has been reduced to closet drama,

---

* *The initial effect of the application of home rule to Ireland would be a war, or at least a major social conflict between Catholic and Protestant. So accustomed are the Irish now to living in a state of political unrest, that the question of land ownership would be enough to banish all internal peace, perhaps for many centuries.*

    In order to introduce such a change safely, one should wait until the times are more settled.

bookishness—to use Corkery's term of censure. However, no one can accuse Synge of penning bookish drama. The hand that once wrote *When the Moon Has Set* has since taken dictation from the living speech of Ireland, adding quaint curlicues of its own. But the embellishments to the language rarely stray far from genuine colloquial Hiberno-English; by the same token, Synge's plotting, characterization and imaging are seldom worlds removed from everyday country life. On the surface, at least; we have seen that the plays whisper of sinister, archetypal forces at work behind the fractious conduct of Synge's more exuberant *dramatis personae*. If Synge has harked back to other times, then he has done so through symbolism, antithesis and allusion, and not by calling up on the stage the ghosts of Ireland's pre-Christian past, as Yeats has done. Until now.

And yet, it is fair to say that Synge's vision is not very different from that of Yeats's, despite the latter's passion for the heroic. Both men are moved by a personal longing: Yeats for marriage and a son, Synge for marriage only. The hero Cuchulain, about whom the elder playwright has already woven two plays, is Yeats's spiritual son; Maud Gonne has appeared in various guises. Synge's explorations of human union—from the nun and the poet; Nora Burke and her three men; Sarah Casey and Michael Byrne; Mary and Martin Doul, to Christy Mahon and Pegeen Mike—have been his dramatic trial marriages. If 'all art is collaboration', then these good people have collaborated in Synge's dramaturgical love-life.

As has Ireland herself. Yeats will aver, in 'The Municipal Gallery Revisited', that Synge, Lady Gregory and he thought that

> All that we did, all that we said or sang
> Must come from contact with the soil, from that
> Contact everything Antaeus-like grew strong.

Of the troika, Synge resembles most the son of Poseidon and Gaia. The mountains and glens of Wicklow are his refuge in times of stress, and he thinks nothing of mounting his bicycle and cycling there and back to Glendalough House, in any weather. In his youth, he tells Molly, he 'nearly always got a wild impulse to wander off and tramp the world' like a wild goose. 'We're all wild geese, at bottom,' he insists, 'all we players, artists, and writers, and there is no keeping us in a back yard like a barndoor fowl.'

Synge is overjoyed to have found a kindred spirit in Molly, to be able to satisfy, at once, his love for her and for Gaia, the soil of Ireland. Many are the assignations John and Molly make at Westland Row railway station. Many are the train journeys they undertake together to Bray, and many are the intimate hours they spend making love in the hills behind Bray.

They have toured together: Wexford, Dundalk, Scotland, England—but always in the company of the other actors. The Abbey Players embark on an extended British tour, from 11 May to 17 June, bringing Synge and *The Playboy* with them. Molly, in the role of Pegeen Mike, is the toast of the London celebratory parties. Molly blooms; Synge seethes with jealously. He will share his prize with no one; he must have her to himself. 'Dearest treasure,' he writes to her, 'you don't [know] how you have changed the world to me. Now that I have you I don't care twopence for what anyone else in the world may say or do.' Synge fears that until he and Molly can spend an extended period of time together, he cannot rightly claim to 'have you'. The moment has come for him and his beloved to enjoy an entire vacation together.

V

See John and Molly exploring the haunts of his adolescence and youth. The summer of 1907 is fickle, but wind, rain and mist have never deterred Synge. His mother has rented Tomriland House again, bringing Florence Ross as her companion. Synge has not joined her this time. Instead, he has taken a cottage for a month in Glencree, a rift-valley in the shadow of Mount Kippure, a good day's tramp northwards from Tomriland. He has chosen this spot because Molly, at his persuasion, had secured—also in Glencree—another cottage, close to Lough Bray, for her and her sister Sara. The Allgood women are less than a kilo-metre from Synge's summer house. One holiday cottage for all three would be unthinkable—his mother would find it highly improper.

Molly has not only fallen in love with John, but with Wicklow, too. So much so that Synge worries about her health. Last autumn, the 'old tramp' and his 'changeling' spent many delightfully long days in the countryside; so long, in fact, that Molly's constitution may have been weakened. She has been suffering chronic eye pain and menstrual difficulties. He will be careful not to take her on too many long hikes this year.

John's own health is as worrying as ever, 'still rather uncertain', as he says himself. He had to shelve his plan for a cycling tour of Brittany, in the company of Henri Lebeau. He and Synge had maintained a correspondence, following Lebeau's visit to Dublin in 1906. Synge will not see France again. When the company went on the British tour, he could not join them at once. Instead, he recuperated for a week in Devon, at the home of Jack B. Yeats, going on to London from there. The artist had produced an excellent series of line drawings to accompany Synge's text of *The Aran Islands*. It was published, at last, in April 1907, by Maunsel and Elkin Mathews.

The swellings on Synge's neck remain his principal concern; he is beginning to suspect the worst, even though Dr Parsons has given his lungs a clean bill of health. But the physician believes something ought to be done about the neck; he thinks another operation is necessary, and arranges it for September. Synge agrees; only when confident of his health will he feel free to marry Molly. His changeling has accepted him; the young lady has said 'yes'.

————————

They follow their own 'nook road' along the valley through which the river Dargle runs. Molly is John's acolyte, a girl still not used to the countryside. The 'little purple grapes'—*frachans*, bilberries that grow among the heather—have become an emblem of his love for her. Synge and Molly leave the lane and climb up to where the berries grow. He notes with dismay that such a short climb tires him. His neck throbs; the glands are much enlarged and he is very self-conscious of them, feeling 'rather queer with this unsightly lump in my lug'.

John and Molly are passionate lovers. The tinkerwoman Sarah Casey's springtime thoughts gave way to Christy and Pegeen 'gaming in a gap of sunshine'. The growing explicitness in the language of Synge's drama reflects the progress of his sexual relations with Molly Allgood. Listen to Deirdre:

> It's a long time we've had, pressing the lips together, going up and down, resting in our arms, Naisi, waking with the smell of June in the tops of the grasses, and listening to the birds in the branches that are highest . . . .

There is no other Deirdre but Molly Allgood. This is not to say that Synge is kneading the Celtic heroine to suit his loved one; he puts neither himself nor his friends in his plays. He is, rather, creating a role which will bring out Molly's finest acting, a role very different from Pegeen in *The Playboy*: 'quiet and stately and restrained and I want you to act in it.'

Almost daily, Synge prepares her for the part, smoothing the rough edges of her speech, personality and education. He gives her books to read, 'improving' books; he wants to teach her Italian so that he can read to her the love-poems of Dante and Petrarch. Synge is delighted that she is taking an interest in opera; he brings her to art galleries and introduces her to the great painters. Synge scolds her mercilessly when she does not live up to his expectations; he tells her about the letters he has received from Annie Horniman, whose continuing benevolence 'depends—as to future tours—on the impression she gets of the acting and what she calls the "*discipline*" of the company'. The troupe's discipline is indeed poor, and Molly is one of the worst offenders; Synge is pleased to hear that Willie Fay has fined her for unpunctuality at rehearsals. Eliza Doolittle has still much to do in Synge's eyes; she must be ready to take on the part of a queen.

VI

Burgeoning fame brings, as it sometimes does, burgeoning dissension. The Abbey Theatre is not spared. The trouble began in March 1907 with news that Charles Frohman, a New York impresario and producer, was coming to Dublin. America was taking note of what was happening in Irish theatre. Frohman has plans for the Abbey Players to tour the United States, and he wished to see a selection of 'suitable' plays.

The Playboy riots had done untold damage to Synge's reputation; Frohman was hesitant about including any of his work. To Synge's dismay, Yeats and Lady Gregory sided with the New York producer. Willie Fay broke the bad news to him; Synge's letter to Molly brims over with his hurt and anger:

> I hear . . . that they are showing Frohman ONE play of mine 'Riders', five or six of L[ady] G[regory]'s and several of Yeats. I am raging about it . . . . I suppose after the P.B fuss they are afraid of stirring up the Irish Americans if they take me. However I am going to find out what is at the bottom of it and if I am not getting fair play I'll withdraw my plays from both tours English and American altogether. It is getting past a joke the way they are treating me. I am going to write to [Agnes Tobin] again to tell her how I am getting on [Synge was still convalescing], and let her know incidentally what is going on here . . . . She, I imagine, does not worship Lady G.

Synge had good reason to be disappointed with his fellow-directors. Only a month before, Yeats was reported as stating that he, the author of *Kathleen ni Houlihan*, 'holding what he believed to be right, refused to give up the work of one whom he believed to be a man of genius . . . because the mob cried at him'. Now he would allow Frohman to view only the 'safest' of Synge's plays, *Riders to the Sea*. It is one thing not to pander to the mob, but quite another, it seems, for Yeats to risk jeopardizing the Abbey tour for the sake of his fellow director's artistic integrity.

And what of Lady Gregory? Where did she stand? She had had doubts about *The Playboy* from the outset, demanding that much of the 'bad language' be cut. Yet she has been Synge's friend and ardent supporter through thick and thin, when his other plays came under attack from the press. All the same, Synge wondered if Lady Gregory was not furthering her own dramatic career at the cost of his. He had written to Frank Fay, he told Molly, requesting

> a list of how many times 'Spreading the News' [by Lady Gregory], 'The Shadow' 'Kathleen' and 'Riders' and 'Baile's Strand' have been played in the Abbey since we opened. I expect their pieces have been done at least three times as often as mine. If that is so there'll be a row. I am tied to the company now by your own good self otherwise I would be inclined to clear away to Paris and let them make it a Yeats-Gregory show in name as well as in deed. However it is best not to do anything rash. They have both been very kind to me at times and I owe them a great deal.

Frank Fay replied that *Riders to the Sea* had, in fact, been staged 'very frequently'. But this was cold comfort to Synge; Fay made no mention, by name, of *The Shadow of the Glen* or *The Well of the Saints*. Instead, he confirmed Synge's worst suspicions. 'When you write uncontroversial pieces,' he told him, 'you will get plenty of show . . . . There is a strong feeling in the company against *The Playboy*, and I doubt if they will agree to take it to [the United States].'

Sure enough, when Charles Frohman arrived in Dublin, Yeats and Lady Gregory staged a 'festival' of Abbey plays, which ran throughout Easter Week 1907. The two directors played safe: *Riders* was the only Synge play Frohman was permitted to see. The New Yorker was entertained with no less than six of Lady Gregory's plays—lightweight, one-act comedies and tragedies—and Yeats's *Kathleen ni Houlihan* and *Deirdre*. Synge remained sanguine, however. Fays's letter served to remind him of how the company had stood by *The Playboy* during the week of rioting. In truth, the only act of treachery among the actors and playwrights had been committed by William Boyle. Subsequently, he published an article in London's *Catholic Herald* attacking Synge and his play. This was reproduced in Dublin's *Evening Telegraph* in the week of Frohman's visit. It was a near thing, but Frohman went away satisfied. Synge wrote to Molly that he 'would like to wring Boyle's neck'.

It was, all things considered, a disillusioning time for Synge, summed up in a letter he wrote to Stephen MacKenna on 9 April. Boyle's treachery and the Frohman incident served only to increase his despondency. He repeated his desire to cut his losses and return to Paris:

> I sometimes wish I had never left my garret in the rue d'Assas . . . . the scur[r]ility, and ignorance and treachery of some of the attacks upon me have rather disgusted me with the middle class Irish Catholic. As you know I have the wildest admiration for the Irish Peasants, and for Irish men of known or unknown genius—do you bow?—but between the two there's an ungodly ruck of fat-faced, sweaty-headed, swine. They are in Dublin, and Kingstown, and alas in all the country towns . . . they stink of porter on every board of Guardians . . . . Do you know that the B[oard]s of Guardians all over the west and south have been passing resolutions condemning me and the French Government? Irish humour is dead, MacKenna, and I've got influenza.

The following month, May 1907, Synge came close to resigning his directorship. His quarrel was with Yeats, and *The Playboy* was the *casus belli*. When planning the British tour, Yeats had decided that the play was too volatile to be given anywhere but Oxford and London; he had learned of an organized plot to disrupt the performances. He ordered Ben Iden Payne, the new Abbey director, and Willie Fay not to play it in Birmingham, for fear of demonstrations. What Synge did not know at the time was that the company had only with difficulty acquired a licence to mount the play in

England. Yeats felt that any disturbance it might cause would result in the censor's withdrawing the permit.

Synge's threat of resignation angered Yeats. He and Lady Gregory, he told Synge, 'considered [*The Playboy*'s] being brought to Oxford and London of the utmost importance . . . . While we are fighting your battles is hardly the moment to talk of resignation.' Synge capitulated.

Payne's appointment had placed Fay in a lesser position than he had come to enjoy, and he resented Yeats's high-handed treatment of him. His bitterness reached its flashpoint during the company's tour of Manchester, Glasgow and Edinburgh in November. A rather unruly group at the best of times, the Abbey Players overstepped the mark in the course of the tour, and Fay made the unusual demand that each member be put under contract to him; he could fire at will. Yeats's response was to draw up a plan empowering the company to elect a committee of three, who would liaise with the directors and players. In effect, this meant that the players might refuse to perform a contentious work such as *The Playboy*. Both Yeats and Synge were, it seems, unaware of this danger. Synge, wishing to preserve the democratic nature of the company, turned against his old friend Willie Fay. The Fay brothers resigned at the start of 1908, a year which will spell tragedy and dashed hopes for J. M. Synge.

VII

The flat is at 47 York Road, Rathmines. It is a set of three rooms, not big, but the rent is only thirteen shillings and sixpence per week. It is to be the first home of John and Molly; he is determined that they will marry soon, come what may. All the same, he wonders whether he is not deluding himself.

He touches the side of his neck and his fingers examine the second scar, now healed. The growth is gone, excised at the Elpis—a nursing home on Lower Mount Street, Dublin—on 13 September 1907 by the surgeon Charles Ball, after consultation with Synge's family doctor, Alfred Parsons. The sutures, long since removed, have drawn together the lips of the wound. The flesh below has contracted, like the subsidence of a grave. To caress the depression is morbidly fascinating; it sometimes aids the creative process.

There is much that Synge and his family do not know about the growth; Ball and Parsons are not telling. Nor is Oliver St John Gogarty, poet and surgeon, whom Synge happened to meet on the street a few weeks before the operation, although 'he says I ought to get the glands out as soon as ever I can and that I will be all right then'. It is Gogarty, oddly enough (he is an ear, nose and throat specialist), who makes the correct diagnosis. It is not tuberculosis, he insists to Ball, because the glands in his neck are located *posteriorly*. This is cancer, Hodgkin's disease.

'The enlarged lymph glands that formed such an ugly lump in the neck were', according to J. B. Lyons, 'possibly only "the tip of the ice-berg".' He proceeds to give an almost lyrical description of the creeping horror of the disease that is killing Synge:

> . . . the malign and subtle process . . . had invaded Synge's tissues, spreading, perhaps, through chains of glands into the centre of the chest, transforming those homogeneous structures into grey or pink masses resembling fish-flesh.
>
> The diseased glands if viewed by an inexpert microscopist might appear as baffling as an abstract painting until the pleomorphic cellular infiltration was pointed to by a pathologist and explained as a disorderly assembly of cells, varied in size and shape, replacing the normal, stolid lymphocytes; an apparently purposeless usurpation by large cells with blistered nuclei, by pink eosinophils, by mononuclear cells with indented nuclei and by giant cells equipped with many large nuclei . . . a sinister, morbid extravaganza to delight some Des Esseintes of the laboratory for whom a plasma cell is no less beautiful than a topaz, who sees disease and distress objectively as the tax exacted by nature for the infinite wonders inherent in protoplasm, a dreadful excrescence governed by its own laws and periodicities.

Synge had gone to Ventry, Co. Kerry, for a short rest in October; an attack of asthma cut the visit even shorter. The attack was a symptom of the spreading cancer, the metastasis that is altering the cells in his chest.

He went to Alfred Parsons in December for a check-up; the physician pronounced him 'grand'. His neck and chest were, he informed Molly, 'very satisfactory. I had not been quite well this week with queer pains in a portion of my inside, but he couldn't find anything the matter so I hope it is nothing'. It was not; the pain got steadily worse.

But thoughts of marriage to Molly help to alleviate his anxiety. He stands in the sitting-room of the flat in Rathmines and inspects his belongings and the pieces of old furniture which Mrs Synge has given him. Some are slick from the rain; Synge curses silently the driver of the cart, who had helped with the removal from Glendalough House. He had loaded it crookedly, and the tarpaulin was skimpy and badly secured.

'You should have let me do the loading,' says Edward Stephens, shaking his head. 'Willie Belton showed me how when we moved Grandmother's things to Castle Kevin.'

Synge sighs. 'At least the books are dry.'

'And the pictures,' his nephew adds cheerfully.

The pictures include an etching by Synge's cousin Edward, entitled 'A Courtyard, Venice'. He is glad that this particular piece has survived the journey intact. It was a gift, given at the time of Edward's first exhibition at the Royal Hibernian Academy in April 1907. Molly chose it, so, in a way, there is something of hers already here in their future home.

Synge goes to the bow window. It faces north, and catches some of the afternoon sun, even if the view is marred by the blank, grey wall of a neighbouring house. The rain has stopped, leaving the winter grass and shrubs of the gardens sparkling with moisture. Out on the road, water vapour rises from the blanket of a slow-moving carthorse. The cart is overtaken by a motorcar, whose engine noise rattles the panes of Synge's window. He is far from the glens of Wicklow. But the Abbey—and Molly—are near. Synge is buoyant.

VIII

Molly Allgood is close to tears. She feels her world crumbling about her. There is no more talk of marriage, no honeymoon in the west of Ireland. They were so close to fulfilment; even Mrs Synge had resigned herself to the match. Since their first meeting in 1906, she and Molly have grown to like and respect one another. It is important to John that the two best-loved women in his life should be on intimate terms.

It does not seem to matter now. The little flat in Rathmines is bare once more; Synge's belongings and Molly's favourite etching have been moved back to Glendalough House. It has been a sad spring for the Synges. First, there was John's mother.

She developed a lump in her groin at the beginning of the year, and underwent an operation at the Elpis Nursing Home. The doctors discovered that the swelling—or 'rupture', as she called it—was more malign than they had supposed. It resembled, in fact, the tumour they had taken from John.

Then, in April 1908, John himself suffered a relapse. When he visited his convalescent mother, she was shocked by his pallor. They went to her bedroom after lunch

> and, there, he told her the news that he had held back in order to save her for as long as was possible from distress and anxiety. He had been growing steadily worse, and lying awake until three in the morning with pains in his stomach and back. He had been twice to Dr. Parsons, but his mother said that he had borne the pain too long in a lonely lodging with no proper food. John said that the doctor had found a small lump in his side, but that the pain did not seem to be connected with it.

Of course it was. Charles Ball and his colleagues operated on 4 May. What they found confirmed the earlier diagnosis: the cancer was too far gone; the tumour was inoperable. The surgeons more than close the wound and alert John's next-of-kin of the implications. Mrs Synge knows, Molly knows, his friends at the Abbey know. Synge himself may or may not suspect the truth.

He was discharged from Elpis on 6 July, and went to stay at the Stephens's home, just around the corner from Glendalough House; Mrs Synge had again taken Tomriland. He did little that summer but potter around the garden, worrying about his mother's health, fretting about the wound in his side which was shut one day and open the next.

Now he worries about *Deirdre of the Sorrows*. With febrile effort, making up for lost time, he produces draft after draft. They are far from satisfactory.

His mother had returned in September, and Synge had moved back to Glendalough House. Molly joins him often, when rehearsals allow. Together they take walks by the sea or day-excursions to Bray. He is not yet strong enough for the mountains. Perhaps, suggests Dr Parsons, a change of air might be beneficial. Synge decides to pay another visit to Germany.

———————

The leaves of Oberwerth have taken on the reds, golds and yellows of October. John Synge's step is light as he tramps the woodland paths he remembers. His breathing is easier.

He misses Molly terribly, but she is needed at the Abbey Theatre. She has the leading role in a new play, *The Suburban Grove* by W. F. Casey, and the Dublin critics acclaim her performance. Norreys Connell, another new playwright, has also joined the company. As yet, there is no replacement for the Fays; William Poel, the founder of the Elizabethan Society, was brought to Dublin in the summer, in order to coach the players. John Quinn, the Abbey's American friend, has bought the *Playboy* manuscript. Yeats has Synge's poems for safe keeping; they are not to be released until after his death.

Death, death and decay. Even the vigour of the once so lively von Eicken sisters has faded; 'poor things they are most of them getting old'. Life is mimicking art: Synge, thinking of *Deirdre*, finds it hard not to see himself as the ageing High King. Lines come, as the autumnal colours fill his vision: 'There's one sorrow has no end surely, that's being old and lonesome,' says Conchubor, and: 'I've let build rooms for our two selves Deirdre, with red gold upon the walls, and ceilings that are set with bronze.'

Death announces itself on 26 October through a telegram sent to the von Eicken's boarding-house by John's brother Robert. Mrs Synge, that remarkable woman who had stood by her youngest son through all his waywardness, is dead.

He cannot go to her funeral; his health would surely give out. He must grieve in private, in a foreign country. His letter to Molly carries his eulogy; no better obituary is possible for Kathleen Synge:

> People like Yeats who sneer at old fashioned goodness and steadiness in women seem to want to rob the world of what is most sacred in it. I cannot tell you how unspeakably sacred her memory seems to me. There is nothing in the world better or nobler than a single-hearted wife and mother . . . . It makes me rage when I think of the people who go on as if art and literature and writing were the first thing in the world. There is nothing so great and sacred as what is most simple in life.

IX

'Will you go to my funeral?' John asks Molly.

'No,' she replies, 'for I could not bear to see you dead and the others living.'

The doctors at the Elpis Nursing Home have decided not to operate. They, and the continual stream of visitors to Synge's room, know it is hopeless. Synge has given up his feverish battle to finish *Deirdre of the Sorrows*. He has handed the manuscript to his brother Robert; posterity shall never know how perfect the completed play was to be.

They have given him a room with a window facing south. When the March drizzles let up, he can gaze out at the softly rounded peaks of the Wicklow hills. He is very pale and thin; but not gloomy. He gives the impression, Lady Gregory thinks, of peaceful courage.

The nurses are greatly distressed; distressed to see the deterioration in the man who had brightened their lives during his previous visits. They loved his gentleness and easy conversation. He is so frail, he cannot raise himself on his arm in bed, and at night can sleep only with the help of drugs. There are no longer any books; Synge is too weak to read. He cannot even read his letters.

On 22 March 1909, Molly returned from a week's engagement in Manchester. Now, worn and haggard from dividing her time between the stage and long hours spent at John's side, her health too is poor. Whenever members of the Synge family come to visit, they comfort Molly; John's illness has forged a link between them.

The pain has ebbed, mercifully. Synge's favourite nurse—his 'tidy nurse', as he calls her—finds a book in brown paper on his locker. She opens it while he is asleep. It is a Bible; he has been reading it in secret. She smiles, thinking of the prayers she and Synge have said together night and morning. Mrs Synge's prayers have been answered too. 'God have mercy on me,' the nurse has heard him say; 'God forgive me.' Poor Johnnie had long ago returned to the fold.

At five-thirty on the morning of 24 March 1909, the same nurse is keeping vigil at Synge's bedside. She notices his breathing has taken on a new note. Putting her book aside, she leans closer to the sleeping man. The breathing stops.

See the hearse and its four black horses halting at the gates of Mount Jerome cemetery. See the mourners alight from the carriages. The men remove their bowler hats as the coffin is borne the short distance to the chapel. There is another group of mourners there: Lady Gregory in her customary black; W. B. Yeats; the Fays; the close friends; a few playwrights; some actors and actresses; Sara Allgood . . . . Her sister Molly mourns elsewhere, in private.

I asked if I got sick and died, would you
With my black funeral go walking too,
If you'd stand close to hear them talk or pray
While I'm let down in that steep bank of clay.

And, No, you said, for if you saw a crew
Of living idiots, pressing round that new
Oak coffin—they alive, I dead beneath
That board,—you'd rave and rend them with your teeth.

See the wreaths that are laid on Synge's grave. There are wreaths from the family. One from the Abbey company reads: 'To our Leader and Friend, Good Bye'. There is one from Lady Gregory, a personal message: 'In memory of his courage and gentleness', and this sentence from Proclus, 'The Lonely returns to the Lonely, the Divine to the Divinity'. The coffin is let down the steep bank of clay. The headstone is not new.

Not for John Synge a Parisian tomb surmounted by a winged sphinx by Epstein; or a burial under bare Ben Bulben's head, complete with admonitions to grim, apocalyptic horsemen; the greatest dramatist of the Irish Literary Revival is laid to rest in a grave already occupied. For one who, throughout his brief life, felt most at ease in the company of women, it is perhaps fitting that Synge's name is found sandwiched between those of his Aunt Jane and sister-in-law Mary. On his death, when his work is getting set to conquer two continents, Synge's relatives can find no epitaph more fitting than:

ALSO
JOHN MILLINGTON SYNGE
BORN APRIL 16 1871
DIED MARCH 24 1909

Struggling with a
Dead Language

I

John Millington Synge was, maintains David H. Greene, 'a strange man whose personality has always struck me as being unchangingly enigmatic'. Greene, co-author of *J. M. Synge, 1871–1909*, is aware that this is 'an unusual admission for a biographer to make', and such candour is refreshing. Synge is a 'puzzle-the-world'.

Looking back at his life, we see a man unable to make up his mind what he wanted to be: naturalist, antiquarian, musician, composer, language tutor, philologist, translator, photographer, art and literary critic, poet, novelist, dramatist, theatre director. Unlike 'myriad-minded' men such as George Russell, Oliver St John Gogarty or William Wilde, John Synge did not—generally speaking—pursue his interests contemporaneously; if he despaired of achieving greatness in one, he turned to another. When he decided that music came more easily to the Germans than to him, he set his sights on literature. When Yeats told him that 'Arthur Symons will always be a better critic of French literature', Synge changed horses again. He found his niche at last in the writing of the comic, peasant plays which secured his reputation for all time. And yet, we cannot say with anything approaching certainty that Synge's career might not have taken an unexpectedly different turn after *The Playboy* and *Deirdre*, had death not intervened; we cannot even say that Synge would have continued playwriting. We have no way of knowing how many strings he might have had to his bow.

I digress. A list of his talents and accomplishments brings us no nearer to an understanding of the man. One would think that

those who knew him should be in a position to supply enlightenment. This is not the case, as Greene discovered:

> Very few people in Synge's life came even reasonably close
> to knowing him well. His mother quite clearly did not
> understand him, although she seems to have thought she
> did. Other members of his family saw only one side of this
> complex man. As a creative artist he was completely outside
> their world . . . .
>
> Synge was a silent man, and silence is not one of the
> normal forms of communication. Masefield and others con-
> firm the fact of his reticence. To Yeats he was 'meditative'.

Greene's meeting with Molly Allgood in 1939 did little to lift the
veil on Synge. 'Her recollections', he reports, 'seemed indistinct,
although I was aware of the possibility that she preferred to keep
them to herself.' To Greene's dismay, none of the people to whom
he talked—Molly and Sara Allgood, Jack Yeats, Willie Fay, Richard
Best—'seemed able to give me any very clear impression of what he
was really like'.

So not even Molly Allgood, Synge's most intimate companion,
is of much help to us. We have only his letters to her—a one-sided
correspondence; Molly's own letters have not survived—and not
his talk. But there was not much talk to begin with; Synge, Greene
learned, was 'a silent man'.

Or was he? To examine his prose is to think otherwise.

Talk occupies a large percentage of Synge's prose works. *The
Aran Islands* is almost continuous dialogue, either reported speech
or reference to speech, connected by short descriptive passages in
which the landscape remains secondary to the people. It is dialogue, not monologue; Synge is far from silent. A builder talks *with*,
not *to* Synge during his first crossing to Inishmore; he returns the
jovial greeting of a group of island girls; he discusses the procuring
of a tutor with Mrs Costello; he makes it clear that, when Old
Mourteen came to visit him, 'we talked' for many hours. And this is
only the first day. 'I said . . . he said . . . he told me . . . I asked
her . . . .' The talk continues to flow, up to the final paragraph of

the book, when Synge 'could hear in the intervals of *our* talk that a number of men had come in to treat some neighbours from the middle island' (my italics). Moreover, Synge has just played his fiddle for the islanders. Clearly, the image of the 'silent man', the 'meditative' man, is in need of some revision.

Let us accompany Synge from Aran to Wicklow. He thinks nothing of entering a cottage and making himself at home, as he records in 'An Autumn Night in the Hills'. In 'People and Places', he regrets the fact that he and an old woman 'were both too weary to talk for very long'. In 'The Vagrants of Wicklow', the inverted commas proliferate, many of them enclosing Synge's own words. The articles on Kerry, and the Congested Districts of Connacht likewise, reveal a Synge far from averse to a lively chat. In short, there is little sign of the 'reticence' which John Masefield attributes to him. Far from sounding reticent, Synge sounds almost garrulous.

This is all rather confusing; almost, indeed, as if Masefield had known another John Synge. And perhaps he had.

Synge devoted much of his life to the exploration of societies and communities other than his own. He did so by getting closer to the people than did, say, W. B. Yeats, who may have urged Synge to go to Aran and live a life there 'as if you were one of the people themselves', for the simple reason that Yeats himself was reluctant to share the squalor and filth of the islanders' cottages—stately Coole and its creature comforts held infinitely more attraction for him. Synge had no such reservations; for him, assimilation into the peasant communities was all-important to his work.

It seems to me that, in order to achieve his end, to circumvent the natural reserve of the countryman towards the 'outsider', Synge became something of a chameleon, adopting the speech and mannerisms of each milieu in which he found himself. When in Aran, he became an Islander. (True, Lady Gregory, on seeing Synge there in 1898, identified him at once as a visitor, but Synge can have spent no more than a fortnight in Aran by that time; integration came later.) When fraternizing with the vagrants of Wicklow and Kerry, he adapted to their ways and speech.

This is why Synge's characterizations ring so true: when he

wrote dialogue, he was simply setting down words that he himself employed; they were first-, not second-hand; they came from his own lips. He did not invent the 'Synge-song' for stage use only; he himself made full use of his own creation, when the situation called for dialect speech. When reading his accounts of conversations he had with the Irish country people, it is sometimes difficult to believe that the Synge speaking is the youngest son of a middle-class Protestant land-owning family. In the Wicklovian essay, 'The People of the Glens', which Synge wrote for *The Shanachie* in 1907, we read:

> 'Well, it's a great wonder,' I said, 'to think you're that age, when you're as strong as I am to this day.'

We could be listening to Michael Dara, Martin Doul, Christy Mahon—in fact, to any of a number of Syngeian characters. Yet this is Synge himself (or, at least, how Synge chose to portray himself). Another old man, who appears in the essay 'In West Kerry', apparently is fooled into thinking that Synge is a local man:

> He asked first if I belonged to Dingle, and I told him I did not.
>
> 'Well,' he said, 'you speak like a Kerry man, and you're dressed like a Kerry man, so you belong to Kerry surely.'
>
> I told him I was born and bred in Dublin, and that I had travelled in many places in Ireland and beyond it.
>
> 'That's easy said,' he answered, 'but I'd take an oath you were never beyond Kerry to this day.'

We are not told what language was being spoken, English or Gaelic (the fishing town of Dingle marks the eastern boundary of the present-day *gaeltacht*). If it was Gaelic, then Synge's mastery of the language is astonishing, if not wholly incredible. It is more plausible to conclude that the conversation was conducted in English. That being the case, Synge's accent and cadences must have been extraordinarily authentic; Kerry ears are unusually sensitive to attempts by outsiders to mimic the speech of that county. The encounter took place in September 1906, by which time Synge had spent, between 1903 and 1906, no more than a total of fifteen weeks in Kerry. As a chameleon, Synge was doing very well indeed.

II

'What a pity that, when thrown among strangers,' Mrs Synge wrote to her son Robert in 1894, 'we only show ourselves as amiable and agreeable and taking everything in good part—while at home we show ourselves sometimes in a very unpleasant aspect, and temper often spoils our comfort, and certainly the comfort of those we live with.' She was alluding to her youngest son John, who had just written to her in glowing terms about his new friends in Germany, the von Eicken sisters. Mrs Synge was hurt, and probably justifiably so.

It cannot have been easy for John and his mother to live under the same roof. Indeed, one suspects that Synge continued living in Crosthwaite Park partly because he could not afford to move out. He and his mother had very little in common. To be sure, Mrs Synge played piano accompaniments to John's violin, but there were few genteel ladies of her generation who did not learn the piano as a matter of course; it was part of their education. There is little indication that she accompanied her son with anything resembling the enthusiasm shown by the von Eicken sisters.

Synge and his mother loved the countryside, yet we rarely hear about their *sharing* the beauty of Wicklow. Mrs Synge rented a summer house each year and, when circumstances allowed, John stayed with her—as a lodger, little more. They went on few walks together; they rarely conversed as intimates. Holiday photographs show Mrs Synge posing with relatives and friends—and a rather reluctant-looking John; he seems to be there on sufferance.

Was Synge a difficult man to live with? A sifting of the accounts of life in Orwell Park and Crosthwaite Park throws up very few instances of bad behaviour on his part. He could be inconsiderate, though; his brother Samuel remembers how he used to see Mrs Synge 'settle the table for [John] with a kind of half smile before he came down' and that Synge 'often did not come down to breakfast till we had finished'. In fact, the evening meal was probably the only occasion of the day when Synge and his mother spoke at any length. He kept very much to himself, was away for many hours at a time, hiking or cycling. He stayed clear of his mother's Bible readings too. Edward Stephens recalls an incident when Synge interrupted such a session; his mother forbade the youthful participants to continue until he had left the room. No, it cannot have been easy for a woman as devout as Mrs Synge; every profane comment from her son, every mention of 'queer literature' and immodest theatre life must have been construed as an affront to her faith and morals. We can imagine an uneasy truce and a minimum of communication, two people living alongside one another; small wonder that she resented Synge's gushing letter from Germany. And yet, mother and son were deeply devoted to one another.

Samuel Synge may have known John well as a boy; in later life, when the elder brother had taken up medical missionary work in China, they had grown so apart that John was almost a stranger. The reviews of John's plays he read in the newspapers were the closest he came to understanding his brother's work: none of the Synges ever visited a theatre. Samuel saw nothing of John's extramural activities; he had but a vague notion that John was living the life of an artist, travelling in the west of Ireland, mixing with the intellectual set in Paris. His many efforts to rekindle the faith in his brother met with rebuffs—or silence. Samuel, too, believed that there was little talk in John.

He also believed that Synge was both a teetotaller and a nonsmoker. In 1915, he told his daughter Edith that

> it was also during the years at Orwell Park that your Uncle John signed the Church of Ireland Temperance Pledge. This he held for many years . . . . I believe [he] sometimes took a little alcoholic drink when living among the country folk in Ireland down in the far west, just to please them. . . . He knew well the evil drink is in Ireland, but he wanted, when living among the people, to live as they did as far as

possible. I have never seen him smoke, and have never seen him take any alcoholic drink except once for some weeks when ordered to specially by his doctor.

If John Synge 'took a little alcoholic drink' just to please the country folk, then he tried to please a lot of the country folk a lot of the time. This, at least, is the conclusion I draw from his writings. Here is Synge on Great Blasket:

> I awoke the next morning about six o'clock, and not long afterwards the host awoke also, and asked how I did. Then he wanted to know if I ever drank whisky; and when he heard that I did so, he began calling for one of his daughters at the top of his voice. In a few moments the younger girl came in, her eyes closing with sleep, and, at the host's bidding, got the whisky bottle, some water, and a green wine-glass out of the kitchen. She came first to my bedside and gave me a dram, then she did the same for her father and brother, handed us our pipes and tobacco, and went back to the kitchen.

Cheap whiskey and a strong pipe at six in the morning must have been rather unsettling for a teetotaller and non-smoker. But Synge apparently took it in his stride, because a day or two later he and the local lads were discussing their respective capacities for drink-taking:

> Then they asked me how much porter I could drink myself, and I told them I could drink whisky, but that I had no taste for porter, and would only take a pint or two at odd times, when I was thirsty.

Thirst was no stranger to Synge when in Aran, and the pipe was always to hand. Naturally, he did not leave a record of each and every occasion when he indulged in these earthy pleasures, but a cursory perusal of his text suggests that the occasions were many:

> When we had had our drink I went down to the sea . . . .
> (*CW II*, 139). We had had a good dinner and drink and

were wrought up by this sudden revival of summer to a dreamy voluptuous gaiety, that made us shout with exultation . . . . (ibid., 142).

A clear-cut case of a not-so-sober Synge. The drinking, smoking and merrymaking continue:

> When we had finished our whisky . . . (*CW II*, 145). After the dancing and excitement we were too stirred up to be sleepy, so we sat for a long time round the embers of the turf, talking and smoking by the light of a candle. (ibid., 154). . . . they talked to me and gave me a little poteen and a little bread . . . (ibid., 162). A couple of Sundays ago I was lying outside the cottage in the sunshine smoking my pipe . . . (ibid., 162). We had another round of porter and whisky, and then the old man . . . gave us a bit of a drinking song . . . . (ibid., 183).

Nor was Synge, when tramping the roads and byways of Wicklow, averse to a glass of whiskey or beer—especially when a shared drink encouraged the country talk he relished so much. 'After a while I stopped at a lonely public-house to get a drink and rest,' he relates in 'The People of the Glens'. He spots a woman he knows and 'when I had been given a glass of beer, I sat down on a barrel near her, and we began to talk'. On another occasion, he invites an old man to have a drink of whiskey with him, in order that they might discuss horse-racing.

Samuel was partially right: drinking brought his brother closer to the country folk; but there is little doubt that John enjoyed it too. A pipe or a cigarette were likewise welcome—as the rest of the family knew: his sister Annie once sent him a gift of 'an elegant little silver Match Box to hang on his watch chain large enough to hold wax matches'. Mrs Synge tut-tutted: 'I told her the money would have been of more use!' (John was relatively penniless in Paris at the time.)

It should be obvious by now that the John Synge whom Samuel saw differed hugely from the John Synge whom others remember. Samuel was flabbergasted when he learned that the dialogue in his brother's plays had offended Dubliners so much. He had never, he informed his daughter, heard John swearing:

> What are the worst words that I ever heard your Uncle John use? . . .
>
> Sometimes I heard him say, 'Bad luck to it,' or 'Bad luck to you . . . .'
>
> He also had some expression, such as 'Holy Moses!' when getting a little older . . . .
>
> In after years did he get the habit of sometimes using stronger expressions than these? If so, could it have come from so often putting them into the mouths of those about whom he wrote? . . .

No doubt many of John's letters to Stephen MacKenna would have shocked Samuel beyond measure. Even the worldly MacKenna found some of their contents a little hard to take; he censored the offending passages with scissors and green ink. In one instance, Synge refers to someone—the name is obliterated—as an 'abortion'. If MacKenna let this word stand, then it is intriguing to speculate about those words he erased.

All this is not to say that Synge was anything other than the gentle, mild-mannered man, as portrayed by Lady Gregory, Edward Stephens, John Masefield, and other contemporaries. I wish only to show that the author of *The Playboy of the Western World* did not live in an ivory tower, but was closer to his subject-matter than his friends and family believed him to be. They saw only a side of him that Synge wished them to see, and, in consequence, many lopsided depictions of him have come down to us. Synge was a well-rounded man, as balanced—and as lively, talkative, boisterous and profane—as the best of the comic plays he wrote. If the lopsided view has tended to inform unduly our image of the man, then Synge must bear some of the blame for this: the chameleon was strong in him. He was also loath to engage in any form of self-aggrandisement; he left the promotion of J. M. Synge and his Works in Yeats's hands.

There was nothing that Yeats liked more.

III

I t started, of course, on that bleak December day in Paris, when Yeats dispatched Synge to the Aran Islands. John Synge fitted in completely with Yeats's ambitious plans, and when he urged the young man to go west, he was, Robert O'Driscoll suggests, 'making possible the means by which a part of his own nature could find dramatic expression, for Yeats saw his contemporaries and the figures of myth and history as a projection of his own personality'. I think Yeats was justified in doing so; his task, that of launching the Irish Literary Renaissance, was formidable, and without Synge he might not have succeeded. He may have been justified, too, by his lights, in turning the man Synge into a figure of myth, a symbol, were it not for the fact that, in so doing, he obfuscated that part of Synge which I consider essential: his intense humanity.

Yeats wrote—and spoke—liberally about Synge, both before and after 1909. To survey this body of prose and poetry is to see the old chestnuts of Synge's silence and reticence come tumbling out of the pyre. From the very start, it seems, Yeats was determined to fashion an image of Synge which would accommodate his need of a *pícaro*, a larger-than-life figure that embodied habits, mannerisms and qualities which could contrast with, and supplement, his own. As late as 1924, Yeats was still sustaining his myth, despite the existence of published material which plainly contradicted it. Thus did he describe to the Royal Academy of Sweden that first, fateful meeting at the Hôtel Corneille:

> I was very poor but he was much poorer. He belonged to a very old Irish family and though a simple courteous man, remembered it and was haughty and lonely. With just enough to keep him from starvation and not always from half starvation, he had wandered about Europe, travelling third class or upon foot, playing his fiddle to poor men on the road or in their cottages. He was the man that we needed because he was the only man I have ever known

incapable of a political thought or of a humanitarian purpose. He could walk the roadside all day with some poor man without any desire to do him good or for any reason except that he liked him. He was to do for Ireland, though more by his influence on other dramatists than by his direct influence, what Robert Burns did for Scotland.

There is so much wrong here that one hardly knows where to begin. It is probably more expedient to ignore the obvious half-truths and to focus instead on Yeats's most damning accusation, viz. that Synge was 'incapable of a political thought or of a humanitarian purpose'. If the first part of that statement is true, why then did Yeats invite Synge to join him and Maud Gonne in their *L'Association Irlandaise* at its inauguration, less than five months later? And was he forgetting the active role that Synge played in that movement up until his resignation?

Yet it is the second part—Synge's lack of a humanitarian purpose—which is the more damaging charge. Yeats cannot have been ignorant of Synge's interests at the time, because they dovetailed, to a large extent, with Maud Gonne's: the fight for home rule and the land struggle. Yeats's family were not landowners, so he had, in consequence, nothing of material value to lose through the Irish tenants' acquisition of basic rights. But Synge had, and Yeats knew this. 'What would become of us', John's mother had asked, 'if our tenants in Galway stopped paying rents?' Answer: they would have been considerably less affluent than they were when Yeats met Synge. Why he failed to perceive—and acknowledge—Synge's participation in the land agitation as an unselfish, *humanitarian* effort is puzzling, to say the least. Moreover, if Yeats had missed reading Synge's prose before 1909, then he had ample opportunity to do so when he became his posthumous editor. He must surely have noted Synge's mission of mercy involving a dog in 'An Autumn Night in the Hills'; or Synge's giving a shilling (a large sum to a man as poor as he; it was all he had in his pocket at the time) to a tramp, for a table he did not want, as told in 'The Vagrants of Wicklow'. These are just two small examples of Synge's humanitarianism.

Yet, to Yeats, the memory of Synge was that of a man so caught up in his work that he spared not a thought for others. 'He had', we are given to understand, 'that egotism of the man of genius which Nietzsche compares to the egotism of a woman with child.' Lady Gregory concurs: 'I have never heard him praise any writer, living or dead.' Very true, Yeats agrees; Synge was hardly aware of the existence of other writers—neither I nor Lady Gregory had ever a compliment from him'. Really? Why then did Synge tell Lady Gregory that 'your *Cuchulain* is a part of my daily bread', and can she possibly have overlooked his review of that same work? 'On the whole,' Synge sums up, 'although it would be possible to criticise certain details in her work, Lady Gregory has done what was required with tact and success.'

Nor had Yeats sufficient grounds for thinking that Synge had neglected *his* work. Synge's tribute in 'Le Mouvement Intellectuel Irlandais' could hardly have been more flattering:

C'est surtout dans l'oeuvre de M. W. B. Yeats, écrivain de génie à la tête de la nouvelle école de la poésie irlandaise, qu'on voit la portée de cette amélioration. Chez lui, le sentiment national, tout en restant aussi profond que celui de ses prédécesseurs, se borne à donner un caractère distinctif à l'atmosphère dans laquelle s'épanouissent les créations délicates de son imagination. De l'autre côté, ses rythmes, composés avec une simplicité curieusement savante, font preuve d'une rare connaissance de la langue anglaise.*

Yet Yeats and Lady Gregory persisted in the illusion of Synge the solitary genius, the dour man of few words, 'always too self-

---

* *It is principally in the work of Mr W. B. Yeats, that writer of genius at the forefront of the new school of Irish poetry, where one sees the extent of this amelioration. Although the national sentiment runs as deeply in him as in his predecessors, he harnesses it for the purpose of imbuing his delicate, imaginative creations with a distinctive character and brilliance. Moreover, his verses, whilst penned with a curiously erudite simplicity, display, nevertheless, an exceptional knowledge of the English language.*

absorbed to think much of others.' And perhaps it was an illusion created by Synge himself, an illusion that he was happy to cultivate. For there is no denying that Synge was more than willing to have Yeats champion his work. At the drop of a hat, Yeats sprang to the public defence of Synge's plays; he revelled in debate, the noisier the better. Synge's dramas, far and away the most controversial of the Abbey's first offerings, afforded Yeats a ready-made platform from which he could assail the philistinism of Ireland's new middle class. He could attack, while remaining for the onlookers a paragon of patriotism: 'The author of *Kathleen ni Houlihan* appeals to you!' (This was cynicism, of course; long before the first performance of *The Playboy*, Yeats had moved far from the unsubtle nationalism of *Kathleen*.) In short, Synge's plays were a godsend to Yeats: a stick with which to beat his enemies.

Synge was happy to stand in the wings and allow his work to be defended by Yeats's histrionic performances, even when his health permitted him to mount his own defence. He bowed to the master. It is also reasonable to assume that Synge was in awe of Yeats's erudition; indeed, he may have been in awe of Yeats's intellectual circle. Masefield remembered seeing Synge for the first time at one of Yeats's famous soirées in London:

> I had known a good many Irish people; but they had all been vivacious and picturesque, rapid in intellectual argument, and vague about life. There was nothing vivacious, picturesque, rapid or vague about Synge. The rush-bottomed chair next to him was filled by talker after talker, but Synge was not talking, he was answering. When someone spoke to him he answered with the grave Irish courtesy. He offered nothing of his own. When the talk became general he was silent. Sometimes he went to a reddish earthenware pot upon the table, took out a cigarette and lit it at a candle. Then he sat smoking, pushed back a little from the circle, gravely watching.

The behaviour, in fact, of a man who feels a little lost in a gathering of strangers whose witty and bright conversation is concerned with topics outside his orbit. Synge was new to London; he had 'skipped over it', in favour of Germany, Italy, Paris and Brittany. News and gossip about the Rhymers Club, Max Beerbohm, Oscar Wilde and the other luminaries of London would hardly have interested him. Had Masefield seen Synge in a rural Irish setting, then his opinion of him would surely have been very different. This applies, too, to Yeats and Lady Gregory—and, indeed, to Synge's brother Samuel. What they saw was but a narrow band of the spectrum of Synge's personality. None of them had ever accompanied Synge on his travels.

But Jack B. Yeats had. His short memoir, 'With Synge in Connemara', pulsates with the joy of being with Synge on his own turf. He could do little wrong in Jack's eyes: 'Synge was fond of little children and animals . . . . Children knew, I think, that he wished them well . . . . I remember a little girl in the crowd [who] clutched Synge by the hand . . . . ' And there was plenty of talk too. 'I remember him holding a great conversation in Irish and English with an innkeeper's wife . . . . Synge must have read a great deal at one time, but he was not a man you would see often with a book in his hand; he would sooner talk . . . . '

Jack Yeats sketches a portrait of a man who exulted in the vibrancy of country life: 'Synge was always ready to go anywhere with one, and when there to enjoy what came . . . . I think the Irish peasant had all his heart . . . but the western men on the Aran Islands and in the Blaskets fitted in with his humour more than any; the wild things they did and said were a joy to him . . . . He loved mad scenes.'

The time has surely come for a radical reassessment of this 'unchangingly enigmatic' man. But if Synge is an enigma, then I suggest that our impression of him has been coloured by a false composite, built up of the mere fragments of his complex personality which he allowed his friends and acquaintances to see. W. B. Yeats may have guessed the truth when he said of Synge that 'the external self, the mask, the persona, was a shadow; character was all.'

There is still a great deal of work to be done on Synge the

man. The clues are there, and many of them are sprinkled throughout his body of writing. In this context I am inclined to believe that it is out of the prose, and not the plays or poems, that the real J. M. Synge emerges. When he told Yeats in Paris that 'we should unite stoicism, ascetism and ecstasy', he may have been alluding to more than his writing. 'Two of them have often come together,' he said, 'but the three never.' Tone-deaf Yeats was not to hear that vital last note of the triad on which Synge based the symphony of his life.

IV

'D o you know, Maddy,' says Dan Rooney to his wife, 'sometimes one would think you were struggling with a dead language.' Maddy agrees that 'it will be dead in time, just like our own poor dear Gaelic'. Samuel Beckett knew, when writing *All That Fall*, that romantic hyperbole, the overblown phrase, the poetic exaggeration—call it what you will—is no longer acceptable. The joyless and pallid words have won.

They have won in the real world, the world beyond the theatre, because no Irish counterpart of Samuel Johnson or Noah Webster has, at the time of writing, come to the rescue of Hiberno-English. Its richness, as Tom Paulin points out,

> appears at the present moment to be in a state of near anarchy. Spoken Irish English exists in a number of provincial and local forms, but because no scholar has as yet compiled a *Dictionary of Irish English* many words are literally homeless. They live in the careless richness of speech, but they rarely appear in print. When they do, many readers are unable to understand them and have no dictionary where they can discover their meaning. The language therefore lives freely and spontaneously as speech, but it lacks any institutional existence and so is impoverished as a literary medium. It is a language without

a lexicon, a language without form. Like some strange creature of the open air, it exists simply as *Geist* or spirit.

Whether the joyless and pallid words have won in the Irish theatre is a matter of opinion. What we can say with certainty, though, is that Syngeian Hiberno-English died with Synge. This is not to say that dialect died. Far from it; Lady Gregory and Synge had pointed the way in which the Abbey would go for many decades to come. But the dialect of writers like William Boyle, T.C. Murray and George Shiels was real, and not an artefact like that of Synge. Moreover, realistic drama—long the norm in Irish theatre—was the tide that Synge's innovatory work sought to turn. Upon his death the dykes were breached, and the Abbey went with the tide. Realistic drama became a hallmark of the Abbey Theatre, a tradition that has—with a few brave instances of mould-breaking—continued up to the present day. It is a tradition that has flown in the face of modernism, that great movement of which Synge was a staunch disciple. The only playwright of note who, before the 1920s, deviated from the path of realism was George Fitzmaurice, a Kerryman whom Yeats and Lady Gregory very foolishly neglected. His best work—*The Dandy Dolls* in particular—bears more than a passing resemblance to Synge's, a fact which led Austin Clarke to wonder how the two Abbey founders 'could have failed to recognise the energy, vehement rhythm and imaginative reality of its two short acts'. But Fitzmaurice was very much a part of the minority; the people wished for representational art, and the Abbey obliged.

In effect, then, the Irish Literary Renaissance, as Yeats had conceived it, had failed. With the death of Synge, Yeats had lost the dramatist who could embody his dreams. The light did not go out; but the glow was that from a succession of peasant hearths, each rekindled from the still-warm embers of its predecessor.

The torch which Synge had set aflame was finally, after more than a decade of sputtering in damp darkness, caught and held by John Casey. Canny observers knew that the torch had passed, for Sean O'Casey—his gaelicized *nom de guerre*—was a trouble-maker, an iconoclast. He was a militant in his early twenties: a member of the Irish Republican Brotherhood and secretary of the Irish Citizen

Army. Yet, by 1916, he had renounced violence and had resigned from both organizations when an armed struggle for Irish independence was advocated. Like Synge, he was a Dublin Protestant; like Synge, he was a Gaelic speaker. Unlike Synge, he grew up in relative poverty in working-class areas of north Dublin.

O'Casey rattled Dublin in 1926. *Juno and the Paycock*, with its robust language and socialist-pacifist ideology, should have given fair warning of what was to come. But *The Plough and the Stars* proved to be too much, even for a new generation of Abbey Theatre patrons. The Easter Rising, the War of Independence and the Civil War were fresh memories—the General Post Office in O'Connell Street, within strolling distance of the theatre, still stood broken and desolate, as a result of howitzer-fire from a makeshift (though fearfully destructive) British gunboat. O'Casey set his drama during Easter Week and so disregarded the conventional pieties that he allowed the republican tricolour—by 1926 the national flag—to be carried into a public house, one of whose customers was Rosie Redmond, a prostitute. The audience rioted.

Yeats, the old war-horse, unaccustomed through long years to excitement, caught once more the whiff of powder in his nostrils. 'You have disgraced yourselves again!' the silver-haired, sixty-two-year-old poet thundered at the mob, and the mob knew well his meaning: Synge was back.

He was back with a different accent—a Dublin one—but the *flavour* of the dialect was of Wicklow and the west of Ireland. O'Casey's Paycock strutted and boasted like Christy Mahon before his unmasking. Yet more than the ridiculous figures and the heaped-up bombast of the lines was the similarity between the version of reality that was portrayed there on the stage and its Syngeian antecedent. It was a heightened reality, and the audiences knew that O'Casey was showing them The Dream—and tearing it asunder in front of their very eyes. His parody of Padraic Pearse was grotesque and vicious. Pearse had seen himself as the supreme martyr:

Voice of the Man. Comrade soldiers of the Irish Volunteers and the Citizen Army, we rejoice in this terrible war

[World War I]. The old heart of the earth needed to be warmed with the red wine of the battlefields . . . . Such august homage was never offered to God as this: the homage of millions of lives given gladly for love of country. And we must be ready to pour out the same red wine in the same glorious sacrifice, for without shedding of blood there is no redemption!

Grotesque though it was, this was a close paraphrase of one of Pearse's own polemical essays and easily recognized as such by a Dublin audience. If that was not cutting enough, O'Casey made certain that his audience was aware that the sacrifice was needless, futile, when it meant nothing to the woman in the street:

Rosie. . . . Well, 'flash in th' pan, or no flash in th' pan,' says I, 'they're not goin' to get Rosie Redmond,' says I, 'to fight for freedom that wouldn't be worth winnin' in a raffle!'

And then he was gone—or as good as gone. O'Casey is remembered principally for his three earliest plays: *The Shadow of a Gunman, Juno and the Paycock* and *The Plough and the Stars*. After the last, he went to England, and his subsequent plays never managed to recapture the wit and cruel honesty that informed his first offerings. It was largely the wit that had dried up; O'Casey's plays no longer offended; and truly good humour, 'charged with outlandish hooks and unexpected jabs is', Mordecai Richler reminds us, 'bound to offend, for, in the nature of things, it ridicules our prejudices and popular institutions.'

But England has the good fortune to be separated from France only by a very narrow body of water; it was across the English Channel that O'Casey passed the torch.

V

In August 1902, George Russell wrote an excited letter to Lady Gregory. 'Tell Willie', he said, 'that the thing I prophesied to him has already come to pass. A new generation is rising, to whose enlightened vision he and A.E. are too obvious, our intelligence backward and lacking in subtlety. The first of the new race called on me a couple of days ago.'

He called on Synge, too, in Paris in 1903, having been introduced to him by Lady Gregory the previous November. Synge impressed James Joyce, and the pair delighted in arguing in bistros, for hours at a time, about the revival of the Irish language, and the tragic quality of *Riders to the Sea*. So impressed was Joyce, in fact, that he translated Synge's play into Italian. That done, their brief relationship was at an end.

But Joyce, in later years, had an acolyte and sometime amanuensis, whose principal interest lay in drama. This was Samuel Beckett, perhaps the last of the great Anglo-Irish writers.

Besides their Protestant middle-class background, Synge and Beckett had in common a reverence for the classical forms of drama. There were other lines of intersection. Their reading had been far-ranging; both were concerned with the human condition, the pathetic attempt by man to impose pattern on a seemingly disinterested and chaotic cosmos. They were agnostics; the two were Trinity men; both had had sojourns in Germany and France, and had been moulded by foreign societies and languages.

It is, perhaps, the last which sets Beckett apart from most of his fellow-Irishmen, and brings him even closer to Synge. Such was Beckett's dissatisfaction with the English language alone as a medium for art that he harnessed French for a considerable body of his writing. Beckett became, to his intents and purposes, a Frenchman; he fought alongside the Resistance during World War II, passing as a farm labourer in order to escape capture by the Gestapo. He became a chameleon, as Synge could assume the guise of an Aran Islander or a Kerryman.

Samuel Beckett is best known for his treatment of the absurd; that is, the absence of meaning in man's perception of the physical world. It is the terror of the Void, the absurdity of attempting to impose a human sense of justice on an utterly hostile and uncaring universe. The realization that there is 'nothing to be done', and everything to be endured, places *Waiting for Godot* uncomfortably near *Riders to the Sea* and its aetiologically destitute 'we must be satisfied'. Beckett's landscapes are not those of Synge, yet there is contiguity of approach, as Katharine Worth observes:

> Beckett's characters are not drawn from the Gaelic-speaking peasants of Aran, but he is very much in tune with Synge and often echoes him. Even if he had not spoken of his special feeling for *The Well of the Saints* we should know it from the atmosphere and setting of his own imagined world with its many Synge-like beings; those tramps and homeless wanderers who meet under trees in country lanes, are familiar with the inside of ditches, take lonely journeys through sparsely-peopled countryside, telling tall tales, if only to themselves. The dangerous closeness to unconscious self-parody in Synge's idiom was something Beckett could use . . . .

Self-parody, both conscious and unconscious, is heard in abundance in that most Irish of Beckett's plays, *All That Fall.* (We can note, too, in passing, that Beckett echoes Synge's work, in as much as his title is also taken from Scripture: 'The Lord upholdeth all that fall and raiseth up all those that be bowed down.') It is no accident that this is a radio play, and the absence of sight recalls strongly *The Well of the Saints*. In this instance, however, it is we, the audience, who are blind. But Beckett compounds the deprivation by making Dan Rooney, Maddy's husband, sightless too. In contrast with Martin Doul, Dan (who displays some of the traits of Dan Burke of *The Shadow*), longs for death. Maddy, like her husband, is old. She is childless and bitter, but she clings to life, despite the many disappointments it has brought her. Maddy believes in The Dream, as her language makes clear; it is full of the rhetoric we

231

could almost associate with a Syngeian character. Beckett felt that Hiberno-English, like Gaelic, would not survive, and he was determined to save it. He brought it to a foreign country, and preserved it in an altered state.

VI

Beckett and Joyce transplanted English to another environment in order to rescue it from the pallid words. For a time, it seemed that exile was the only decent course open to the Irish writers. The Free State failed to live up to its name. Yeats knew, argued Hubert Butler, that 'Irish independence was primarily the notion of a small Protestant minority. It is in stark opposition to the imperialist universalism of the English and to the Catholic universalism of the Irish and derives from a handful of unpopular Trinity students and a few Belfast radicals.'

The Irish Free State was conceived free of the burden of an ideology (assuming that anglophobic negativism falls short of true ideology). This is not to say that *all* those who agitated for a republic lacked a template. James Connolly, for one, envisioned a socialist state; he had, tragically, been felled by the executioners in 1916, and Ireland's opportunity of becoming a socialist republic died with him. The regime that emerged was one which embraced the bourgeois values of the old rulers; in fact, it proved to be more reactionary than Britain had ever been. Censorship was imposed on literature (though not, surprisingly enough, on drama). Beckett was so incensed by literary censorship that he banned the production of his plays in Ireland during the Dublin International Theatre Festival of 1958.

For a time, it seemed as if the mark of the great Irish writer was the volume of his or her work which was banned. Very few of his compatriots actually read the works of James Joyce during his lifetime and, though he has long been rehabilitated, there still clings an odour of insalubrity to his books. Emigration, for over a century the lot of the Irish poor, appeared to be the only course of the aspiring literato. The prerenascent Anglo-Irish writers had chosen London; newly independent Ireland did not look favourably on their native Irish supplanters.

But times changed. The Irish Free State became the Republic of Ireland, and took its place in Europe and the world. A new generation of 'Antaeus-like' playwrights found sustenance in their native soil. Men like John B. Keane drew extensively on their local landscapes, their local dialects, and found receptive ears in Ireland and abroad. Brian Friel stayed at home, too, venturing forth only to collect his international awards.

What became of John Synge's work was, in its way, inevitable. His peasant communities were already an anachronism when he celebrated them in his drama. Now they are history, folklore. A Synge revival attracts audiences composed largely of nostalgia-seekers; they come to laugh and wonder at the quaint, comic antics of Sarah Casey, Christy Mahon and the Tramp. The satiric bite is gone; the old enemies are long buried and forgotten; the social issues are no longer relevant.

The danger, like the threat of the seas off Aran, has passed.

VII

In the 1990s, as Ireland moves towards the *fin* of another *siècle*, the traveller can fly to the Aran Islands. They are served by their own domestic airline, and each island has its own airstrip and terminal.

The descent to Inishmore on a cloudless day gives the traveller the topographical view of this strange western world. The island and its smaller neighbours appear as patchworks of tiny, rock-strewn fields bounded by loose stone walls whose patterns seem arbitrary at first sight; a second sight might well attach a mystical, alien significance to their twistings and convolutions. The walls cluster about small groups of houses and solitary cottages; they surround and sometimes merge with the grey-white limestone rock that vies with the green of the grass; they fan out from ancient churches and the remains of countless diminutive monastic settle-ments; they skirt the slopes leading to the Bronze Age *dúns*. Seen from the sky, little of Aran has changed in one hundred years.

But the traveller who approaches Inishmore from the sea no longer encounters red petticoats and pampooties on the pier at Kilronan. There are still horse-drawn taxis, but they face stiff com-petition from a small fleet of minibuses which times its arrival to coincide with the docking of the ferryboat from Galway. The boat brings, in all seasons, certain visitors whose purpose in coming to Aran owes less to leisure than to scholarship; many come in search of John Millington Synge. Their languages are occidental, oriental, and often those in between; Synge's work has long moved beyond the frontiers of English.

Some of these visitors—the islanders still call all visitors *strain-séirí*—find lodgings at what was once Mrs Costello's Atlantic Hotel. Should they come in the summer months, they have the opportu-nity to see Robert J. Flaherty's *Man of Aran*, screened twice weekly in the nearby community hall. They may wonder what Synge might have thought of the 'life that has never found expression' as seen through the eyes of the cinematographer. Perhaps they may find themselves agreeing with Tiger King, the islander who played the starring role in the film: 'Yerra, we knew well it was bullshit but what did we care.'

Many of the visitors will opt for bed and breakfast offered by the landladies of Inishmore, in cottages furnished with the modern conveniences of telephone and television. The radio in the kitchen will be tuned, as like as not, to Raidió na Gaeltachta, broadcasting news, talk shows and phone-ins in the Irish language, interposed by traditional tunes that would surely have gladdened the hearts of the founders of the Gaelic League. For the Irish language did not die in Aran, as Synge supposed it would. On the contrary, it has pros-pered, and would prosper even more if 'the Mainland', Britain and North America did not continue to lure away Aran's young people. The islands' population declines inexorably with each passing year.

But the English of Aran disappoints the seeker after the exotic. The colourfully individualistic Hiberno-English of Synge's day has yielded ground to RTE-speak and the parlance of American and Australian soap operas—though the traveller may imagine he hears echoes of Christy Mahon and Pegeen Mike in the speech of Aran's elders. Aran remains a place of imagining.

The little ten-seater touches down on the airstrip of Inishmaan, the whine of its deceleration scattering a flock of hooded crows. Four-wheel-drive vehicles convey the passengers over the uneven, fuchsia-flanked road to their destination: the MacDonagh cottage, now sign-posted *Teach Synge*, Synge's House. The travellers duck through the low entrance, intrigued to see at first hand the miserable conditions in which John Millington Synge lived with the ancestors of the cottage's present owners. It is all there, lovingly preserved—only the dirt, the animals, the smells and sicknesses are missing.

The day is fine, with just a suggestion of wind blowing in from the Atlantic; fine enough to visit Synge's Chair, a pile of rocks far out on the cliff edge, overlooking Gregory's Sound.

'This is where he wrote *Riders to the Sea*,' a man with a Cornish accent whispers *sotto voce* to his wife. She nods sagely and records him on video, seated on the rock in a Syngeian pose. *Yerra, we knew well it was bullshit* . . . .

Under the limestone cliffs, the surf pounds relentlessly. As a breaker recedes, making room for its successor, it deposits human flotsam no more ominous than a battered German beer can.

The travellers, satisfied, stroll back towards Inishmaan's sole public house, leaving the gulls to cry above the green stones of the shore.

Chronology

1871   Born 16 April to John Hatch Synge and Kathleen Synge née Traill, at 2 Newtown Villas, Rathfarnham, Dublin.

1872   Synge's father dies of smallpox. Mrs Synge and children move to 4 Orwell Park, Rathgar, Dublin.

c. 1881   Attends Mr Harrick's Classical and English School, Dublin.

c. 1884   Attends school at Aravon House, Bray, Co. Wicklow.

1884–8   Private tutoring three times a week. Attends Bible classes at Zion Church, Rathgar.

1885   Joins the Dublin Naturalists' Field Club.

1887   Begins taking violin lessons from Patrick J. Griffith.

1888   Passes entrance examinations for Trinity College, Dublin.

1889   First lectures at TCD. Attends lectures in violin, musical theory, and composition at the Royal Academy of Music, Dublin.

1890   Death of John's grandmother; Mrs Synge and family move to Crosthwaite Park, Kingstown, Co. Dublin.

1891   Joins the students' orchestra at the Academy. Plays in concert in March. Florence Ross's mother (Mrs Synge's sister Agnes) dies; Florence joins Synge household.

1892   Awarded scholarship in counterpoint at Royal Academy. Receives pass degree from TCD.

1893   His sonnet 'Glencullen' is published in *Kottabos*, TCD. Falls in love with Cherrie Matheson. First stay in Oberwerth, Germany.

1894   Studies violin and piano in Würzburg, Germany. Drafts 'Plan for a Play'. At Castle Kevin with Cherrie Matheson and Florence Ross. Stays at Oberwerth, studies German and French.

1895   Lodgings in Paris. Enrols at Sorbonne. Begins exchange of language lessons with Thérèse Beydon. Begins lessons in Italian in Dublin.

1896   Rooms at Hôtel Corneille, Paris. Takes Italian lessons. Sojourns in Rome and Florence. Studies art and Italian; befriends Maria Zdanowska and Hope Rea. Stays at Hôtel de l'Univers, Paris. Rejection of marriage proposal by Cherrie Matheson. Meets Stephen MacKenna, W. B. Yeats and Maud Gonne. Studies at Sorbonne.

1897   Joins L'Association Irlandaise, 1 January; resigns on 6 April. First
       operation on neck in Elpis Nursing Home, Dublin. Writes
       'Under Ether'.

1898   Stays at Hôtel St Malo, Paris. Attempts novel. Meets Richard
       Best. Enrols at Sorbonne. Meets Margaret Hardon. First visit to
       Aran Islands. Stays at Coole Park. 'A Story from Inishmaan'
       published in *New Ireland Review* in November. Moves into
       permanent rooms in Paris. Begins studying Breton.

1899   Publishes 'Anatole Le Braz' in *Daily Express*. Visits Brittany.
       Second visit to Aran. Returns to Paris.

1900   Publishes 'A Celtic Theatre' in the *Freeman's Journal*. Third visit
       to Aran.

1901   Publishes 'The Last Fortress of the Celt' in *The Gael*, New York.
       At Coole with Lady Gregory and W. B. Yeats. Fourth visit to
       Aran.

1902   Publishes 'La Vielle Littérature irlandaise' in *L'Européen*. Begins
       writing *Luasnad, Capa and Laine* and *A Vernal Play*. Writes two-act
       version of *When the Moon Has Set*.* Publishes 'Le Mouvement
       intellectuel irlandais' in *L'Européen*. Reviews Lady Gregory's
       Cuchulain of Muirthemne in *The Speaker*. Writes *In the Shadow of the
       Glen* and *Riders to the Sea*; begins *The Tinker's Wedding*. Publishes
       'The Old and New in Ireland' in *The Academy of Literature*. Fifth
       visit to Aran.

       * *Date of writing unknown. In 1907, Synge informed the journalist and
       playwright Leon Brodsky that 'I wrote one play—which I never
       published—in Paris, dealing with Ireland of course, but not a peasant
       play, before I wrote* Riders to the Sea.' *It seems likely, then, that* When
       the Moon Has Set *was written at or about the same time as his verse
       plays.*

1903   Takes rooms in London. Is introduced to Yeats's London
       friends. Gives up room in Paris; meets James Joyce. Publishes
       'An Autumn Night in the Hills' in *The Gael*. Publishes 'A Dream
       of Inishmaan' in *The Green Sheaf*. Sojourn in West Kerry. *Riders to
       the Sea* is published in *Samhain*. First Dublin performances of *In
       the Shadow of the Glen*.

1904   First Dublin production of *Riders to the Sea*. Publishes 'A Dream of Inishmaan' in *The Gael*. Present at performances of *The Shadow* and *Riders* in London. Reviews d'Arbois de Jubainville's *The Irish Mythological Cycle* in *The Speaker*. Helps Lady Gregory revise *Kincora* at Coole. Second visit to Kerry. Visits Mayo. *The Shadow* is published in *Samhain* and New York. Revival of *The Shadow* in Abbey Theatre, December.

1905   Publishes 'An Impression of Aran' in *Manchester Guardian*. Performances of *The Well of the Saints* (with Molly Allgood). Maunsel publishes *The Well of the Saints*. 'The Oppression of the Hills' in *Manchester Guardian*. Elkin Mathews publishes *The Shadow* and *Riders*. Tours the Congested Districts with Jack B. Yeats; publishes twelve articles in *Manchester Guardian*. Visits Kerry, including Blasket Islands. Becomes director of Abbey. On English tour with players.

1906   Max Meyerfeld's translation of *The Well of the Saints* performed in Berlin. Karel Mušek's translation of *The Shadow* performed in Prague. Tours in Ireland and Britain with company. Visits Kerry. Publishes 'The Vagrants of Wicklow' in *The Shanachie*. Visits Edward Synge in Surrey.

1907   First performances of *The Playboy* in Dublin. Maunsel publishes theatre edition. John Quinn copyrights *The Playboy* in New York. 'The People of the Glens' published in *The Shanachie*. Maunsel and Elkin Mathews publish *The Aran Islands*. 'At a Wicklow Fair' is published in *Manchester Guardian*. With Jack Yeats in Devon; joins company on British tour. Publishes 'In West Kerry' in *The Shanachie*. Vacations with Molly in Glencree. 'A Landlord's Garden in County Wicklow' published in *Manchester Guardian*. Second operation in Elpis Nursing Home. *The Tinker's Wedding* is published by Maunsel.

1908   Publishes 'Good Pictures in Dublin: The New Municipal Gallery' in *Manchester Guardian*. Rents flat in Rathmines, Dublin. Elpis; tumour is inoperable. Convalesces at home of Annie Stephens. Sojourn in Germany. Death of Mrs Synge. Publishes 'In Wicklow. On the Road' in *Manchester Guardian*.

1909   Final illness; dies in Elpis Nursing Home on 24 March.

Select Bibliography

The following are the principal works consulted during the preparation of this biography. Most of this material, together with incidental sources, is referred to in the *Notes and Comments*, with the relevant page numbers appended.

WORKS BY JOHN MILLINGTON SYNGE

The Collected Letters of John Millington Synge, I, Ann Saddlemyer, ed., Oxford: Clarendon Press 1983.

The Collected Letters of John Millington Synge, II, Ann Saddlemyer, ed., Oxford: Clarendon Press 1984.

Collected Works, I: *Poems*, Robin Skelton, ed., London: Oxford University Press 1962.

Collected Works, II: *Prose*, Alan Price, ed., London: Oxford University Press 1966.

Collected Works, III: *Plays, Book I*, Ann Saddlemyer, ed., London: Oxford University Press 1968.

Collected Works, IV: *Plays, Book II*, Ann Saddlemyer, ed., London: Oxford University Press 1968.

Letters to Molly: John Millington Synge to Maire O'Neill, Ann Saddlemyer, ed., New York: Harvard University Press 1971.

My Wallet of Photographs, Lilo Stephens, ed., Dublin: Dolmen Press 1971.

WORKS DEVOTED WHOLLY TO JOHN MILLINGTON SYNGE

Bickley, F. L., *J. M. Synge and the Irish Dramatic Movement*, London: Constable 1912.

Bloom, Harold, ed., *John Millington Synge's The Playboy of the Western World*, New York: Chelsea House 1988.

Bourgeois, Maurice, *John Millington Synge and the Irish Theatre*, New York and London: Benjamin Blom 1913 (Reprint).

Bushrui, S. B., ed., *Sunshine and the Moon's Delight: A Centenary Tribute to John Millington Synge*, Gerrards Cross: Colin Smythe 1972.

Corkery, Daniel, *Synge and Anglo-Irish Literature*, Cork: Cork University Press 1931.

Gerstenberger, Donna, *John Millington Synge*, New York: Twayne 1964.

Greene, David H. (and Edward M. Stephens), *J. M. Synge, 1871-1909*, New York: Macmillan 1959.

Grene, Nicholas, *Synge: A Critical Study of the Plays*, London: Macmillan 1975.

Harmon, Maurice, ed., *J. M. Synge Centenary Papers 1971*, Dublin: Dolmen Press 1972.

Howe, P. P., *J. M. Synge: A Critical Study*, London: Secker 1912.

Johnston, Denis, *John Millington Synge*, New York: Columbia University Press 1965.

Kiberd, Declan, *Synge and the Irish Language*, revised edition, Dublin: Gill & Macmillan 1993.

Kilroy, James, *The 'Playboy Riots'*, Dublin: Dolmen Press 1971.

King, Mary C., *The Drama of J. M. Synge*, London: Fourth Estate 1985.

Mikhail, E. H., ed., *J. M. Synge: Interviews and Recollections*, London: Macmillan 1977.

Price, Alan, *Synge and Anglo-Irish Drama*, London: Methuen 1961.

Saddlemyer, Ann, *J. M. Synge and Modern Comedy*, Dublin: Dolmen Press 1968.

Skelton, Robin, *J. M. Synge*, Lewisburg: Bucknell University Press 1972.

— *J. M. Synge and His World*, London: Thames and Hudson 1971.

— *The Writings of J. M. Synge*, London: Thames and Hudson 1971.

Stephens, Edward M., *Life of J. M. Synge*, TS in University College Dublin.

— *My Uncle John: Edward Stephens's Life of J. M. Synge*, Andrew Carpenter, ed., London: Oxford University Press 1974.

Strong, L. A. G., *John Millington Synge*, London: G. Allen and Unwin 1941.

Synge, Rev. Samuel, *Letters to My Daughter: Memories of John Millington Synge*, Dublin and Cork: Talbot Press 1931.

Yeats, W. B., *Synge And The Ireland Of His Time*, Dublin: Cuala Press 1911.

WORKS DEVOTED PARTLY TO JOHN MILLINGTON SYNGE

Carney, James, *The Playboy and the Yellow Lady*, Swords: Poolbeg Press 1986.

Carpenter, Andrew, ed., *Place, Personality and the Irish Writer*, Irish Literary Studies 1, Gerrards Cross: Colin Smythe 1977.

Colm, Padraic, *The Road Round Ireland*, New York: Macmillan 1930.

Coxhead, Elizabeth, *J. M. Synge and Lady Gregory*, London: Longmans 1962.

— *Lady Gregory: A Literary Portrait*, London: Secker & Warburg 1966.

Cronin, Anthony, *Heritage Now: Irish Literature in the English Language*, Dingle: Brandon 1982.

Donoghue, Denis, *We Irish: Essays on Irish Literature and Society*, New York: Alfred A. Knopf 1986.

Dunleavy, J. E. and G. W. Dunleavy, *Douglas Hyde: A Maker of Modern Ireland*, Berkeley and Los Angeles: University of California Press 1991.

Eliot. T. S., *On Poetry and Poets*, London: Faber and Faber 1957.

Fay, Gerard, *The Abbey Theatre*, London: Hollis & Carter 1958.

Fay, William G. and Catherine Carswell, *The Fays of the Abbey Theatre*, London: Rich & Cowan 1935.

Flannery, James W., *Miss Annie F. Horniman and the Abbey Theatre*, Dublin: Dolmen Press 1970.

Gallagher, S. F., ed., *Women in Irish Legend, Life and Literature*, Irish Literary Studies 14, Gerrards Cross: Colin Smythe 1983.

Gregory, Augusta Lady, *Our Irish Theatre*, New York: Oxford University Press 1972.

— *Seventy Years*, Colin Smythe, ed., Gerrards Cross: Colin Smythe 1974.

Harmon, Maurice, ed., *The Celtic Master: Contributions to the First James Joyce Symposium*, Dublin: Dolmen Press 1969.

Hogan, Robert (with R. Burnham and D. Poteet), *The Abbey Theatre: The Years of Synge, 1905-9*, Dublin: Dolmen Press 1978.

Howarth, Herbert, *The Irish Writers, 1880-1940: Literature Under Parnell's Star*, London: Rockliff 1958.

Kenner, Hugh, *A Colder Eye: The Modern Irish Writers*, New York: Alfred A. Knopf 1983.

Kohlfeldt, Mary Lou, *Lady Gregory: The Woman Behind the Irish Renaissance*, London: André Deutsch 1985.

Krutch, J. W., *'Modernism' in Modern Drama: A Definition and an Estimate*, New York: Cornell University Press 1953.

Lyons, J. B., *'What Did I Die of?': The Deaths of Parnell, Wilde, Synge and Other Literary Pathologies*, Dublin: Lilliput Press 1991.

Maxwell, D. E. S., *A Critical History of Modern Irish Drama, 1891-1980*, Cambridge: Cambridge University Press 1984.

McCann, Sean, ed., *The Story of the Abbey*, London: New English Library 1967.

Nic Shiubhlaigh, Maire, *The Splendid Years: Recollections of Maire Nic Shiubhlaigh*, as told to Edward Kenny, Dublin: James Duffy 1955.

Saddlemyer, Ann, ed., *Theatre Business: The Correspondence of the First Abbey Directors: W. B. Yeats, Lady Gregory and J. M. Synge*, Gerrards Cross: Colin Smythe 1982.

Sekine, Masaru, ed., *Irish Writers and Society at Large*, Irish Literary Studies 22, Gerrards Cross: Colin Smythe 1985.

Skelton, Robin, *Celtic Contraries*, Syracuse: Syracuse University Press 1990.

Waters, Maureen, *The Comic Irishman*, Albany: State University of New York Press 1984.

Watson, G. J., *Irish Identity and the Literary Revival: Synge, Yeats, Joyce and O'Casey*, London: Croom Helm 1979.

GENERAL WORKS

Atkins, H. G., *Johann Wolfgang Goethe*, London: Methuen 1904.

Beckett, Samuel, *The Complete Dramatic Works*, London and Boston: Faber and Faber 1986.

Bell, Michael, *The Context of English Literature: 1900-1930*, London: Methuen 1980.

Boyd, Ernest A., *Ireland's Literary Renaissance*, Dublin: Maunsel 1916.

Brown, Malcolm, *The Politics of Irish Literature: From Thomas Davis to W. B. Yeats*, Seattle: University of Washington Press 1972.

Clarke, Austin, *The Plays of George Fitzmaurice*, Dublin: Dolmen Press 1967.

Connolly, Peter, ed., *Literature and the Changing Ireland*, Irish Literary Studies 9, Gerrards Cross: Colin Smythe 1982.

Deane, Seamus, *A Short History of Irish Literature*, London: Hutchinson 1986.

Ellis-Fermor, Una, *The Irish Dramatic Movement*, London: Methuen 1939.

Fallis, Richard, *The Irish Renaissance*, Syracuse: Syracuse University Press 1977.

Field Day Theatre Company, *Ireland's Field Day*, Notre Dame:
University of Notre Dame Press 1986.

Flannery, Mary Catherine, *Yeats and Magic: The Earlier Works*, Irish
Literary Studies 2, Gerrards Cross: Colin Smythe 1977.

Foster, R. F., *Modern Ireland: 1600-1972*, London: Allen Lane 1988.

Goethe, J. W., *The Autobiography of Johann Wolfgang Goethe*, Chicago
and London: University of Chicago Press 1974.

Gregory, Augusta Lady, *Collected Plays*, Vols. I-IV, Ann Saddlemyer, ed.,
Gerrards Cross: Colin Smythe 1970.

— *Cuchulain of Muirthemne*, London: John Murray 1902.

Gwynn, Denis, *Edward Martyn and the Irish Revival*, London: Jonathan
Cape 1930.

Hogan, Robert, *After the Renaissance: A Critical History of the Irish Drama
since 'The Plough and the Stars'*, London: Macmillan 1968.

— (with James Kilroy), *The Irish Literary Theatre, 1899-1901*, Dublin:
Dolmen Press 1975.

— (with James Kilroy), *Laying the Foundations: 1902-1904*, Dublin:
Dolmen Press 1976.

— *The Rise of the Realists, 1910-15*, Dublin: Dolmen Press 1979.

Hone, Joseph, *The Life of George Moore*, New York: Macmillan 1936.

— *W. B. Yeats, 1865-1939*, London: Macmillan 1962.

Hyde, Douglas, *Love Songs of Connacht*, London: Fisher Unwin 1893.

Jackson, Holbrook, *The Eighteen Nineties*, London: Grant Richards
1913.

Jeffares, A. Norman, *Anglo-Irish Literature*, London: Macmillan 1982.

— *W. B. Yeats: A New Biography*, London: Hutchinson 1988.

Joyce, P. W., *English as we speak it in Ireland*, Dublin: Wolfhound Press
1991.

Kenny, Herbert A., *Literary Dublin: A History* (new and revised
edition), Dublin: Gill and Macmillan 1991.

King, Bruce, ed., *Literatures of the World in English*, London and Boston:
Routledge & Kegan Paul 1974.

Krause, David, *Sean O'Casey: The Man and His Work*, London:
McGibbon & Kee 1960.

MacDonagh, Thomas, *Literature in Ireland: Studies Irish and Anglo-Irish*,
Dublin and Cork: Talbot Press 1916.

Martin, Augustine, ed., *The Genius of Irish Prose*, Cork and Dublin:
Mercier Press 1985.

McCann, Sean, ed., *The World of Sean O'Casey*, London: New English Library 1966.

Meisel, Martin, *Shaw and the Nineteenth-Century Theater*, Princeton: Princeton University Press 1968.

Moore, George, *Hail and Farewell: Ave, Salve, Vale*, Richard Cave, ed., Gerrards Cross: Colin Smythe 1976.

O'Casey, Sean, *Three Plays: The Shadow of a Gunman, Juno and the Paycock, The Plough and the Stars*, London: Macmillan 1957.

Ó hEithir, Breandán and Ruairí, eds, *An Aran Reader*, Dublin: Lilliput Press 1991.

O'Rahilly, T. F., *Early Irish History and Mythology*, Dublin: Institute for Advanced Studies 1976.

Owens, Graham, ed., *George Moore's Mind and Art*, London: Oliver and Boyd 1968.

Pochin Mould, Daphne D. C., *The Aran Islands*, Newton Abbot: David & Charles 1972.

Pyle, Hilary, *Jack B. Yeats*, London and Boston: Routledge & Kegan Paul 1970.

Summerfield, Henry, *That Myriad-Minded Man: A Biography of George William Russell "A.E." 1867-1935*, Gerrards Cross: Colin Smythe 1975.

Ward, Margaret, *Maud Gonne: Ireland's Joan of Arc*, London: Pandora Press 1990.

Worth, Katharine, ed., *Beckett the Shape Changer: A Symposium*, London and Boston: Routledge and Kegan Paul 1975.

Yeats, W. B., *Autobiographies*, London: Macmillan 1955.

— *The Bounty of Sweden*, Dublin: Cuala Press 1925.

— *Essays and Introductions*, London: Macmillan 1961.

— *Explorations*, London: Macmillan 1962.

— *The Letters of W. B. Yeats*, Allan Wade, ed., London: Rupert Hart-Davis 1954.

— *Memoirs*, Denis Donoghue, ed., London: Macmillan 1972.

— *Uncollected Prose*, II, John P. Frayne and Colton Johnson, eds, New York: Columbia University Press 1975.

Notes and Comments

A Wilder Altar

1   GIVE UP PARIS . . . J. M. Synge III, *Collected Works*, Ann
Saddlemyer, ed., London: Oxford University Press 1966, 63. The
four volumes are under the general editorship of Robin Skelton;
the individual editors are: *CW I, Poems*, Robin Skelton; *CW II, Prose*,
Alan Price; *CW III, Plays Book 1*, Ann Saddlemyer; *CW IV, Plays
Book 2*, Ann Saddlemyer. Hereafter, all references to this collection
will be referred to by *CW*, volume and page number.

     The above is contained in a preface, written by W. B. Yeats, to
the first edition of *The Well of the Saints*. It has been pointed out that
Yeats may have been exaggerating his role in Synge's decision to
visit Aran. Robin Skelton, in *The Writings of J. M. Synge*, London.
Thames and Hudson 1971, p. 24, takes the view that Yeats's words
'may reasonably be regarded as much as a comment upon what
Synge did as an accurate memory of what he told Synge to do'.
AS IF YOU WERE ONE . . . Ibid., p. 63.
OLD MOURTEEN . . . *CW II*, p. 50. Synge had the good fortune
to have been introduced by his landlady to one of Inishmore's
more colourful storytellers, Martin Coneely, known locally as Old
Mourteen. We meet the same man in the writings of Arthur
Symons. In his *Cities and Sea-Coasts and Islands* (1897), Symons
writes that 'one of our party . . . came in with a singular person
whom he had picked up on the way, a professional story-teller, who
had for three weeks been teaching Irish to [Franz N. Finck] who
had preceded us on the island. He was half blind and of wild
appearance; a small and hairy man, all gesture, and as if set on
springs, who spoke somewhat broken English in a roar. He
lamented that we could understand no Irish, but, even in English,
he had many things to tell . . . .' (Cited in *An Aran Reader*,
Breandán and Ruairí Ó hEithir, eds, Dublin: Lilliput Press 1991,
88.)

2   THE DIRTIEST MAN IN DUBLIN . . . W. B. Yeats, in *Autobiographies* (London: Macmillan 1955, p. 137), recalls 'an old Dublin riddle' relating to Wilde's lack of personal hygiene: '"Why are Sir William Wilde's nails so black?" Answer: "Because he has scratched himself".'
AS WE TALKED . . . *CW II*, p. 50.
MAG TUIRED . . . Thomas F. O'Rahilly, *Early Irish History and Mythology*, Dublin: Institute for Advanced Studies 1976, 388–90.

3   STRONG, WELL-BUILT MAN . . . *The Collected Letters of John Millington Synge, Vol. I*, Ann Saddlemyer, ed., Oxford: Clarendon Press 1983, ix.
I AM LORD OF ALL . . . Rev. Alexander Synge to his brother Edward, 14 July 1851, MS 6200, f. 4, Trinity College, Dublin.

4   WENT TO THEM . . . Ibid., 19 August 1851, f. 5.
MET WITH OPPOSITION . . . From news items printed by *The Galway Vindicator*, 1852–1853, cited in *An Aran Reader*, pp. 34–8.
BROGUE OF GALWAY . . . *CW II*, p. 50.

5   MISSIONARY MONKS . . . T. J. Westropp, *Proceedings of the Royal Academy, Vol. XXVII, Section C, No. 11*, Dublin: Hodges Figgis 1910, 177–8.
WOMAN OF SLIGO . . . *CW II*, pp. 56–7.

6   I FLED FROM ALL . . . *CW I*, p. 15.

7   INGENIOUSLY DESIGNED . . . Edward M. Stephens, *The Life of J. M. Synge*, f. 987. This is the TS on which David H. Greene drew. A new biography was commissioned by Stephens's widow, 'made up entirely from my husband's TS and reflecting his particular views'. The result was *My Uncle John: Edward Stephens's Life of J. M. Synge*, Andrew Carpenter, ed., London: Oxford University Press 1974.

8   I HAVE NOTICED . . . *CW II*, p. 54n.
HARMONIZE WITH THE LIMESTONE . . . Ibid., p. 54n.
I SAW SUDDENLY . . . Ibid., p. 54n.

9   AS RELIEF . . . Ibid., p. 54n.
MEDIOCRE TALENT . . . Greene and Stephens, p. 74.
EDMUND JOHN MILLINGTON SYNGE . . . He was christened Edmund John, but it seems that Edmund was never used.

10   THE BRETHREN . . . 'The attempt to establish Protestant control of education was particularly vigorous in Wicklow where the evangelical movement acquired great strength among the settler Protestant farmers . . . . Its strength was due, in part at least, to the

ministry of the Rev. John Nelson Darby . . . . He had not long been working in the Wicklow mountains before his bishop published a call to the clergy of the dioceses to oppose Catholic emancipation on the ground that it would be dangerous to the temporal interests of the church. The young curate regarded this view as mundane, went into public opposition to his bishop, and left for England as a leader of the Brethren, afterwards known as the Plymouth Brethren' (Stephens, f. 35).

11   THE NEED TO EARN THEIR OWN LIVING . . . 'The general fall in the incomes of country estates . . . was causing a migration of people belonging to the landlord class. Dublin's suburbs [came to be] occupied by people who had lived in mansions looking out on gravel sweeps, wide lawns and fine trees' (ibid., f. 131).

THOUSAND FORMS OF WICKEDNESS . . . Dr Traill's notebook reads: 'The [Roman Catholic] priests, trained in their Satanic school, and nurtured in Jesuitism and deceit, are well skilled in all the wily policy of their apostate church' (ibid., ff. 123–4).

12   SEEN AND NOT HEARD . . . Ibid., f. 178.
SAINTS . . . Ibid., f. 178.
WAS ABOUT FOURTEEN . . . *CW II*, pp. 10–11.

13   RENOUNCED CHRISTIANITY . . . Ibid., p. 11. Edward Stephens notes that Synge, after he had 'accidentally opened *The Origin of Species* at the page on which he read Darwin's comparison of a man's hand, a monkey's paw and a bird's wing [had] not come to rest in any settled religious belief . . . . After he had regained his composure he had begun to read works on Christian evidence: [John] Locke's [*Essay Concerning the*] *Human Understanding*, [William] Paley's *Evidences of Christianity*, and [Samuel] Butler's *Analogy*' (Stephens, ff., 320–1).

ONE NIGHT I THOUGHT . . . CWII., p. 4.

14   PAINFULLY TIMID BOY . . . Ibid., p. 4.
THE WELL-MEANT . . . Ibid., pp. 4–5.
ALEISTER CROWLEY . . . Aleister Crowley, *The Confessions of Aleister Crowley*, John Symonds and Kenneth Grant, eds, London: Routledge & Kegan Paul 1979, 18 and *passim*. See also *The Letters of W. B. Yeats*, Allan Wade, ed., London: Rupert Hart-Davis 1954, 340.

15   UNITE THE RADICAL TRUTHS . . . W. B. Yeats, *Memoirs*, Denis Donoghue, ed., London: Macmillan 1972, 124.

16   RANSACKING IRELAND . . . W. B. Yeats, *Letters*, pp. 256–7. Eva
      Gore-Booth was the younger sister of Constance (later Countess
      Markievicz), who played an active part in the Easter Rising of 1916
      and the Irish Civil War.
      L'ASSOCIATION IRLANDAISE . . . The New Ireland Society (or
      League) should not be confused with the Young Ireland movement
      of the 1840s, a group of young nationalists led by Thomas Davis,
      Charles Gavan Duffy, John Mitchel and James Fintan Lalor. They
      favoured more drastic action than Daniel O'Connell—founder of
      the Catholic Association—advocated. Their official organ was *The
      Nation* newspaper. The movement collapsed following an abortive
      armed uprising in 1848.
      THE ULTIMATE GOAL WAS HOME RULE . . . 'John
      mentioned his membership of the Irish League in a letter to his
      mother. His joining such an organization seemed to his relations
      an incomprehensible change in his allegiance, for they
      remembered his collecting [in February 1893] signatures to a
      petition against Home Rule. The political programme of the Home
      Rule movement had not attracted him, because it seemed to him
      devised to satisfy religious aspirations which he did not feel. At
      home he had listened so often to the phrase "Home Rule means
      Rome Rule", that it had clouded in his mind the issues raised by
      the advocates of Irish self-government. Unexpectedly he had
      found, in Paris, an opportunity for supporting the national
      movement in a way to which religious beliefs were irrelevant'
      (Stephens, ff. 820–1).
      SIX YEARS AGO . . . *CW II*, p. 63.
18   ARMENIAN SCIENTIST . . . Michel Elmassian, a biologist who later
      distinguished himself at the Institut Pasteur, and 'whose complete
      ignorance of English obliged Synge to practise his French' (Maurice
      Bourgeois, *John Millington Synge and the Irish Theatre*, New York and
      London: Benjamin Blom 1913, 42).
      PLOTINUS . . . MacKenna (1872–1934) was awarded a gold medal
      in 1924 by the Royal Irish Academy for his translation. He refused
      it for political reasons, disapproving of an Irish institution that still
      called itself 'Royal'.
19   HAS GONE BACK TO PARIS . . . Stephens, f. 811. Mrs Synge
      continues: '. . . and for that possibility [John] is giving up

everything. He says he is not selfish or egotistical but quite the reverse. In fact he writes the most utter folly.'

TALKED DAYS AND NIGHTS . . . Stephen MacKenna in a letter to *The Irish Statesman*, 3 November 1928, p. 169.

MONTH OF APRIL . . . Stephens, ff. 845–6. Stephens gives a conflation of the versions told by Maurice Bourgeois, Arthur Lynch and Edwin Dodds. Lynch, a journalist and fellow-member of *L'Association Irlandaise*, fought on the Afrikaner side during the Boer War; Dodds, also a member, edited *Journal and Letters of Stephen MacKenna*, (London: Constable 1936). Synge's diary of 23 April 1897 reads: 'Soir, Society Irlandaise'.

SYNGE WAS, AFTER ALL . . . Greene and Stephens, p. 62.

FENIAN TURN . . . W. B. Yeats, *Memoirs*, p. 107.

ENGLAND WOULD ONLY . . . Ibid., p. 107. Yeats claimed that this was 'the only political sentence I ever heard on his lips'. In *Synge And The Ireland Of His Time* (Dublin: Cuala Press, 1911, p. 11), he writes that 'Synge seemed by nature unfitted to think a political thought, and with the exception of one sentence [see above], spoken when I met him in Paris, that implied some sort of nationalist conviction, I cannot remember that he spoke of politics or showed any interest in men in the mass, or in any subject that is studied through abstraction and statistic.' Stephens, on the other hand, writes (f. 824) that 'John was interested in politics generally . . . . '

20   MANIFESTATIONS . . . MS 4418, TCD, f. 52. The entry reads simply: 'Meeting Irish League. Saw manifestations.'
     I'M AN INITIATED MYSTIC . . . *CW II*, p. 42.
     ANOTHER PAROXYSM . . . Ibid., p. 42.

21   SHAPES TREMBLING . . . W. B. Yeats, 'Rosa Alchemica', in *Mythologies*, London: Macmillan 1959, 285.
     NO DOUBT PARIS . . . Greene and Stephens, p. 69.

22   CHRONIC ILL-HEALTH . . . When he was thirteen, Synge attended another school at Aravon House, Bray, Co. Wicklow. Ill-health forced a return to private tuition after a year.
     COULD NOT FEEL CERTAIN . . . Stephens, f. 178.

23   FULLY AROUSED . . . Ibid., f. 245.
     JOHNNIE'S EAR . . . Ibid., f. 314.

24   SOON AFTER I HAD . . . *CW II*, pp. 13–4.

26   FOR NO MONEY AT ALL . . . Ibid., p. 62.

A FEW COMMENTS . . . MS 4385, TCD, f. 66.

27 IT GAVE ME . . . *CW II*, p. 65.

THE MERCY OF SOME OF THE NATIVES . . . Ibid., p. 95.

28 MORE TO ARABIA . . . Synge visited the Somali village at the International Exhibition held in Dublin in 1907. He commented to Molly Allgood that a 'bit of the war-song the niggers were singing was exactly like some of the keens on Aran'. (Synge, *Letters I*, pp. 343–4.)

AM I NOT LEAVING . . . MS 4385, TCD, f. 49. Edward Stephens notes the contents of Synge's portmanteau: '[Fr Owen] O'Growney's small paper-covered Irish Grammar, and the epic tales published by the Irish Texts Society . . . He had also taken with him to Aran a number of books he had been reading in Paris—*The Life of Guy de Maupassant*, *The Earth Breath* [by AE], *Madame Bovary*, *Le Trésor des Humbles*, *Les Grandes Initiés*, *Aucassin and Nicolette*, [Dante Gabriel] Rosetti's *Poems*, and the works of [Emanuel] Swedenborg and Pierre Loti' (Stephens, f. 1004).

TROIKA

29 LADY GREGORY ASKS ME . . . Yeats to Synge, 21 June 1898, in *Theatre Business: The Correspondence of the First Abbey Theatre Directors: W. B. Yeats, Lady Gregory and J. M. Synge*, Ann Saddlemyer, ed., Gerrards Cross: Colin Smythe 1982, 27.

GATHERING FOLK-LORE . . . Lady Gregory, *Our Irish Theatre*, New York: Oxford University Press 1972, 73.

30 ONE OR TWO POEMS . . . *CW III*, p. 63.

DRIFTING, SILENT MAN . . . W. B. Yeats, *Memoirs*, p. 203.

THE RUSHING UP . . . Ibid., p. 223.

A SLEEPING BEAUTY PALACE . . . Elizabeth Coxhead, *Lady Gregory, A Literary Portrait*, London: Secker & Warburg 1966, 22.

THERE HAS ALWAYS BEEN . . . Lady Gregory, *Seventy Years*, Colin Smythe, ed., Gerrards Cross: Colin Smythe 1974, 25.

THROUGH THE LONG YEARS . . . Ibid., pp. 25–6.

31 COOLE HAS RATS . . . Coxhead, p. 22.

HOUSE ITSELF DISAPPOINTED . . . Ibid., p. 22.

32 TURNING THE PEOPLE . . . *Seventy Years*, p. 16. Elizabeth Coxhead notes that 'It is difficult for a non-Irish and non-Catholic

reader to appreciate the depth of bitterness with which [the] accusation of proselytism is still made in Ireland; to have been an evictor is almost preferable. It has its roots, of course, in the famine years, when a starving peasantry "turned" for a bowl of soup' (Coxhead, p. 3).

COW BARNS, DAIRIES . . . Mary Lou Kohlfeldt, *Lady Gregory, The Woman Behind the Irish Renaissance*, London: André Deutsch 1985, 16.

FIGURES FROM THE EIGHTEENTH CENTURY . . . W. B. Yeats, *Autobiographies*, London: Macmillan 1955, 393.

33   KILLALA . . . The Rising of 1798 was organized in various parts of the country by the United Irishmen. A fleet under the command of General Jean Humbert landed in Killala Bay, Co. Mayo, but, by the time it arrived, the main rising had been crushed. There followed a short campaign in Connacht which culminated in the inevitable French defeat and surrender. Wolfe Tone's brother Matthew, who had accompanied them, was hanged in Dublin. Maud Gonne laid a commemorative plaque at the landing-place at Kilcummin in 1898.

FENIAN BOOKS . . . 'Shopkeepers in market towns all over Ireland were doing a brisk trade in the songs of Young Ireland, which they usually called "Fenian" literature—giving the name of the current resistance movement to the previous one' (Kohlfeldt, p. 24).

THEN OF A SUDDEN ONE MORNING . . . *Seventy Years*, pp. 14–5.

34   STANDISH HAYES O'GRADY . . . O'Grady (1846–1928) published a *History of Ireland: Heroic Period* in 1878. It was not a conventional history book; it included translations of Celtic literature, myths and legend. The work was an inspiration to many Irish writers of the period, and it could be said that the Irish Renaissance dated from the year of its publication. O'Grady later became a journalist, and campaigned vigorously for home rule.

SPENDING HER TIME AS WOMEN . . . Kohlfeldt, p. 35.

35   DREARY CANNES . . . Ibid., p. 36.

A LOCAL REBELLION . . . Egypt was ruled by the Turkish Khedive Ismail, a corrupt despot who, with the connivance of the British and French, had amassed an enormous personal fortune. Colonel Ahmed Arabi, a commander of Egyptian peasant stock, rebelled against the corruption. The British sent a fleet to bombard his forces at Alexandria, and Arabi was taken prisoner. He would have been hanged, had not Wilfrid Scawen Blunt and the Gregorys championed his cause; the sentence was commuted to exile in Ceylon, Sir William's former governorate, where he could be assured of a kind reception. 'The parallel with British treatment of Irish nationalist leaders', observes Elizabeth Coxhead (p. 27), 'was not one that could be lost on an intelligent woman [like Augusta Gregory].'

IT WAS PERHAPS . . . W. B. Yeats, *Autobiographies*, pp. 390–1.

36   THE LANGUAGE OF THE SERVANTS . . . In fact, few of William Gregory's servants were Irish; he liked to recruit them abroad, generously in France and Italy.

A NATIONAL THEATRE . . . Richard Fallis, in *The Irish Renaissance* (Syracuse: Syracuse University Press 1977, pp. 88–9), comments: 'The idea of regular performances of serious Irish plays by Irish playwrights was indeed a new and attractive one, but drama had existed in Ireland for centuries . . . . Dublin's first theater had gone up in 1637, and it was there that the first historical play on an Irish subject, James Shirley's *St. Patrick for Ireland*, had been staged in 1640. In the latter part of the seventeenth century and on through the eighteenth, Dublin had a lively theatrical tradition . . . . After the Act of Union in 1800, Ireland had become increasingly a theatrical backwater. Dublin was an important stopping place for traveling companies from England, and most of the major Irish towns had their occasional theatrical presentations, but what Irish drama there was existed primarily for the English stage.'

It is necessary, though, to see the rebirth of Irish drama in the context of that which was happening elsewhere. In England, for example, the theatre was largely stagnant up until 7 June 1889, when Charles Charrington produced Ibsen's *A Doll's House* in London. This was effectively the beginning of the English dramatic renaissance, the 'new drama'. The movement was, according to Holbrook Jackson, 'so radical in its demands that it had first to create conditions in which it could exist . . . . The new drama already existed on the Continent in the plays of Ibsen, Hauptmann, Maeterlinck, Sudermann, Strindberg and others; and both theatres and audiences were coming into existence in support of it. But here [in England], save for Bernard Shaw and Oscar Wilde, we possessed

no native plays at all comparable with these foreign ones . . . .'
(Holbrook Jackson, *The Eighteen Nineties*, London: Grant Richards
1913, pp. 209–10).

TULLIRA CASTLE . . . There are variant spellings of the name of
Martyn's ancestral home: Tulira (W. B. Yeats); Tillyra (A. Gregory
and G. Moore). This last is probably a poke at the family's Dutch-
seeming variation on the surname Martin.

37   EDWARD MARTYN AND HIS SOUL . . . An idle threat which
Moore never carried out, though he did write a letter to Martyn on
the subject. He said, according to Yeats, that the pamphlet 'was the
best opportunity I ever had. What a sensation it would have made!
Nobody has ever written that way about his most intimate friend'
(Yeats, *Autobiographies*, p. 415).

38   MAGICAL PSEUDONYM AE . . . The first syllable of the word
Æon had a magical significance for Russell. See Henry
Summerfield, *That Myriad-Minded Man: A Biography of George William
Russell "A.E." 1867–1935*, Gerrards Cross: Colin Smythe 1975, pp.
14–5. When writing to the journal *Lucifer* in 1888, Russell used Æon
for the first time. The printer could read only the block capital, so
he split the diphthong for his convenience. Thereafter, Russell
became AE.

A CLOCK . . . In 1900, Synge sent a present of a clock to his hosts,
the MacDonagh family, on Inishmaan. David H. Greene comments
that the timepiece 'must have been a fairly useless but novel
possession on the island'.

A COMFORTABLE GUEST . . . *Seventy Years*, p. 388.

39   ARTICLES ON IRISH FOLKLORE . . . Ann Saddlemyer thinks it
likely that these were 'Yeats's publications on Irish folklore, written
with the help of Lady Gregory and published in the *New Ireland
Review*, which later (November 1898) published Synge's "A Story
from Inishmaan"' (Synge, *Letters I*, p. 48n).

CELTIC AND IRISH PLAYS . . . *Our Irish Theatre*, p. 20. Lady
Gregory explains the unusual nomenclature: 'I think the word
"Celtic" was put in for the sake of Fiona Macleod whose plays
however we never acted, though we used to amuse ourselves by
thinking of the call for "author" that might follow one, and the
possible appearance of William Sharp in place of the beautiful
woman he had given her out to be, for even then we had little
doubt they were one and the same person' (ibid., pp. 20–1). Fiona

Macleod was Sharp's 'spirit love' with whom he had regular spiritualist communication in Yeats's rooms in Woburn Buildings, London.

40   WILLIAM LECKY . . . W. E. H. Lecky (1838–1903), though a Trinity College graduate, was an ardent campaigner for a Catholic university in Dublin. His most famous work is *A History of England in the Eighteenth Century* (1893), of which five volumes are devoted to Ireland.

A POOR AND PRETENTIOUS PIECE . . . Todhunter was the doctor-playwright friend of W. B. Yeats. The play in question, *The Comedy of Sighs*, was howled off the stage.

41   HIS PLAY NEITHER PLEASED . . . George Moore, *Hail and Farewell: Ave, Salve, Vale*, Richard Cave, ed., Gerrards Cross: Colin Smythe 1976, 78.

THE STRIKE AT ARLINGFORD . . . The play was given on 21 February 1893 and published by Walter Scott the same year. It was much admired by William Archer, the celebrated London critic and author of *The Theatrical 'World' of 1893–1897*.

A MUTUAL CONTEMPT . . . As is frequently the case, Yeats's recollections are faulty here. In *Hail and Farewell*, Moore paints a loving portrait of Martyn, and leaves little doubt that his fondness for his relative was reciprocated.

AN ESTATE OF 12,371 ACRES . . . Yeats writes that Moore came, like Augusta Gregory, 'from a house where there was no culture, as [Arthur] Symons and I understood that word . . . .' (W. B. Yeats, *Autobiographies*, pp. 404–5). There was little love lost between Yeats and Moore; they parted company—to all intents and purposes—in 1902.

LAND LEAGUE . . . Michael Davitt (1846–1906) formed the Land League of Mayo in 1878 (and the National Land League a year later). The Leagues combined agitation for home rule and land reform, not always by peaceful means.

A MUMMER'S WIFE . . . The book greatly impressed the young novelist and literary critic Arnold Bennett, and was to influence profoundly his own work. In his review he states that 'Moore has produced a masterpiece . . . beautiful with the terrible beauty which hides itself in the ugliness of life'. W. B. Yeats, in 'Easter 1916', borrowed Bennett's phrase 'terrible beauty', with stunning effect.

PARNELL AND HIS ISLAND . . . Moore published a revised version in 1887 in which he reworked several scenes contained in *A Drama in Muslin.*

IRELAND IS A BOG . . . George Moore, *Parnell and His Island*, London: Swann Sonnenschein 1887, 37.

43   ABOVE THE WALL . . . *CW II*, pp. 230–1.

STILL, THIS CLASS . . . Ibid., p. 231n. The article, as it was published in the *Manchester Guardian* of 1 July 1907, did not include this sentence.

44   BUCK WHALEY . . . Thomas Whaley (1766–1800) was a descendent of Oliver Cromwell. His memoirs include an account of his celebrated visit to Jerusalem in 1788/89, a journey he made on foot to win a wager.

CHARACTER OF IRELAND . . . *Buck Whaley's Memoirs*, Edward Sullivan ed., London: Alexander Moring 1906, xiii.

45   CHURCH OF IRELAND . . . R. F. Foster, *Modern Ireland: 1600–1972*, London: Allen Lane 1988, 156.

46   EMERGENCY MEN . . . Synge's enduring contempt of such men is clear in his poem 'The Mergency Man' (1908), *CW I*, p. 58. Maurice Bourgeois, in *Synge and the Irish Theatre* (p. 24), describes how Synge's eyes 'flashed with anger when the conversation turned upon the brutality of the police in Ireland; . . . he told someone how he had been on the point of letting loose a mad bull or cow that was in a field close to where an eviction was taking place. The only thing that prevented him from doing so was fear lest women and children should be injured. Mingled with his manly indignation against the police there was a boyish delight in the thought of the havoc the wild animal would have wrought if let loose upon them.'

47   CAME FROM WITHIN AND OWED MORE . . . Declan Kiberd, 'The Perils of Nostalgia: A Critique of the Revival', in *Literature and the Changing Ireland*, Peter Connolly, ed., Gerrards Cross: Colin Smythe 1982, 20. Kiberd's thoughtful essay complements Synge's theory contained in 'A Landlord's Garden in County Wicklow'.

AYE . . . Synge sometimes spells it 'ay'.

48   THE ENGINEERS WHO BEGAN . . . Stephens, f. 231.

I HAVE MET AN OLD VAGRANT . . . *CW II*, p. 195.

49   THE HEAVENS THEMSELVES RUN . . . Robert Burton, *The Anatomy of Melancholy*, A New Edition, London: Chatto and Windus 1881, 336–7. This edition enjoyed tremendous popularity in

Synge's time. Robin Skelton also draws our attention to Synge's knowledge of the work of Christopher Marlowe, and the 'Marlovian vigour in *Luasnad, Capa and Laine*' (*J. M. Synge and his World*, London: Thames and Hudson 1971, p. 74). Certainly Marlowe's *Tamburlaine the Great* prefigures Burton and Synge: 'Nature that fram'd us of four elements/ . . . Doth teach us all to have aspyring mindes;/ . . . And measure everie wand'ring planetes course/ . . . And alwaies moving as the restless spheares /Will us to weare ourselves and never reste . . . .'

There is a strong likeness in passages of Synge's verse play. For example: 'The gods have never made us. They have gotten/ Our first grey seed upon the slime of earth/. . . We are one/ With all this moon and sea white and the wind/ That slays us. And our passions move when we die/Among the stars that wander or stand quiet/In the great depths of night' (*CW III*, p. 203).

GOOD HUMOUR . . . *CW II*, p. 202.

THIS PECULIAR CLIMATE . . . Ibid., p. 209.

HAS PRESERVED THE DIGNITY . . . Ibid., p. 196.

LAST COTTAGE AT THE HEAD . . . Synge places Nora Burke in such a cottage in *The Shadow of the Glen* (*CW III*, p. 31).

50   AND MY SOUL WAS SICK . . . 'The Parting', *CW I*, p. 20.

THE YOUNG LADY SAYS 'NO'

51   SCHOOL AT THE AGE OF TEN . . . This was Mr Harrick's Classical and English School, 4 Upper Leeson Street, Dublin.

52   WE HAD A LARGE ESTABLISHMENT . . . *CW II*, p. 6. Synge and Florence liked to breed rabbits. He observed that the offspring of sickly parents were not strong, and concluded that he, being a sickly boy, could never sire healthy children. See p. 73.

ALWAYS PRIMITIVE . . . Ibid., p. 7.

PROBABLY THE HAPPIEST . . . Ibid., p. 7.

FINDING BY EXPERIENCE . . . Stephens, ff. 241–2.

53   QUICK OF GESTURE . . . Ibid., f. 603.

LOW CHURCH . . . The Synges were members of the Church of Ireland, a Church within the Anglican Communion. Anglicans distinguish between the High Church party, which places greatest stress upon symbolic ritual, liturgical elaboration and episcopalian authority, and those of Low Church views, who emphasize evangelicalism, unadorned simplicity in church furnishings and worship and a general distancing of the Church from Roman Catholic forms and practices. The general temper of the Church of Ireland was Low Church.

54 JOHN HAD SET HIS HEART . . . In November 1889, Synge enrolled at the Royal Academy of Music, Dublin, and studied violin, theory and composition for three years. He joined the Academy orchestra in January 1891 and played a concert in March, an experience he cherished; a female violinist seated near him took his fancy.

55 ORGANIZE A CONCERT . . . The piano recital was held on 17 April 1893 in the Antient Concert Room, Dublin (the venue that was to host the first offerings of the Irish National Theatre Society). Synge booked the hall, took charge of the publicity, and arranged for three musicians to accompany Cousin Mary. *The Irish Times* carried an excellent review of the performance.

£40 A YEAR . . . Mrs Synge's income from the Galway estate was £400 per annum. Synge's paternal uncle Edward, who had been a missionary in the Australian bush, had left him £100; Edward's sister Jane, who died a spinster, bequeathed her furniture to John's brother Edward, and £500 to John. Synge's brother-in-law, Harry Stephens, invested the money at 6 per cent interest, and this, together with his allowance from the family estates, produced for Synge £40 a year for the remainder of his life (Stephens, f. 699).

56 SMALL AND FULL OF VIOLENCE . . . Ibid., ff. 593–4. Mary Synge was 53 when John accompanied her to Germany.

57 THE LOVE AFFAIR APART . . . Daniel Corkery, *Synge and Anglo-Irish Literature*, Cork: Cork University Press 1931, 34.

OLIVER GOLDSMITH . . . Corkery compares Synge and Goldsmith: 'Both were emotional rather than intellectual' (p. 35). Few would agree with this evaluation of Synge. Corkery neglects to mention the fact that Goldsmith went to Edinburgh, then to Leiden, to study medicine; only when he became a reviewer for a magazine in London did he begin to take an interest in writing. That said, Corkery's parallel of Synge's and Goldsmith's European experiences is a valid one.

FROM SHERIDAN TO SHAW . . . Ibid., p. 35.

58 HUGH LANE'S MUSEUM ... Hugh Percy Lane (1874–1915) was a nephew of Lady Gregory. He was an avid art collector, and made a fortune in the London art world. It had always been his ambition to found a gallery of modern art in Ireland, in order to house—among his other pieces—his excellent collection of French Impressionists. Lane had plans drawn for the venture, the most noteworthy being an ambitious design for a bridge-gallery across the Liffey. Dublin Corporation refused his offer, so Lane lent his pictures to London's National Gallery instead. He was appointed a director of the National Gallery of Ireland in 1914. Lane drowned the following year when the *Lusitania* was torpedoed off the coast of Cork. He had inserted a codicil in his will, bequeathing his collection to the Irish National Gallery, but this had not been witnessed. Lady Gregory and Yeats fought a legal battle to recover the paintings but, in the end, an arrangement was made whereby Dublin and London would take turns in holding them. Part of the Lane collection went towards the foundation of the Municipal Gallery of Modern Art, which opened on 20 January 1908 in Harcourt Street, Dublin (it was moved later to Parnell Square). Synge published a piece—'Good Pictures in Dublin' (*CW II*, pp. 390–2)—in the *Manchester Guardian* of 24 January 1908, commending the gallery.

THE DAY OF VALESKA ... '*lá Valesca*', MS 4414, TCD, f. 106. Of the women in Synge's life, Valeska von Eicken is the most elusive. Very little of their correspondence is extant, and the handful of letters and fragments that remain give us few clues to her character. They provide even fewer clues to her relationship with John Synge. Was there sexual attraction, or was it simply a case of two intelligent and talented people delighting in each other's company? Probably the second, because Cherrie Matheson remained strongly in John's thoughts throughout his first stay in Germany. Nevertheless, his friendship with Valeska and her sisters provided Synge with an overseas base, a retreat to which he was welcome to return at any time. Ann Saddlemyer, considering the 'freedom, gaiety and decorum' of their correspondence, sees Valeska in the role of a young aunt of Synge's.

BOARDING-HOUSE ... The building was part of an old convent. The sisters took turns in running the boarding-house; at the time of Synge's first visit, four were on the premises.

59 EUROPEAN CO-RELIGIONISTS ... In the late nineteenth
century, the number of Catholics living in Rheinland-Pfalz (the
German province containing Koblenz) exceeded that of
Protestants. The percentages remain unchanged today: Catholics,
c. 7 million; Protestants, *c.* 5 million.

60 COLOGNE MIGHT PROVIDE ... Stephens, f. 631.

61 THEIR ENVIRONMENTS ... Ibid., f. 636. Stephens makes
much of perceived parallels in the lives of Synge and Goethe. He
quotes, in this context, the appraisal of Goethe's friend Heinrich
Merck: 'The line or purpose from which you cannot deviate is to
give poetic form to reality' (ibid., f. 637). Stephens notes also a line
from Goethe's *Autobiography*, which states that 'Every province loves
its dialect, for it is really the element in which the soul breathes'
(*The Autobiography of Johann Wolfgang Goethe, Vol. II*, trans, John
Oxenford, Chicago and London: University of Chicago Press 1974,
p. 224). This statement may have influenced Synge's work more
than any other part of Goethe's writings.
MYSTERY OF THE 'ETERNAL FEMININE' ... H. G. Atkins,
Johann Wolfgang Goethe, London: Methuen 1904, 32.

62 INTELLECTUAL PERPLEXITY ... Stephens, f. 636. Stephens
also notes that Synge had 'peculiar sympathy' with the Goetheian
story of Fredericka Brion, the daughter of a vicar, and that Synge
evidently saw resemblances in her home-life and that of Cherrie
Matheson (ibid., 637–8).
ACT IV ... *CW III*, p. 182.

63 HE STUDIED LANGUAGES ... Ann Saddlemyer, 'Synge and
the Doors of Perception', in *Place, Personality and the Irish Writer*,
Andrew Carpenter, ed., Gerrards Cross: Colin Smythe 1977, 102.
HIS NOTEBOOK ... MS 4372, TCD, f. 3–52. See also below.
NOW, AS LONG AS ... Stephens, f. 642.

64 I HAD A LONG LETTER ... Ibid., f. 633.
LIEBES FRLN VALEWSKA ... Synge, *Letters I*, pp. 14–16. Apart
from drafts such as this one, no letters of Synge to Valeska von
Eicken have survived.

65 VERY FINE LOVELY DAY ... Rev. Samuel Synge, *Letters to my
Daughter*, Dublin and Cork: Talbot Press, 1931, p. 199.
JOHN OCCUPIED HIS TIME ... Stephens, f. 673.
A MOUNTAIN FLOWER .... *CW I*, p. 4.

66 WIND AND STREAM ... *CW II*, p. 20.

67 THESE BOYISH VERSES . . . MS 4372, TCD, f. 1. Synge scribbled this in blue pencil on the cover of a notebook of poems which he wrote in Germany in 1893/94. 'Boyish' is an afterthought. Nevertheless, at least one of his verses, 'To Keats', is not without merit: 'Thou happiest of poets, thou, for whom/ Our sad sweet mother hath soft pity shown,/ And ta'en thee early to her restful tomb,/ Where woe and joy and pain are all unknown./ Thou in thine early death supremely blest,/ Great is thy privilege of perfect rest! // The mastery of life, the long, slow pain;/ The agony of waking, day by day,/ To hear the dripping of the mist and rain,/ To know that sorrow standeth in the way./ All this didst thou escape in youthful years,/ By lot the happiest of all thy peers.'

68 JE VOUS REMERCIE . . . Synge, *Letters I*, p. 20.

69 IT WAS NOT UNTIL 1946 . . . Ian Littlewood, *Paris: A Literary Companion*, London: John Murray 1987, 56.

70 WET WINDS AND RAIN . . . 'In the City Again', *CW I*, p. 16. Synge revised it in 1907, then rewrote it in 1908, with the title, 'Winter', and subtitle 'With little money in a great city' (ibid., p. 63).

    This rewritten version is, if possible, even more Anglo-Saxon in flavour: 'There's snow in every street/ Where I go up and down,/ And there's no woman, man or dog/ That knows me in the town./ I know each shop, and all/ These Jews, and Russian Poles,/ For I go walking night and noon/ To spare my sack of coals.'

71 SHE WAS A DEVOUT PROTESTANT . . . Stephens, f. 711. Alfred Dreyfus (1859–1935) was a captain in the French army in 1894, when charged with selling secret documents to the German government. He was sent into exile on Devil's Island, off the coast of French Guiana. Later he was retried and sentenced to prison for ten years. It transpired that Dreyfus had been the victim of an anti-Semitic conspiracy. Emile Zola led a campaign on his behalf, and Dreyfus was pardoned by the president. In 1916, a higher court declared him innocent; he was restored to the army and later made an officer of the Legion d'Honneur.

72 IT IS VERY AMUSING TO ME . . . C. H. Houghton née Matheson, 'John Synge as I Knew Him', in *The Irish Statesman* II, no. 17, 5 July 1924, p. 534.

VISITING ART EXHIBITIONS . . . Cherrie, by this time, had become an accomplished water-colourist. In later years, she was to exhibit at the Paris Salon. The area in and around Patrick Street was Synge's favourite part of Dublin.

Stephens (f. 181) makes an amusing observation about the cathedral's incumbent dean: 'To avoid their being confused with Catholics, who always bore the names of saints, it was quite usual for Protestants to give their children at baptism the names of ancient pagan heroes. The son of the dean of St Patrick's [Dr West] had been christened Hercules.'

73   I CURSE MY BEARING . . . *CW I*, p. 14.

CHERRIE MARRIED . . . Cherrie's own recollections of the love affair with Synge differ markedly from those of Synge and Stephens. In a memoir written for *The Irish Statesman* (see above), she discloses nothing of a romantic relationship, or of a proposal of marriage. Possibly she felt that mention of such matters might be unseemly for a married woman. She dismisses their love affair thus: 'Shortly after [Synge's first operation] I went to France, and on my return I did not see him so frequently, as in the meantime I had become engaged to be married.'

74   ZDANOWSKA . . . Stephens calls her, variably, Zdowska and Zdanowska. The latter is the more likely spelling.

75   CONVENTIONAL BUT FRIENDLY . . . Stephens, f. 768.
THERE IS NO GOD . . . Ibid., f. 786.
EGREGIO SIGNORE . . . Synge, *Letters I*, p. 36.

78   GREAT GAP . . . Ann Saddlemyer, 'In Search of the Unknown Synge', in *Irish Writers and Society at Large*, Masaru Sekine, ed., Gerrards Cross: Colin Smythe 1985, 194.
WHAT DO WE HAVE ON RECORD . . . Ibid., p. 195.

79   WE ARE DEPENDING . . . Ibid., p. 196.

80   SIR JOHN AND SCHERMA . . . This seems to have been a dramatized version of his love affair with Cherrie Matheson. 'Scherma' was a nickname he coined for her.

FIRST BLOOD

81   THE DRAWING-ROOM AT COOLE PARK . . . See George Bernard Shaw's photograph (plate 16).
OF SLIGHT MERIT . . . *Our Irish Theatre*, p. 76.

82 THE BENDING OF THE BOUGH . . . This was Moore's revision of Edward Martyn's play *The Tale of a Town*, a comic five-act satire about the English method of 'divide and rule' as applied to Irish local politicians. Having read it, Moore told Martyn: 'There is not one act in the five you have sent me which, in my opinion, could interest any possible audience—Irish, English, or Esquimaux.' Alice Milligan (1866–1953) was a poet and playwright. She wrote the dramatic trilogy *Oisín and Pádraic* (1899, 1904). Yeats said about *The Last Feast of the Fianna* that 'if it were acted without scenery it would resemble a possible form of old Irish drama' (W. B. Yeats, *Uncollected Prose, II*, John P. Frayne and Colton Johnson, eds, New York: Columbia University Press 1975, p.202). Edward Martyn's *Maeve* was performed together with Milligan's play. Lady Gregory commented that, though 'we didn't think [*Maeve*] a Nationalist play at all, [it] has turned out to be one, the audience understanding and applauding the allegory' (*Our Irish Theatre*, p. 29).
SMOULDERS DISMALLY . . . Nicolas Grene, *Synge: A Critical Study of the Plays*, London: Macmillan 1975, 4.
EVERY LIFE IS A SYMPHONY . . . TS 4351, TCD, f. 1. Ann Saddlemyer believes this two-act version to be the one read by Yeats and Lady Gregory in September 1901. Synge revised the play some time after 1902. He toyed with the idea of expanding it to three acts, changed his mind and cut it to one; later it again became a two-acter. The text contained in *CW III* (pp. 153–177) is a conflation of two one-act versions; I have quoted from TS 4351 throughout.
IF ART IS THE EXPRESSION . . . Ibid., f. 40. The version contained in *CW III* (p. 177) omits these lines.

83 FROM THE ASCETICISM . . . Mary C. King, *The Drama of J. M. Synge*, London: Fourth Estate 1985, 162.
HAS AS ITS THEME . . . Ibid., p.165. King refers to a relationship contained in the later two-act version. In this instance, the woman, Mary Costello, is still alive; she is also insane, and appears on stage. Nevertheless, this relationship is identical to the one involving the uncle and Aunt Biddy.
ÉTUDE MORBIDE . . . This was written *c.* 1899, and revised *c.* 1907. Synge also made use of passages from *Vita Vecchia* in the two-act version of *When the Moon Has Set*.
CHOUSKA/CELLINIANI . . . The two female principals are probably based on real people. The Chouska may be Maria

Zdanowska. A letter from Rome, from Miss Capps to Synge, hints at a possible model for the Celliniàni; she writes that 'Miss Chiellini never came to table and seldom left her room until she went to Venice the first of July' (Stephens, f. 786). Nothing more is known about this mysterious Signorina Chiellini.

A MORBID THING . . . *The Collected Letters of John Millington Synge II*, Ann Saddlemyer, ed., Oxford: Clarendon Press 1984, 155. This volume contains letters dating from 1 July 1907 to 19 February 1909; Synge's letters to Molly Allgood are found in the two volumes. Synge wrote to Yeats on 4 May 1908, prior to an operation, to say that he was 'a little bothered about my "papers"', and requesting Yeats to get 'someone—say MacKenna who is now in Dublin—to go through them for you and do whatever you and Lady Gregory think desirable'. He did not want 'my good things destroyed, or my bad things printed rashly'. He included *Étude Morbide* among the latter (ibid., 155).

TOO OBVIOUSLY A VEHICLE . . . Skelton, p. 18.

84   GREEN WEDDING DRESS . . . Synge had a fascination with green dresses; he dubbed Margaret Hardon 'La Robe Verte'. The colour of the dress may be an attempt to symbolize the pagan aspect of the wedding ceremony, and related to the Green Man of springtime nature-worship.

IN THE NAME OF THE SUMMER . . . TS 4351, TCD, f. 42. These words conclude the play in all versions.

FAIRY HERO . . . The principal in *Maeve* dreams of a fairy hero of Celtic romance, who finally visits her in her last sleep.

THE OUTRAGE TO A TOMB . . . *CW II*, p. 89. Synge had just witnessed a series of evictions on Inishmaan.

I WISH TO BE EMPHATIC . . . From a Memorandum to Synge's executors, 1909, *CW III*, p. 155n.

85   SYNGE HAD BEEN TOLD . . . Edward Stephens writes: 'Although the operation had been successful the doctors must have known the nature of the disease and that its symptoms might recur. My father, as one of the owners of the Mount Street Nursing Home, may have been aware of their anxiety, but John and the other members of Mrs Synge's family remained in ignorance of his danger' (Stephens, f. 944). It should be said, however, that this comment is not reliable. Stephens appears to be name-dropping: his claim about his father is rather unlikely.

NUMBER OF OINTMENTS . . . Synge was first treated in Paris by a friend whom he had met in 1896: Dr James Cree, a Dubliner, who was connected with the Collège des Irlandais. Cree's prescription only exacerbated the condition. The Synge family physician, Dr Alfred Parsons, administered medications in May 1901, which brought down the swelling.

MY UNCLE IS A BIT . . .TS 4351, TCD, f. 5.

86   MRS BYRNE . . . This character does not appear in later versions.

THUDDING THREE-STRESS . . . Hugh Kenner, *A Colder Eye: The Modern Irish Writers*, New York: Alfred A. Knopf 1983, 139. Kenner cites several instances of Synge's use of a 'pattern—three syncopated measures, then a thudding three-stress termination— we may come to think it omnipresent': examples, 'for a wed I ding I day'; 'in the years I gone I by'; 'of the Judge I ment I Day'; all taken from *The Playboy of the Western World*.

I HAVE HEARD . . . TS 4351, TCD, ff. 33–4.

87   IT IS NATURAL FOR OLD MEN . . . Ibid., f. 25.

YOUR SOUL HAS BEEN . . . Ibid., f. 41.

EVERY LEAF AND FLOWER . . . Ibid., f. 32.

NOT A GOOD PLAY . . . Lady Gregory thought it was 'not good at all', *Our Irish Theatre*, p. 76.

A MIXTURE OF VERSE AND PROSE . . . T. S. Eliot, *On Poetry and Poets*, London: Faber and Faber 1957, 73–4.

88   JOYLESS AND PALLID WORDS . . . From Synge's preface to *The Playboy of the Western World, CW IV*, p. 53.

NO TWO JOURNEYS . . . *CW II*, p. 151.

THE GIRL WHO WAS SPINNING . . . Ibid., p. 158n.

89   A YOUNG MAN WHO HAD DIED . . . Ibid., p. 160.

THIS LAST MOMENT OF GRIEF . . . Ibid., p. 161.

90   QUEER THINGS IN IT . . . Ibid., p. 161.

WE MUST BE SATISFIED . . . I give Declan Kiberd's translation of the words used by Martin McDonagh in a letter to Synge on 1 February 1902. See *Synge and the Irish Language* (Dublin: Gill and Macmillan 1993, pp. 205–7) for his interesting comments on the perils of translation.

A RATTLETRAP . . . *A Colder Eye*, p. 113.

91   COTTAGE KITCHEN . . . *CW III*, p.5.

WHERE IS SHE? . . . Ibid., p. 5.

92   THE WHOLE PIECE . . . Skelton, p. 80.

ARE JESTING . . . *CW III*, p. 198.

SIX FINE MEN . . . Ibid., p. 21.

93   PLAIN STOCKING . . . Ibid., p. 15.

GREAT ROARING . . . Ibid., p. 7.

WIND IS RAISING . . . Ibid., p. 9.

BLACK HAGS . . . Ibid., p. 17.

BLACK NIGHT IS FALLING . . . Ibid., p. 11.

BLACK CLIFFS . . . Ibid., p. 15.

WERE LOST IN . . . Ibid., p. 21.

AFTER SAMHAIN . . . Ibid., p. 25.

A BLACK KNOT . . . Ibid., p. 15.

THE PIG WITH THE BLACK FEET . . . Ibid., p. 9.

GREEN HEAD . . . Ibid., p. 11.

94   TYPOLOGICALLY RELATED . . . King, p. 55.

A CLEAN BURIAL . . . *CW III*, p. 27.

HALF OF A RED SAIL . . . Ibid., p. 21.

WATER DRIPPING . . . Ibid., p. 21.

THEY'RE ALL GONE NOW . . . Ibid., pp. 23, 25.

95   MANTEAU DE . . . Alfred de Vigny (1797–1863), 'Le Mont des Oliviers', in *Alfred de Vigny: Poèmes Choisis*, E. Allison Peers, ed., Manchester: Manchester University Press 1918. In 'Le Mont', de Vigny enquires whether Jesus was not in fact abandoned by God. In 'Le Déluge: mystère', he speaks of God's destroying mankind without discrimination. Although no record exists of Synge's having known the work of this Romanticist, there are parallels. De Vigny's mother reared him in a stern, semi-Jansenistic environment. He was lonely as a boy, reading widely and in solitude. He wrote a number of plays, novels and articles. His themes and symbols are sometimes classical or contemporary, but rely heavily on the Bible, the Old Testament in particular. He looked after his English wife, an invalid, for thirty years, during which he had a love affair with the actress Marie Dorval. Anatole France published a biography of de Vigny in 1868.

96   MARY KINSELLA . . . *CW II*, p. 188.

REAPING IN THE GLEN . . . Ibid., pp. 209–10.

97   INFLUENCE OF A PARTICULAR . . . Ibid., p. 209.

SO FEW GIRLS . . . Ibid., p. 210. 'The Oppression of the Hills' was written between 1898 and 1902, and published in the *Manchester Guardian* of 15 February 1905.

98   WHO WOULD WALK THROUGH . . . *CW III*, p. 47.
NEVER A LAMB . . . Ibid., p. 47.
CITY OF DUBLIN . . . Ibid., p. 47.
YEAR THAT'S GONE . . . Ibid., p. 37.
IN THE SHADOW . . . Synge entitled it firstly *In the Glen*; then *In the Shadow of the Glen*, and finally *The Shadow of the Glen*. See *CW III*, p. 29n.

99   A WONDERFULLY SIMPLE . . . 'An Epic of Ulster' in *The Speaker*, 7 June 1902, cited in *CW II*, p. 367.
THE PEASANT NOTE ALONE . . . *CW II*, pp. 367–8.
A COMPARISON . . . Ibid., p. 361.

100   PECULIAR HOMOGENEOUSNESS . . . This extends to the story told to Synge on Inishmaan (*CW II*, p. 159). It concerned a woman who had been taken by the fairies. She instructed the men to lie in wait until the fairy band pass by on four or five hundred horses on the 'Oidche Shamna' (Hallowe'en; *Samhain*, Yeats's periodical, owed its title to this pagan feast). She would ride a grey horse, behind a young man. If the islanders could 'throw something on her and on the young man' they would be liberated of the fairy spell. This coincides, in all but the finer details, with the English legend of Tam Lynn.
GOLDEN BOUGH . . . Synge also saw, in Aran, a verification of Frazer's observations of primitive societies and nature: 'A savage hardly conceives the distinction commonly drawn by more advanced peoples between the natural and the supernatural. To him the world is to a great extent worked by supernatural agents. That is, by personal beings acting on impulses and motives like his own, liable like him to be moved by appeals to their pity, their hopes and their fears' (James George Frazer, *The Golden Bough*, London: Macmillan 1978, p. 33). Frazer may also have influenced *Luasnad, Capa and Laine*.
ONE EVENING WHEN . . . *CW II*, p. 10.

101   TO BE SITTING ALONE . . . *CW III*, p. 41.

102   HY BRASIL . . . Thomas Johnson Westropp, 'A Study of the Fort of Dun Aengusa in Inishmore, Aran Islands, Galway Bay', cited in Daphne D. C. Pochin Mould, *The Aran Islands*, Newton Abbot: David & Charles 1972, 120–1.

103   DARK GLENMALURE . . . It can hardly have escaped Synge's attention that the name can easily be rendered as Glen *Malheur*,

which is, given the circumstances of *In the Shadow of the Glen*, most appropriate.

LOOKING OUT FROM A DOOR . . . *CW III*, p. 49.

SITTING HERE IN THE WINTER . . . Ibid., p. 49.

104   WAS ALWAYS COLD . . . Ibid., p. 35.

PEGGY CAVANAGH . . . Ibid., p. 51.

BEGGING MONEY . . . Ibid., p. 53.

POWER OF MEN . . . Ibid., p. 49.

105   DEPICTING THE TRAMP . . . Alan Price, *Synge and Anglo-Irish Drama*, London: Methuen 1961, 122.

BLOW WITH THE STICK . . . *CW II*, p. 72. *CW.*

WILL FOLLOW YOU . . . *CW III*, p. 53.

COME ALONG . . . p. 57.

106   WITH THE SUNSHINE . . . Ibid., *CW I*, p. 32.

IT'S A FINE LIFE . . . *CW III*, p. 53.

BULLOCKS AND SHEEP . . . *CW II*, p. 225. 'At a Wicklow Fair' was written between 1902 and 1905, and published on 9 May 1907 in the *Manchester Guardian*.

107   SKILL IN DIPPING . . . Ibid., p. 228.

ONE TIME HE . . . Ibid., p. 228.

THE PRIEST SAID . . . Ibid., p. 228.

THEY WENT OFF THEN . . . Ibid., pp. 228–9.

108   TINKERS . . . Edward Stephens writes (f. 149) that Synge's experience of tinker life dates from his childhood years in Rathgar: 'A stone's throw from the house [in Orwell Park] the road from Dublin dipped and crossed the Dodder bridge. Beyond the bridge a by-road turned up by the unfenced grassy bank of the river, and crossed a level open space where John often went with his nurse or his mother. Tinkers sometimes used it as a camping place, and their horses grazing kept the grass a sward.'

USELESS PARASITES . . . Ibid., f. 1483.

NORA/SARAH . . . *CW IV*, p. 6n.

MAYDAY FOLLY . . . King, p. 87.

CAN'T YOU SPEAK A WORD . . . *CW IV*, p. 7.

109   GETTING AN AGED WOMAN . . . Ibid., p. 37.

KEEP YOU MINDING . . . Ibid., p. 49.

PLAYING CARDS . . . Ibid., p. 13.

THE NIGHT BEFORE LARRY WAS STRETCHED . . . A Dublin ballad written in the late eighteenth century. Synge includes a snatch of it that is very anti-clerical: 'And we asked him what way he'd die,/ And he hanging unrepented,/ "Begob," says Larry, "that's all in my eye,/ By the clergy first invented."' (*CW IV*, p. 17.).

The disrespect for the clergy and love of drink that pervade another of its verses might have appealed to Mary Byrne: 'Then the clergy came in with his book,/ He spoke him so smooth and so civil; Larry tipped him a Kilmainham look [rhyming slang for 'left hook'],/ And pitched his big wig to the devil;/ Then sighing, he threw back his head/ To get a sweet drop of the bottle . . . .

SOME KIND OF HERO . . . Price, p. 132.

110   MARY [*PENSIVELY*] . . . *CW IV*, p. 19. The final version reads: 'MARY [*with compassion*]'.

OLD BITTER MAN . . . Ibid., p. 19. 'Bitter' is deleted from the final version.

IT'D BREAK MY HEART . . . Ibid., p. 19.

111   INISHEER . . . This was Synge's last visit to Aran. He spent three weeks, from 14 October to 8 November 1902, on Inisheer. He had been there the previous year, from 1 until 19 October.

MASTERPIECES . . . *Our Irish Theatre*, p. 76.

THE TINKER'S WEDDING . . . Yeats and Lady Gregory were extremely reluctant to produce the play in Ireland; Synge himself thought it would have created an even greater disturbance than *The Playboy*. It was eventually published by Maunsel, Dublin, on 23 December 1907. Ann Saddlemyer suggests that 'it could well be that Synge's decision to publish *The Tinker's Wedding* was in part at least a result of the furore caused by the first production of *The Playboy* . . . and, as such, was an emphatic reiteration of his flustered reply to the press on that occasion, "I don't care a rap"' (*CW IV*, p. xvi). *The Tinker's Wedding* was never performed during Synge's lifetime; the first production (with an English company) took place in London on 11 November 1909. The first Irish performance was given in the Abbey Theatre during the Synge centenary celebrations in 1971. It played very well.

ON TRIAL

112 SOME CROWDED ROOM . . . W. B. Yeats, 'The Irish Dramatic
Movement', in *The Bounty of Sweden*, Dublin: Cuala Press 1925, 38.
WHEN YOU *READ* A BOOK . . . *The Splendid Years: Recollections of
Maire Nic Shiubhlaigh, as told to Edward Kenny*, Dublin: James Duffy
1955, 43.

113 THE PLOT, STRICTLY SPEAKING . . . Ibid., p. 40.
I DO BE THINKING . . . *CW III*, p. 49.

114 A FEW YEARS AGO . . . *CW II*, p. 239.
BOUCICAULT . . . Dion Boucicault (1822–90) was responsible
for comic plays that reversed the traditional role of the Irishman in
such drama. Far from being portrayed as simpletons, Boucicault's
protagonists were shrewd and patriotic. His plays were much
admired by Bernard Shaw and Sean O'Casey. His best known are
The Colleen Bawn (1860), *Arrah-na-Pogue* (1864) and *The Shaughraun*
(1875). Synge wrote a review of a production of *The Shaughraun* at
the Queen's Theatre, Dublin; see *CW II*, pp. 397–8.

115 SYNGE HAS THE EYE . . . Synge displayed a remarkable aptitude
for photography; his work can compete with that of professionals
of his day. Besides his unerring eye for composition, one of the
features which distinguish his photography was his habit of
shooting against the light, a technique that produced results which
look surprisingly modern. See especially Plate 8.
I CANNOT SAY IT TOO OFTEN . . . MS 4384, TCD, f. 42.
This is the notebook that Synge brought to Aran in 1899. It also
contains a rough draft of a passage in *Riders to the Sea.*
WAS DAN STANDING . . . William G. Fay and Catherine
Carswell, *The Fays of the Abbey Theatre*, London: Rich & Cowan 1935,
138-9.
HIS PUPILS . . . In the first production of *In the Shadow of the Glen*,
on 8 October 1903, Willie Fay played the Tramp; Mary Walker was
Nora Burke; George Roberts played Dan Burke, and P. J. Kelly was
Michael Dara.

116 JOHNNIE TOOK LONG RIDE . . . *Letters to my Daughter*,
p. 247.
MR. SYNGE DID NOT DERIVE . . . *Irish Daily Independent and
Daily Nation*, 8 October 1903, p. 4. Later, the newspaper came to be
known as the *Irish Independent.*

MOTHER TAKES *THE IRISH TIMES* . . . Mrs Synge's paper had long been the *Daily Express*, which invariably took the side of the landlords in questions of property rights. John persuaded her to take *The Irish Times*. 'I took it to please Johnnie,' she wrote to Robert in Argentina, 'but I find it a rebel paper and [it] praises [Daniel] O'Connell, so I gave it up' (Stephens, f. 474).

117   BUT YOU'VE A FINE BIT . . . *CW III*, p. 57.

118   ALL SYNGE'S MOTHER READ . . . Stephens, f. 1606.

119   A FARCICAL LIBEL . . . *Irish Independent*, 9 October 1903, p. 6. EXCESSIVELY DISTASTEFUL . . . *The Irish Times*, 9 October 1903, p. 8. CONVINCING RING . . . *Daily Express*, 9 October 1903, p. 5. NOT AN IRISH PLAY . . . Reply to a letter to the *United Irishman*, 31 October 1903, p. 7. AT THE TIME WHICH SYNGE . . . 'J. M. Synge: The Personal Compulsions and the Political Beliefs', in Robin Skelton, *Celtic Contraries*, Syracuse: Syracuse University Press, 1990, 51.

121   THE IRISH PRESS . . . In constructing Synge's mock-trial, I have drawn on criticism and counter-criticism dating from the first performance of the play in 1903 and the revival on 27 December 1904, as well as some personal observations by Synge's contemporaries. I have conflated the criticisms in the Irish newspapers because those of 1903 did not differ greatly from those of the following year. Most of the quotes are given verbatim; some are paraphrasing. THE DECAMERON . . . *United Irishman*, 17 October 1903, p. 1. SYNGE NEVER BELONGED . . . W. R. Rodgers, in a BBC radio interview in May 1952, cited in *J. M. Synge: Interviews and Recollections*, E. H. Mikhail, ed., London: Macmillan 1977, p. 115. However, Edward Stephens writes (f. 812) that Synge sometimes went to the theatre, and that he saw Sarah Bernhardt in *La Dame au Camelias*. AS WAS THE GENERAL CUSTOM . . . D. J. O'Donoghue, 'John M. Synge: A Personal Appreciation', *Irish Independent*, 26 March 1909, p. 4.

122   I FIRST MET SYNGE . . . John Masefield, 'John M. Synge', in *Contemporary Review*, April 1911, cited in Mikhail, p. 78. SYNGE IS AS UTTERLY . . . *United Irishman*, 17 October 1903, p. 1.

A CHINAMAN . . . Editorial in the *United Irishman*, 7 January 1905, cited in W. B. Yeats, *Memoirs*, p. 211n.

123   NOT LESS NATIONAL . . . W. B. Yeats, 'First Principles', in *Explorations*, London: Macmillan 1962, 157–8.

WE ARE WILLING . . . Arthur Griffith, *United Irishman*, 17 October 1903, p. 1.

I BEG TO SUBMIT . . . From a letter Synge wrote to the *United Irishman* on 1 February 1905, Synge *Letters I*, p. 106. Arthur Griffith did not acknowledge receipt of the letter until W. B. Yeats forced him to do so.

SOME MEN AND WOMEN . . . *United Irishman*, 17 October 1903, p. 1.

HEAVEN FORBID THAT . . . Synge to Stephen MacKenna, 28 January 1904 (Synge, *Letters I*, p. 74).

124   CERTAIN PEOPLE HAVE OBJECTED . . . W. B. Yeats, 'The Dramatic Movement', in *Explorations*, pp. 143–4.

THE OUTCRY AGAINST . . . John B. Yeats in the *United Irishman*, 31 October 1903, p. 7.

125   THE LONG EXPOSURE . . . *The Irish Times*, 26 February 1904, p. 5.

DREADFULLY DOLEFUL . . . Synge, *Letters I*, p. 62.

CHEAP TRICK . . . Arthur Griffith, *United Irishman*, 5 March 1904, p. 1.

WEST BRITON . . . See p. 181.

A NASTY ATTACK . . . Letter to Lady Gregory, 16 December 1903 (Synge, *Letters I*, p. 70).

127   RHYMERS CLUB . . . The club was formed in 1891, and met in an upper room of the Cheshire Cheese public house, near Fleet Street, London. Yeats helped form the club, together with the Welsh poet Ernest Rhys, and the Irishman T. W. Rolleston, who, like Yeats, was a member of the Irish Republican Brotherhood.

SYNGE'S TALK WAS BEST . . . John Masefield, 'John M. Synge', in the *Contemporary Review*, April 1911, cited in Mikhail, pp. 81–2.

MEN USUALLY TALK THEIR BEST . . . Ibid., p. 79. Masefield's view that Synge 'was only gay when he was talking to women' is conjectural. Cf. pp. 224–5.

128   IN HUYSMANS . . . *CW II*, p. 395.

WILLIAM ARCHER AND MAX BEERBOHM . . . William Archer (1856–1924) was a great admirer and translator of Henrik Ibsen.

His books on the theatre include *About the Theatre* (1886) and *Masks or Faces?* (1888). Holbrook Jackson calls him 'the father of modern dramatic criticism' in Britain (*The Eighteen Nineties*, p. 207). Henry Maximilian Beerbohm (1872–1956) succeeded George Bernard Shaw as dramatic critic of *The Saturday Review*. He was also a brilliant caricaturist; one of his wittiest drawings is of 'Mr. W. B. Yeats presenting Mr. George Moore to the Queen of the Fairies', reproduced in his book, *The Poet's Corner* (1904).

ASKING HER IF . . . *Our Irish Theatre*, p. 31.

129 THE PIT WENT AWAY . . . Ibid., p. 32.

A VERY ODD THING . . . Max Beerbohm, *Saturday Review*, 9 April 1904, cited in Stephens, f. 1709.

SINGULARLY BEAUTIFUL . . . *Westminster Gazette*, 28 March 1904, cited in Stephens, f. 1704.

LOCAL ORACLES . . . Frank Fay to Synge, cited in Stephens, f. 1702.

130 PROBABLY TRYING . . . George Moore, *Hail and Farewell*, p. 688n.

WE WENT ALONG . . . Ibid., p. 118.

131 THE LATTER ENGAGES . . . The lease could not be drawn up in Horniman's name because she was not an Irish citizen. The terms of the lease prohibited Lady Gregory from the 'exhibition of wild beasts or dangerous performances or to allow women or children to be hung from the flies or fixed in positions from which they cannot release themselves' (*Our Irish Theatre*, p. 35).

I SPENT LAST WINTER . . . Synge, *Letters I*, p. 87.

132 I HAVEN'T SEEN THE SPRING . . . Ibid., pp. 87-8.

CASTING MY HOROSCOPE . . . Despite Synge's understandable scepticism about such matters, Horniman's horoscope makes fascinating reading. She would, of course, have known a great many things about Synge already. 'Your mental capacities cannot help being good . . . and you should be able to learn languages pretty easily. There is also a certain vigour about your mind which may make you enjoy a healthy pugnacity . . . . Serious & perhaps gloomy ideas attract you & tragic stories please you & you will write them best . . . . You are not liable to insanity because . . . your mind is well-balanced. Strange unexpected events will turn up in your love affairs & spoil them . . . . Being of a very affectionate disposition . . . this is not fortunate. I think that you are very unlikely to marry . . . & if you did she would be eccentric & not a good match, . . . nor a good temper . . . . In regard to popularity it is very obvious that the Church cannot possibly support you, . . . nor would the ordinary people appreciate you; yet a certain amount of success is certain . . . . But your imaginative faculty is of a disturbing nature to other people . . . as well as to yourself. Your sense of beauty . . . is strong and well-balanced, yet you can appreciate the bizarre . . . as well as that which is gentle & mysterious . . . . Your imagination is drawn towards changing vague images . . . which are full of rich beauty, and they are perhaps sombre too . . . . Comparing your planets with those in Mr Yeats nativity I find it clear that his influence has been excellent for both of you . . . and you will add to the prosperity of his theatrical schemes. (Synge, *Letters I*, pp. 89–90n.)

MADAME ESPOSITO . . . Nathalie Pétrovna Klebnikoff was married to the composer Michel Esposito, who later wrote a score to Synge's *Deirdre of the Sorrows*. She supported the Irish Literary Theatre from its early days, sometimes helping to make costumes and taking an occasional part. She translated *Riders to the Sea* into French and Russian. Neither translation was ever published. Louis Pennequin of Douai published a French translation of *Riders to the Sea* in 1913, entitled *La Chevauchée à la Mer*, though it was never performed. In 1938, Maurice Bourgeois staged his own version, *À Cheval vers la Mer*; it was published in 1942, together with translations of Synge's other plays, with the exception of *Deirdre*.

RETAINING WALL . . . Stephens, f. 4 and *passim*.

133   WHERE AFTER A STORMY . . . *CW II*, p. 193.

COLLABORATED WITH YEATS . . . In plays such as *Diarmuid and Grania*, *Where there is Nothing*, and even *Kathleen ni Houlihan*, it is impossible to say whether certain sections of dialogue were written by Yeats or by Lady Gregory.

WITCHES' CAULDRON . . . W. B. Yeats, *Letters*, p. 436.

134   HUMAN SKELETON . . . W. B. Yeats, *Letters*, p. 438.

135   IN MAYO . . . MS 4395, TCD, f. 46.

FOOL OF FARNHAM . . . Ibid., f. 1.

AT AN EPIDEMIC . . . Synge, *Letters I*, p. 94.

OTHER GIRLS AND MEN

136   EXPENSIVE BUSINESS . . . Edward Martyn financed the first
productions of the Irish National Theatre Society.

SARA ALLGOOD . . . She was an ex-pupil of Frank Fay, who gave
elocution lessons before he began work with Synge and colleagues.
Sara Allgood joined the Irish National Theatre company in 1903.
She left Ireland in 1913, and returned in 1923, when she played in
O'Casey's *Juno and the Paycock.*

WORKING-CLASS BACKGROUND . . . Molly's father, George
Allgood, was an Ulster Orangeman who, like Synge's maternal
grandfather, had an antipathy towards Roman Catholicism. He was
a printing compositor—hence artisan class—and insisted that his
children be brought up as Protestants. He died in 1894, leaving his
widow, Margaret, to bring up eight children in reduced
circumstances in Mary Street, Dublin. Like Mrs Synge, Margaret
Allgood accomplished this with the help of her mother (her maiden
name was O'Neill, which Molly adopted as a stage-name), and
instilled in her offspring the beliefs and mores of Catholicism. On
her father's death, Molly had been placed in a Protestant
orphanage; she ran away after eight months. In 1899, she had
herself apprenticed to Annie Duggan, a dressmaker in Capel Street;
she joined the staff of Switzers in 1903. Molly married G. H. Mair in
1911, and gave birth to a son, John, and a daughter, Pegeen, so
named in tribute to her erstwhile lover and her first great acting
role.

SHE WAS SLIGHT IN BUILD . . . Greene and Stephens, p. 200.

137   HE WAS WEARING A WIDE-BRIMMED HAT . . . Stephens,
f. 1994–5.

138   HE SAT SILENT . . . Oliver St John Gogarty, *As I Was Going Down
Sackville Street: A Phantasy in Fact,* London: Rich & Cowan 1937, pp.
283–4.

139   COMES ON TO THE PEOPLE . . . *CW III,* p. 93.

MRS STEWART'S HOUSE . . . Synge took lodgings at 15 Maxwell
Road, Rathgar, on 10 October 1904 until 15 February 1905, when
he moved back to his mother's in Crosthwaite Park; she had been
ill for some time. On 6 February 1906, he moved to 57 Rathgar
Road.

THERE ARE CERTAIN RULES . . . *The Fays of the Abbey Theatre*, pp. 167–8.

140 A MONOCHROME PAINTING . . . Ibid., p. 168.

AND SHE AFTER GOING BY . . . *CW III*, p. 106n. Synge later amended this to 'And she after going by with her head turned the way you'd see a sainted lady going where there'd be drunken people in the side ditch singing to themselves'. (*CW III*, p. 107). We do not know if Willie Fay's arguments convinced him that it was safer to do so, but it seems likely. A letter of Synge's to Fay (1 July 1904), includes this defence: 'What put the simile into my head was a scene I saw not long ago in Galway where I saw a young man behaving most indecently to a girl on the roadside, while two priests sat near by on a seat looking out to sea and not pretending [*sic*] to see what was going on' (Synge, *Letters I*, p. 90).

TELL MISS GARVEY . . . Synge, *Letters I*, p. 91.

MORALITÉ DE L'AVEUGLE . . . This work was part of Synge's reading at the Sorbonne. Maurice Bourgeois (pp. 185–90) explores other possible sources of the plot. These include Clémenceau's *Le Voile du Bonheur*, Chaucer's *The Merchant's Tale*, Maeterlinck's *Pelléas and Mélisande* and *The Sightless*; Zola's and Huysmans' books on Lourdes. 'But who', Bourgeois asks, 'will fail to perceive the inanity of suchlike genealogical investigations? We have no coercive proof that Synge wrote his play under the influence of the above-mentioned works, and the literary pedigree of *The Well of the Saints* could easily be lengthened without certainty or profit.'

141 THE EMOTIONS WHICH PASS THROUGH US . . . *CW II*, p. 3.

142 HAD RECEIVED A STRANGE ASSURANCE . . . Stephens, f. 1239.

'BLIND' AND 'DARK' ARE INTERCHANGEABLE . . . P. W. Joyce, in *English as we speak it in Ireland*, (Dublin: Wolfhound Press, 1991, p. 246), glosses 'dark' as: 'a dark man'. . . . Used constantly even in official and legal documents, as in workhouse books, especially in Munster [in 1910, when the book was first published]'.

143 KNOW SURELY WE WERE THE FINEST . . . *CW III*, p. 73.

MARRIED WITH A WOMAN . . . Ibid., p. 87.

MARTIN DOUL (FIERCELY) . . . Ibid., p. 141.

THEY'RE A BAD LOT . . . Ibid., p. 73.

144　FUNDAMENTALLY SHE IS A MORAL WRITER . . . Coxhead, p. 118.

MR. SYNGE HAS IN COMMON . . . *CW III*, pp. 66–7.

KILTARTAN . . . Kiltartan is a village adjoining the Coole estate. Lady Gregory devoted much of her time to listening to the speech of the villagers and their neighbours. She called the style of dialect that she thus acquired 'Kiltartan'. Ezra Pound was to comment that, for him, the Irish Literary Renaissance had three hues: dove grey, shamrock and Kiltartan.

145　HAPPY 'TIS . . . Douglas Hyde, 'Happy 'tis, Thou Blind, for Thee', in *Love Songs of Connacht*, London, Fisher Unwin 1893, 131.

IRELAND'S LITERARY CRITICS . . . Nicholas Grene (p. 113) draws our attention to some grim humour in Act I, when Mary Doul tells her husband that a thief is due to be hanged, and regrets their missing the spectacle, 'and we not seeing at all'. 'Strange', Grene comments, 'that the audiences who resented the implications of national infamy in *The Shadow* and *The Playboy* should not have seen this passage as a caricature of Ireland as a land of ghouls and drunkards.'

UNE OEUVRE SUBTILE . . . Henri Lebeau in *Dana*, April 1905, cited in Synge, *Letters I*, p. 101.

146　MAX MEYERFELD . . . Meyerfeld (1875–1952) began in May 1905 what was to become a fruitful correspondence with Synge. He was a theatre critic, as well as being the translator of Oscar Wilde and George Moore. Henri Lebeau's excellent review of *The Well of the Saints* sparked off Meyerfeld's interest in Synge. The play was performed in Berlin's Deutsches Theater on 12 January 1906, under the title *Der Heilige Brunnen*, The Holy Well. Synge took great pains to supply Meyerfeld with an extended glossary of the Hiberno-English words that his plays employed.

LAND PURCHASE ACT . . . This Act preceded the Wyndham Land Act of 1903, whereby George Wyndham, the Chief Secretary for Ireland (see also p. 118), introduced the legislation which finally resolved the vexed question of Irish land ownership. It did this by putting in place a scheme which transferred ownership of over 7 million acres of land from landlords to tenants. Landlords were offered a bonus on the sale price as an inducement to sell. Tenants were enabled to purchase by the advance of government funds repayable over 68.2 years at an interest rate of 34 per cent.

147   HEAP THE SAND . . . Jack B. Yeats, 'With Synge in Connemara', in W. B. Yeats, *Synge And The Ireland Of His Time*, p. 39.

         WILLIE'S SKETCHES . . . See the reproductions on p. 13 of A. Norman Jeffares, *W. B. Yeats: A New Biography*, London and Boston: Hutchinson 1988.

         HE FOLLOWED HIS OWN . . . Hilary Pyle, *Jack B. Yeats*, London and Boston: Routledge & Kegan Paul 1970, 35.

148   THE PROBLEM HAD BEEN . . . Ibid., p. 43.

149   HAVING WORKED . . . Ibid., p. 43.

         A MARRIAGE MADE . . . Stephens, f. 1900.

         NOTHING FOR COMFORT . . . 'With Synge in Connemara', p. 42.

150   SYNGE'S ARTICLES . . . Synge complained to Stephen MacKenna that Jack Yeats received more than he did for his work on the twelve articles. J. B. Yeats knew the publishers, and had already agreed a good price for himself. Jack, wrote Synge, 'being a wiser man than I, made a better bargain, and though I had much the heavier job the dirty skunks paid him more than they paid me, and that's a thorn in my dignity! I got £25.4.0 which is more than I've ever had yet and still I'm swearing and damning' (Synge, *Letters I*, p. 116).

         NOT HIS BEST WORK . . . Alan Price notes (*CW II*, p. 283n) that W. B. Yeats thought Synge's articles of inferior quality. After Synge's death, a note was found among his papers, indicating that he had intended publishing them in book form. They appeared in Volume Four of the *Works* in 1910, prompting Yeats to withdraw the introduction he had written.

         OLD BEGGARWOMAN . . . *CW II*, p. 287.

         THE HORSE-BREEDER . . . Ibid., p. 300.

         DRESSED LIKE THE PEOPLE . . . Ibid., p. 287.

151   THERE ARE SIDES . . . Synge, *Letters I*, p. 116.

         UNGODLY RUCK . . . Ibid., p. 330.

152   KING OF THE BLASKETS . . . Whether in jest or in earnest, Synge, when writing to Lady Gregory from Great Blasket on 20 August 1905, gave his address as 'c/o The King, Shawn Keane [Seán Ó Catháin, son of Pádraig], The Great Blasket Island, Dunquin, Dingle, Co. Kerry' (Synge, *Letters I*, p. 122).

         THE YOUNG PEOPLE . . . *CW II*, p. 250.

         A SMALL, BEAUTIFULLY-FORMED . . . Ibid., p. 247.

153   YOU'VE PLUCKED A CURLEW . . . *CW I*, p. 35.

FIGHTING AND KICKING IN . . . *CW II*, p. 251.

THERE WAS GREAT SPORT . . . Ibid., p. 275.

154 ISLAND WITH POPULATION . . . MS 4403 TCD, f. 63. Synge made some notes on the geography of Great Blasket, evidently intending to set *The Playboy* there.

155 MARY WALKER . . . . After the secession of 1905, she returned occasionally to the Abbey Theatre to play certain roles. In her autobiography, Walker writes that 'although most of us who took the course of secession, the action meant the finish of any progress we might have been making individually towards international distinction as Irish players—in my own case it virtually meant the end of a career on the stage which might or might not have taken me away from Dublin altogether in the years that followed—I doubt if many of us had any regrets at the time' (*The Splendid Years*, pp. 72–3).

GEORGE MOORE . . . Moore quarrelled continually with Yeats, Lady Gregory and the Fays. Yeats thought that this stemmed from jealously, and Moore's ambition to direct plays. The last straw was when Moore published a damning article in the September 1904 issue of *Dana*, under the pseudonym 'Paul Ruttledge'.

156 LOST MANY HELPERS . . . Cited in *Our Irish Theatre*, p. 38.

GEORGE RUSSELL . . . AE had resigned his vice-presidency in 1904, but continued to help manage the Abbey's affairs.

FRED J. RYAN . . . Frederick J. Ryan (1876–1913) became secretary to the Irish National Theatre Society in 1903, then treasurer, when the society moved to Abbey. He was the co-founder of *Dana*; he also wrote a play, *The Laying of the Foundations*, which the Irish National Dramatic Society produced in 1902.

157 SISTER CATHLEEN . . . The part had been played by Sara Allgood at the first production of *Riders* on 25 February 1904.

MY NECK . . . Synge, *Letters I*, p. 138.

ROMAN CATHOLICISM . . . Molly's mother, following the death of her husband, reverted to Catholicism. One of her youngest sons, Tom, became a Trappist (Normandic Cistercian) monk.

158 MOLLY'S INTERPRETATION . . . Joseph Holloway notes in his diary, 27 January 1906, that 'her Cathleen was ever and always attuned to the scene—the pathetic stops in the voice, and subdued demeanour of resigned sadness were present in her interpretation'.

HER RICH VOICE . . . Stephens, f. 2018.

IS IT GO AWAY . . . *CW III*, p. 45.

159 MOLLY UNCHAPERONED . . . Molly's grandmother insisted on accompanying her and her sister Sara to all rehearsals.

YOU SHALL MARRY AN OFFICER . . . *Standard Edition of the Works of Bernard Shaw*, London: Constable 1930–1950, p. 224.

TRY HER HAND AT PLAYWRITING . . . Synge's letter to Molly of 21 October 1906 is revealing about his opinion of Lady Gregory's plays, and his own method of conception: 'I've a new idea. Do you think you could write a little comedy to play in yourself; say about your life in the convent school? I could give you a scenario, would not it be fun, and then you'd be able to patronise Miss [Florence] Darragh, and Mrs Bill Fay and the lot of them. I'm sure you've as much humour as Lady Gregory, and humour is the only thing her little farces have. Or could you write a comedy about the women at Kilmacanogue . . . or about some incident of your early career? The one thing needful is to get hold of some little centre of life that you know thoroughly, and that is not quite familiar to every one. I'm sure your old grandmother would be a lovely character in a play. Think about it, little heart, and, when you're acting, notice how the scenes etc. are worked out, one into the other. This is all a wild idea, but it would be fun to try; no one would know but ourselves and of course I'd help and advise you. You could write out your MSS on the typewriter, so all is complete!' (Synge, *Letters I*, 221).

I HEARD ACCIDENTALLY . . . Ibid., p. 176.

IT IS CURIOUS . . . MS 4404, TCD, f. 58. Cf. W. B. Yeats: 'When he had left the Blaskets for the last time, he travelled with a lame pensioner who had drifted there, why heaven knows, and one morning having missed him from the inn where they were staying, he believed he had gone back to the island and searched everywhere and questioned everybody, till he understood of a sudden that he was jealous as though the island were a woman.' ('With Synge in Connemara', in *Synge And The Ireland Of His Time*, p. 21).

160 SYNGE HAD EVERY REASON . . . Greene and Stephens, p. 198.

161 I GET A SORT . . . Synge, *Letters I*, 198.

SORT OF ASTHMA . . . Ibid., p. 199.

GOOD DEAL BETTER . . . Ibid., p. 200.

VERY UNWELL . . . Ibid., p. 203.

MUCH BETTER AGAIN . . . Ibid., p. 205.
NOT BE WELL ENOUGH . . . Ibid., p. 207.
NOT AT ALL WELL . . . Ibid., p. 220.
I WASN'T WELL . . . Ibid., p. 221.
I'VE HAD A BAD TURN . . . Ibid., p. 235.
I AM VERY UNWELL . . . Ibid., p. 236.
IF I AM WELL . . . Ibid., p. 238.
THE DOCTOR SAYS . . . Ibid., p. 240.
I AM GOING ON WELL . . . Ibid., p. 242.

162   RATHER A WORSE ATTACK . . . Ibid., p. 242.
I AM NOT WELL . . . Ibid., p. 244–5.
KICK THE BUCKET . . . Ibid., p. 251.
I HAVE GOT A SORT . . . Ibid., p. 251.
THE ASTHMA HAS . . . Ibid., p. 254.
I LOOK SO THIN . . . Ibid., p. 255.
THAT ACCURSED PLAYBOY . . . Ibid., p. 236.

A SHADOW UPON HER MIRROR

163   CHARGES THEM ADMISSION . . . The Monday night debate
made a profit of £16 for the Abbey Theatre—a not inconsiderable
sum, when one considers that the cheapest seat available for a
performance cost one shilling (there were twenty shillings to the
pound). It was the only night on which the theatre was sold out.
THE FULL STORY . . . James Kilroy in *The 'Playboy' Riots* (Dublin:
Dolmen Press 1971) has amassed a comprehensive collection of
material relating to the events surrounding the riots; it includes
newspaper reviews, letters to the papers, interviews and private
correspondence.
SOME FOUR YEARS ON . . . See *Our Irish Theatre*, Appendix IV,
pp. 222–36. Eleven of the Irish Players (the name adopted by the
touring company) were arrested in Philadelphia on grounds of
sacrilege and obscenity; Lady Gregory received an anonymous
death threat in Chicago.

164   THIS UNMITIGATED . . . *Freeman's Journal*, 28 January 1907,
p. 10.
WE SHALL REGRET . . . *Sinn Féin*, 2 February 1907. A libel
action forced the closure of the *United Irishman* in 1906. *Sinn Féin*

(Gaelic: 'we ourselves') was its successor, and the mouthpiece of the Sinn Féin movement, whose first chairman was Edward Martyn. The movement pursued a policy of self-reliance for Ireland. It played no part in the Easter Rising of 1916 but was mistakenly accused by the British authorities of doing so. Accordingly, the separatist and republican political movement that developed after 1916 took the Sinn Féin name and swept the boards in nationalist Ireland at the general election of 1918, and Éamon de Valera (1882–1975) became prime-minister, with Arthur Griffith as minister for home affairs. By 1921, Sinn Féin had negotiated the Anglo-Irish treaty which established the new Irish state.

TRANSLATING SYNGE . . . 'Synge in Germany', in *Sunshine and the Moon's Delight: A Centenary Tribute to John Millington Synge*, S. B. Bushrui, ed., Gerrards Cross: Colin Smythe 1972, 273–4. Still more unfortunate is Maurice Bourgeois's French translation: *Le Baladin du Monde Occidental*. Gerard Leblanc comments (ibid., 'Synge in France', p. 266) that 'some Irish readers resented [the title] for its suggestion of Christy as a third-rate mountebank'.

166   OH MY GRIEF . . . *CW IV*, p. 173. Synge's eleventh and final draft of the play (draft K) ends differently. Pegeen 'makes a rush out of the door upsetting two chairs', and the CROWD exclaim '[*loudly all together*]. 'Well now' (ibid., p. 175). Synge perceived, in the course of rehearsals, that this ending was dramaturgically less satisfactory than bringing the curtain down on Pegeen's lament.

THE TYPESCRIPT HAS GONE . . . John Quinn (1870–1924) was a New York lawyer and patron of the arts, and a friend of Lady Gregory. He financed American copyright editions of many plays by Synge, Yeats and Lady Gregory. When Quinn offered to buy the manuscript of *The Playboy*, Synge wrote and explained his method of working: 'I work always with a typewriter—typing myself—so I suppose it has no value? I make a rough draft first and then work over it with a pen till it is nearly unreadable; then I make a clean draft again, adding whatever seems wanting, and so on. My final drafts—I letter them as I go along—were 'G' for the first act, 'I' for the second, and 'K' for the third! I really wrote parts of the last act more than eleven times, as I often took out individual scenes and worked at them separately. The MS., as it now stands, is a good deal written over, and some of it is in slips or strips only, cut from the

earlier versions—so I do not know whether it has any interest for
the collector' (*CW IV*, pp. xxxii–xxxiii).

AS IN MY OTHER PLAYS . . . Ibid., p. 53.

167   THAT THE LORD GOD . . . Ibid., p. 125.

SORDID, SQUALID AND REPULSIVE . . . *Freeman's Journal,*
29 January 1907, p. 7.

THIS IS MY PROTEST . . . William Boyle in a letter to the
Freeman's Journal, 1 February 1907, p. 12. Commenting on the
defection, Yeats told the paper that one of Boyle's own plays,
The Building Fund, had been called 'a libel on Irish character'.

168   NOT IN THE LEAST REGRET . . . Stephen Gwynn in a letter to
the *Freeman's Journal,* 2 February 1907, p. 14. Stephen Lucius
Gwynn (1864–1950) was a novelist and travel writer. He was a
director of Maunsel and Company, and was MP for Galway city from
1906 to 1919.

WILLIAM CARLETON . . . John B. Yeats chose an unlikely writer
for his comparison. In the first place, William Carleton
(1794–1869) was a writer of fiction, not a playwright. Though few
of his stories, comments Maureen Waters, 'are unrelieved by
comedy', no writer of his time 'equalled Carleton's ability to convey
the cruel realities of Irish life.' She notes that, in *Wildgoose Lodge,*
'he probably produced the most horrifying tale to come out of
nineteenth-century Ireland' (*The Comic Irishman,* Albany: State
University of New York Press 1984, p. 59).

ANDY ROONEY . . . The eponymous hero of Samuel Lover's 1837
novel *Handy Andy* was the bumptious, rustic clown who, more than
any other, spawned the home-grown Stage-Irishman.

SHE NEVER WITNESSED . . . 'Memories of Yeats' in the
Saturday Review of Literature, 25 February 1939. Cited in Greene and
Stephens, p. 248.

ALL GREAT LITERATURE . . . From an interview with W. B.
Yeats in the *Freeman's Journal,* 30 January 1907, p. 8.

169   NO ONE IS BETTER QUALIFIED . . . *Freeman's Journal,* 26
January 1907, p. 10.

A PLAY WITH A PURPOSE . . . Letter to *The Irish Times,* 31 January
1907, p. 5. Patrick D. Kenny, writing under the byline 'Pat' had
made some interesting comments, i.e. 'In a way there are two plays,
one within another, and unless the inner one is seen, I am not

surprised at the screaming about the outer one, which in itself is repellant, and must so remain until seen in the light of the conception out of which it arises, as when we welcome a profane quotation in a sermon, recognising a higher purpose that it is employed to emphasise' (*The Irish Times*, 30 January 1907, p. 9).

170   HE OFTEN TELLS ME . . . *CW II*, p. 95.

HIS FATHER DRANK HEAVILY . . . Seán Ó Súilleabháin, 'Synge's Use of Irish Folklore' in *J. M. Synge Centenary Papers 1971*, Maurice Harmon, ed., Dublin: Dolmen Press 1972, 21–2. Apropos the Aran story, Synge stated in an interview that he 'knew a young fellow in the Aran Islands who had killed his father'. A curious statement; but poor reporting on the part of the interviewer cannot be ruled out.

171   THE NEW HOTEL . . . Cited in James Carney, *The Playboy and the Yellow Lady*, Swords: Poolbeg Press 1986, 45–6.

173   THE ACHILL PEASANT . . . Ibid., p. 1.

MAYBE HE'S STOLEN OFF . . . *CW IV*, p. 97. Notebook 34 contains a number of alternative lines, intended to 'strengthen girls' scene. Of interest here is: 'I yoked the ass-cart and drove to Keel to see the lad slit the lady's nose in Achill. He was a great devil.' (MS 4397, TCD, f. 31). Furthermore, an early draft of the play (then entitled *Murder Will Out*) makes reference, by name, to James Lynchehaun:

> 3RD MAN. If they found it itself I'm thinking, they'd be afeard to come after him. Sure they never touched Lynchehaun when they knew the kind he was. It's only a common, week-day kind of a murderer them lads would lay their hands to at all.
> (*CW IV*, p. 311)

174   THE NORTHERN SHORE . . . Carney, p. 208.

175   THE CHOUSKA . . . Synge wrote *Étude Morbide* in or about 1899. Maria Zdanowska, whom he had met in Florence in 1895, also has the -ska ending in her surname.

WHAT SYNGE HAS CONCRETELY . . . Stanley Sultan, 'A Joycean Look at The Playboy of the Western World', in *The Celtic Master: Contributions to the First James Joyce Symposium*, Maurice Harmon, ed., Dublin: Dolmen Press 1969, 51-2.

176   ONCE THE NOTION . . . Skelton, p. 119.

WOULD NOT BE WISE . . . Kiberd, p. 120.

CUCHULAIN IN EARLY YOUTH . . . Ibid., p. 116.

IT'S PEGEEN I'M SEEKING . . . *CW IV*, p. 167.

178 BORE HIM THREE CHILDREN ... Captain O'Shea claimed that the three children were his.

THE YOUNG GRADUALLY ... Herbert Howarth, *The Irish Writers, 1880–1940: Literature Under Parnell's Star*, London: Rockliff 1958, 5–6. Writing of Synge (p. 212), Howarth makes the intriguing observation that he was an 'amoralist'.

179 THE WHOLE SPIRIT ... *CW II*, p. 124. The passage concludes Part II, written in 1899.

COUNTY COUNCILLOR ... . MS 4395, TCD, f. 2. Synge's first rough scenario for *The Playboy* is contained in this notebook dating from 1904. Christy is surnamed O'Flaherty. There is reason to suppose that he intended setting the play in Aran, since in 1893 a list of surnames of Aran indicates that the name (O')Flaherty was the most common: 80 occurrences in a total of 458 individuals (Haddon and Browne, 'Ethnography of the Aran Islands, 1893, cited in *An Aran Reader*, p. 53). Synge eventually chose for Christy the surname Mahon, but gave the name Flaherty to Pegeen Mike and her father.

180 SONS AND DAUGHTERS WALKING ... *CW IV*, p. 85.

A MAN NEVER GAVE PEACE ... Ibid., p. 85.

WIDOW QUEEN ... Synge may have had a lifetime's fascination with the words 'queen' and 'quin'; Samuel Synge recalls how he and John played with toys as very young children, and he speaks of 'a pretty little china figure, about two inches high, that ... John called Queeny-Quiny' (*Letters to my Daughter*, p. 11).

DARK ROSALEEN ... One of the traditional allegorical names given to Ireland by poets. Kathleen ni Houlihan is a similar personification.

GO OFF TILL YOU'D FIND ... *CW IV*, p. 155.

181 WEST BRITON ... The term was also applied to a member of the Anglo-Irish communty, perhaps with more pertinence.

IN THE MEANTIME CHRISTY ... Augustine Martin in 'Christy Mahon and the Apotheosis of Loneliness', in *Sunshine and the Moon's Delight*, p. 65.

182 MIXING YOURSELF UP ... Synge struck this out of draft 'G' (*CW IV*, p. 60n).

183 A RAMPANT ... Synge to MacKenna, Synge, *Letters I*, p. 117.

LET YOU WAIT TO HEAR ... *CW IV*, p. 149.

184 SO PERFECTLY HAPPY ... Synge, *Letters I*, p. 359.

PEGEEN DIFFERS . . . Skelton, p. 128.

TOPSY-TURVY MIRROR-IMAGE . . . A comment of Yeats is useful here: 'The fact that he [Synge] reflects the world in a strange mirror—not strange to him, perhaps—makes us also see them for a moment as if we were Adam. He has therefore his double effect; his sincerity that makes us share his feeling, his strangeness that makes us share his vision. He shows us a picture, as a painter might, reversed in a looking-glass, that we may see it as it is. But this strangeness wears off and leaves only his sincerity. Strangeness is, however, more often than not the cause of the first successes of writers as well as the cause of their first failures. Every writer has, however, his mirror, which is the creation of his sincerity. He is different' (Yeats, *Memoirs*, p. 250).

ALSO JOHN MILLINGTON SYNGE

185   I AM A POOR MAN . . . C. H. Houghton, née Matheson, *The Irish Statesman* II, no. 17, 5 July 1924, p. 534.

ANGLO-IRISH THEATRE . . . Pearse's leading article, which appeared on 9 February 1907, was headed, 'The Passing of Anglo-Irish Drama'. Pearse called for a boycott of the Abbey Theatre, holding its directors responsible for Synge's 'propagation of a monstrous gospel of animalism, of revolt against sane and sweet ideals'.

MAZAWATTEE TEA-HEIRESS . . . Annie Horniman's family produced Mazawattee Tea, the up-market favourite. Yet she used some of her shares in the Hudson's Bay Company to underwrite Yeats's theatrical enterprise. The Abbey Theatre was intended primarily for his use, and not for others unconnected with his company. In January 1906, when the seceding Abbey players were threatening to play under the name of the Irish National Theatre Society, Synge and the others changed the name of their company to the National Theatre Company Limited. Annie Horniman then transferred her patronage from Yeats to the new company.

186   WE, THE PLAYERS AND I . . . *Our Irish Theatre*, p. 194.

KHARKI CUT-THROATS . . . *CW IV*, p. 75. This is an overt reference to the khaki-clad British soldiers who had, reportedly, been guilty of atrocities against civilians during the Boer War.

MOTES IN THE EYES . . . Corkery, p. 182.

A NEWSPAPER MAN . . . *Our Irish Theatre*, p. 104.

GERARD LEBLANC . . . 'Synge in France', in *Sunshine and the Moon's Delight*, pp. 266–7.

187 THE WEEK'S RIOTING . . . *Our Irish Theatre*, p. 81.

I AM GLAD . . . Synge, *Letters I*, p. 290.

FAY IS A LITTLE ASS . . . Ibid., p. 295.

188 MOORE AS USUAL . . . Ibid., p. 308.

DISSENTRY . . . Ibid., p. 299. Synge's bad spelling could sometimes contain unintentioned punning.

THE YOUNGER PEOPLE . . . *CW II*, p. 224n.

189 BOOK OF LEINSTER . . . *Synge and the Irish Language*, pp. 179–84.

190 SERIOUSLY PUT FORWARD . . . *CW II*, p. 372. Synge's review appeared in the *Manchester Guardian* of 28 December 1905. Poor though Leahy's translation is, professional jealousy may also account for Synge's scathing comments. He had made his own translation (MS 4341, TCD, ff. 3–61) of *Oidhe Chloinne Uisneach: The Fate of the Children of Uisneach* [or Usna], written in 1740 by the Gaelic scholar Aindrias MacCuirtín. Synge's version was never published.

DURING THE PAST . . . Corkery, p. 205.

GEORGE RUSSELL'S DEIRDRE . . . The first two acts were presented in a private performance given in the garden of the archaeologist George Coffey on 2 January 1902. The full play was first performed publicly on 2 April at the Hall of St Theresa's Total Abstinence Association, Clarendon Street, Dublin.

191 ALTOGETHER TOO MUCH DEIRDRE . . . *Daily Express*, 3 April 1902, p. 5. See Robert Hogan and James Kilroy, *Laying the Foundations: 1902–1904*, Dublin: Dolmen Press 1976, pp. 12–3.

FOLK STORYTELLERS . . . Kiberd, p. 191.

192 POORLY DRESSED . . . *CW IV*, p. 189.

ROYALLY DRESSED . . . Ibid., p. 207.

193 I'M A LONG WHILE . . . Ibid., pp. 194n, 195.

ISN'T IT A LONG WHILE . . . *CW III*, pp. 49, 51.

IT ISN'T LONG TILL . . . *CW IV*, p. 257.

AT DAWN . . . Ibid., p. 370.

194 WHAT IS PRETENTIOUS . . . Grene, p. 167.

BY THE SUN AND MOON . . . *CW IV*, p. 215.

FROM THE KNOWLEDGE . . . Donna Gerstenberger, *John Millington Synge*, New York: Twayne 1964, 100.

195 YOUTH'S SPLENDOUR PASSES . . . Skelton, 149.

DID THAT PLAY OF MINE . . . A curious fact relative to these lines—taken from 'The Man and the Echo'—is Yeats's use of the word 'English'. As Malcolm Brown observes in *The Politics of Irish Literature* (Seattle: University of Washington Press 1972, 321), Yeats never employed 'England/English' in his poetry for the first thirty years of his career. 'England' and 'English' appeared once in 'Easter 1916', and 'English' once in his play *The Dreaming of the Bones*. Brown attributes this to John O'Leary's injunction to his pupil Yeats against the 'canting abuse of England'.

I DO NOT BELIEVE . . . Synge, *Letters I*, p. 74.

196 LE PREMIER RESULTAT . . . Ibid., p. 29. Ann Saddlemyer thinks it possible that this is a French exercise prepared for Thérèse Beydon.

WHAT WE ALL NEED . . . *CW IV*, p. 193.

197 SYNGE FOR MARRIAGE ONLY . . . In his *Autobiography* (*CW II*, p. 9), Synge expresses his concern that his illness may be hereditary, and he 'surmised that unhealthy parents should have unhealthy children'. He decided never to 'create beings to suffer as I am suffering', a resolve which remained with him to the end. See note p. 52.

ALWAYS GOT A WILD IMPULSE . . . Synge, *Letters I*, pp. 300–1.

198 DEAREST TREASURE . . . Ibid., p. 285.

ONE HOLIDAY COTTAGE . . . Molly shared the cottage with her sister for a fortnight. On 23 July she came back alone for another two weeks, which she spent largely in Synge's company.

199 JACK B. YEATS . . . The artist had moved to Devonshire in the 1890s. Lady Gregory told her friend Lord Gough (*Seventy Years*, p. 383) that 'I grudge him to overpainted England and want to keep him in touch with our neglected west country'. She was charmed by his Aran illustrations: 'He paints peasant life with a kind of dramatic fervour . . . .'

200 FEELING RATHER QUEER . . . Synge, *Letters I*, p. 342. He explained to Molly on 12 May that he would rather postpone the operation until after the British tour.

IT'S A LONG TIME WE'VE HAD . . . *CW IV*, p. 231.

QUIET AND STATELY . . . Synge, *Letters I*, p. 250.

DEPENDS—AS TO FUTURE TOURS . . . Ibid., p. 351.

201   THEY ARE SHOWING FROHMAN . . . Ibid., p. 316.

AGNES TOBIN . . . A friend of Synge's with whom he corresponded a good deal. She was a poet, and a translator of Petrarch. It was she whom Charles Frohman approached when arranging the American tour.

HOLDING WHAT HE BELIEVED . . . *Freeman's Journal*, 5 February 1907, p. 6. The journalist is paraphrasing part of Yeats's defence of Synge during the famous debate of the previous evening.

202   A LIST OF HOW MANY TIMES . . . Synge, *Letters I*, p. 318.

VERY FREQUENTLY . . . Greene and Stephens, pp. 257–8.

LADY GREGORY'S PLAYS . . . Because of the dominance of Yeats and Synge in the early history of the Abbey Theatre, Lady Gregory's immense dramatic contribution is sometimes overlooked. 'During the eight years from the opening of the Abbey in 1904 through 1912 she wrote nineteen plays (thirteen one-act tragedies or comedies, one two-act comedy, and five three-act comedies or tragedies) as well as seven translations. Her plays were very popular. From 1904 to 1912 there were 600 performances of her plays at the Abbey or on tour, compared with 245 performances of Yeats's plays, 182 of Synge's, 125 by William Boyle, 78 by W. F. Casey, 65 by Lennox Robinson, 47 by Norreys Connel[l], and 44 by G. B. Shaw' (Kohlfeldt, p. 185). In the light of these statistics, Synge's irritation is understandable.

203   BOYLE'S NECK . . . Synge, *Letters I*, p. 326.

I SOMETIMES WISH . . . Ibid., p. 330.

BEN IDEN PAYNE . . . In February 1907, the Abbey engaged the English actor Ben Iden Payne to produce the verse and classical plays, in order to lessen some of the pressure on the directors. Willie Fay continued as producer of the 'dialect' plays.

OXFORD AND LONDON . . . *Theatre Business*, p. 222.

205   GOGARTY, ODDLY ENOUGH . . . Dr Patrick Kelly, a radiologist, formerly of the Hammersmith Hospital, wrote to Ulick O'Connor: 'This is a very good indication of Gogarty's quality as a physician, even though he was an [ear, nose and throat] specialist. This might seem a small thing in the light of the great advances which have been made in medicine since that time. But in Gogarty's day, when reliance upon clinical findings was paramount

and rarely aided by laboratory assistance, it represented a high degree of competence in diagnosis'. (Cited in Ulick O'Connor, *Oliver St John Gogarty: A Poet and his Times*, London: Granada 1981, 133.)

HE SAYS I OUGHT TO . . . Synge, *Letters II*, p. 33.

THE ENLARGED LYMPH GLANDS . . . J. B. Lyons, *'What Did I Die Of?': The Deaths of Parnell, Wilde, Synge and Other Literary Pathologies*, Dublin: Lilliput Press 1991, 157–8.

206   PRONOUNCED HIM 'GRAND' . . . Synge, *Letters II*, p. 97.

LOADED IT CROOKEDLY . . . Stephens, f. 2962. Willie Belton was a carter whom Mrs Synge often employed for her annual summer vacation.

207   TOLD HER THE NEWS . . . Ibid., f. 3014.

208   VISIT TO GERMANY . . . Andrew Carpenter suggests that Synge's going to Germany so suddenly may indicate his reluctance to face up to his mother's death.

POOR THINGS . . . Synge, *Letters II*, p. 208.

209   THERE'S ONE SORROW . . . *CW IV*, p. 259.

I'VE LET BUILD . . . Ibid., p. 259.

PEOPLE LIKE YEATS . . . Synge, *Letters II*, p. 221.

WILL YOU GO TO MY FUNERAL? . . . Yeats, *Autobiographies*, p. 519.

210   HE IS VERY PALE AND THIN . . . *Seventy Years*, p. 439.

THE NURSES . . . Synge was popular with the nurses at Elpis; after his discharge in 1908, he corresponded regularly with four of them.

NOW SO FRAIL . . . *Seventy Years*, p. 439.

POOR JOHNNIE HAD LONG . . . In Samuel Synge's *Letters to My Daughter* (p. 131), there is a passage which appears to confirm Synge's return to the faith: 'A visit that he paid to a Dublin clergyman about 1908, and the object of the visit, show how God had a place in his thoughts that many of his friends perhaps hardly knew about.' Samuel does not elaborate on 'the object of the visit'.

211   I ASKED IF I GOT SICK . . . *CW I*, p. 64. Molly's reply to Synge's question, 'Will you go to my funeral?' inspired the poem, although Yeats writes (*Autobiographies*, p. 509): 'I believe that some thing I said may have suggested "I asked if I got sick and died".'

TO OUR LEADER AND FRIEND . . . *Seventy Years*, p. 440.

STRUGGLING WITH A DEAD LANGUAGE

212   A STRANGE MAN . . . David H. Greene, 'A Centenary Appraisal', in *J. M. Synge Centenary Papers 1971*, p. 180.

213   VERY FEW PEOPLE . . . Ibid., pp. 180–1.

215   WELL, IT'S A GREAT WONDER . . . Ibid., p. 221.

HE ASKED FIRST . . . *CW II*, p. 278. The long essay 'In Kerry' was published in 1907 in *The Shanachie* in three consecutive numbers: Summer, Autumn and Winter.

216   WHAT A PITY . . . Letter of Mrs Synge to Robert Synge (in Argentina), 29 January 1894 (Stephens, f. 640).

SETTLE THE TABLE . . . *Letters to My Daughter*, p. 145.

217   QUEER LITERATURE . . . Mrs Synge received a letter from John from Paris on 20 November 1899. 'He says', she wrote to Samuel, 'I am to tell Robert to get . . . [G. Borrow's] *The Bible in Spain*, it is very interesting he says, and he picked it up on the quays for 1s/0d. . . . I am thankful among all the queer literature he gathers up that he gets some good books among them' (ibid., p. 160).

NONE OF THE SYNGES . . . Edward Stephens tells of Mrs Synge's grave disapproval of Florence Ross's 'going to any theatre from her house'. She, together with Stephens's brother Frank and cousin Ton Traill, had gone to see W. B. Yeats's *The Hour-Glass* and William Boyle's *The Mineral Workers* in January 1907. Mrs Synge's diary reads: 'Frank, Ton and Florence went to the Abbey—not home till after 12. I lay awake a great deal . . . .' (Stephens, f. 2397).

IT WAS ALSO DURING . . . *Letters to My Daughter*, 29–30.

218   I AWOKE THE NEXT MORNING . . . *CW II*, p. 250.

THEN THEY ASKED ME . . . Ibid., p. 254.

219   AFTER A WHILE . . . Ibid., p. 218.

AN ELEGANT LITTLE SILVER . . . *Letters to My Daughter*, p. 169.

220   THE WORST WORDS . . . Ibid., pp. 140–1.

THOSE WORDS HE ERASED . . . It must not be thought that MacKenna erased bad language only. The evidence seems to indicate that he obliterated unkind references to mutual acquaintances and others. MacKenna felt that such ill-chosen allusions might damage Synge's posthumous reputation.

221 MAKING POSSIBLE THE MEANS . . . Robert O'Driscoll,
'Yeats's Conception of Synge', in *Sunshine and the Moon's Delight*,
p. 161. O'Driscoll mentions, in this context, Yeats's fondness of
quoting Goethe's 'We do the people of history the honour of
naming after them the creations of our minds'.
I WAS VERY POOR . . . W. B. Yeats, 'The Irish Dramatic
Movement', in *The Bounty of Sweden*, pp. 43-4.
ACTIVE ROLE THAT SYNGE PLAYED . . . We learn from Greene
and Stephens (p. 62) that, 'in addition to the regular meetings he
went with the members on St Patrick's day to Versailles to lay a wreath
at the statue of Hoche, the commander of the French forces at Bantry
Bay in 1796, and then visited Hoche's house . . . . He spent a good
deal of time with Miss Gonne and Yeats, when politics and the
activities of the league must have been the chief topic of
conversation'.

223 HE HAD THAT EGOTISM . . . Yeats, *Memoirs*, p. 205.
I HAVE NEVER HEARD HIM . . . *Our Irish Theatre*, p. 76.
NEITHER LADY GREGORY . . . W. B. Yeats, *Autobiographies*, p. 511.
YOUR CUCHULAIN . . . Ibid., p. 75.
ON THE WHOLE . . . *CW II*, p. 368.
C'EST SURTOUT . . . Ibid., p. 379.
ALWAYS TOO SELF-ABSORBED . . . Yeats, *Memoirs*, p. 222.

224 I HAD KNOWN A GOOD MANY . . . John Masefield, 'John M.
Synge', in *Contemporary Review*, April 1911, cited in Mikhail, p. 79.

225 SYNGE WAS FOND . . . *Synge And The Ireland Of His Time*, p. 39.
I REMEMBER HIM HOLDING . . . Ibid., p. 40.
SYNGE WAS ALWAYS READY . . . Ibid., p. 41.
THE EXTERNAL SELF . . . Yeats, *Memoirs*, p. 204.

226 WE SHOULD UNITE . . . Yeats, *Autobiographies*, p. 509.
DO YOU KNOW, MADDY . . . *All That Fall*, Samuel Beckett, *The
Complete Dramatic Works*, London and Boston: Faber and Faber,
1986, 194.
APPEARS AT THE PRESENT MOMENT . . . Tom Paulin, 'A
New Look at the Language Question', in *Ireland's Field Day*, Notre
Dame, Indiana: University of Notre Dame Press 1986, 11.

227 COULD HAVE FAILED TO RECOGNISE . . . Austin Clarke, in
his introduction to *The Plays of George Fitzmaurice* (Dublin: Dolmen
Press 1967, viii). Robert Hogan thinks that it may have been
perceived blasphemy and 'the randy folk-like character' of the

priest in *The Dandy Dolls* that prevented Yeats and Lady Gregory accepting the play, which, in Hogan's opinion, is 'a masterpiece fit to rank with the best of Synge and the later O'Casey' (Robert Hogan, *After the Irish Renaissance: A Critical History of the Irish Drama since 'The Plough and the Stars'*, London: Macmillan 1968, 167).

228   COMRADE SOLDIERS . . . Sean O'Casey, *The Plough and the Stars*, Act II.

229   FLASH IN TH' PAN . . . Ibid.

HE WENT TO ENGLAND . . . The Abbey rejected O'Casey's *The Silver Tassie* in 1928; the rejection prompted his removal to England. The Abbey finally produced the play in 1935, and it caused immediate outraged protests from religious and patriotic factions. In 1957, O'Casey banned professional productions of his plays in Ireland; Samuel Beckett would later follow his lead. Molly Allgood died on 2 November 1952, during rehearsals for a radio version of *The Silver Tassie.*

TRULY GOOD HUMOUR . . . Mordecai Richler in a foreword to *The Best of Modern Humor*, New York: Alfred A. Knopf 1983.

230   TELL WILLIE . . . Lady Gregory, *Seventy Years*, p. 425.

231   BECKETT'S CHARACTERS . . . Katharine Worth in an introduction to *Beckett the Shape Changer: A Symposium*, Katharine Worth, ed., London and Boston: Routledge & Kegan Paul 1975, 5.

232   YEATS KNEW . . . Hubert Butler, *Grandmother and Wolfe Tone*, Dublin: Lilliput Press, 1990, 144.

234   YERRA, WE KNEW WELL . . . '*Ara, bhí fhios againne go maith gur bullshit a bhí ann ach ba chuma linn.*' From a television interview, cited in *An Aran Reader* (p. 208). King was referring to the film-makers' many falsifications of life in Aran, such as teaching the fishermen shark-hunting in order to facilitate a dramatic sequence.

IT HAS PROSPERED . . . Uriel Weinreich has an interesting comment on the failure of a colonial language to supplant a native one: 'Rural populations sometimes develop a hostile attitude (or at least an ambivalent one) toward their urban centers. In the Hebrides . . . the Gaelic language survives in the countryside as a symptom of rural hostility to the Anglicized towns.' (Uriel Weinreich, *Languages in Contact: Findings and Problems*, The Hague: Mouton 1970, 97, 108).

235   RTE-SPEAK . . . Radio Telefís Eireann is the Irish national radio
       and television body. See Desmond Fennell, *Nice People and Rednecks*:
       Ireland in the 1980s, Dublin: Gill and Macmillan 1986, pp. 54–5, 145.
       GREGORY'S SOUND . . . The body of water between Inishmaan
       and Inishmore. The name bears no connection to the Gregory
       family of Coole, but rather to St Gregory or to Pope Gregory the
       Great. See Hubert Butler, 'Influenza in Aran', in *Grandmother and*
       Wolfe Tone, pp. 129–30, for a lively discourse on the name.

Index